Dictionary of Bible Place Names

By the same author :
DICTIONARY OF BIBLE PERSONAL NAMES
DICTIONARY OF BIBLE THEMES

---MAPS---

Eight pages of specially drawn maps appear after page 175 carrying all place names mentioned in the text of this comprehensive volume.

DICTIONARY OF
BIBLE PLACE
NAMES

H. H. ROWLEY

OLIPHANTS

OLIPHANTS
BLUNDELL HOUSE
GOODWOOD ROAD
LONDON S.E.14

ISBN 0 551 00541 6

Printed in Great Britain by
Western Printing Services Ltd Bristol

PREFACE

In this concise dictionary I have sought to include every place name mentioned in the RSV Bible, including the Apocrypha. I have included a few of the more interesting variants in the Jerusalem Bible, but for reasons of space could not systematically include all the variants of this or any other version. A summary of biblical information relating to every place is given, but the scope of the work restricted the extra-biblical information that could be included. Wherever possible an indication of the modern identification of sites is given, but the reader will quickly see how much uncertainty attaches to many of these. The use of bold type indicates another entry in this volume where the reader may find supplementary information. It is, of course, impossible in a work on this scale to include every reference to every place, but it is hoped that enough has been given to enable the reader to see what part each place plays in the Bible story, and that students of every level will find this little volume handy for reference on the less as well as the more familiar place names that abound in the Bible.

H. H. ROWLEY

Stroud, Glos.

ABBREVIATIONS

AV	Authorized Version
JB	Jerusalem Bible
LXX	Septuagint (Greek) Version
LXX^B	The Vatican MS of LXX
MT	The Massoretic (Hebrew) text of OT
NEB	New English Bible
NT	New Testament
OT	Old Testament
RSV	Revised Standard Version
RSVm	Revised Standard Version, marginal note
RV	Revised Version
Vulg.	Vulgate (Latin) Version

Books of the Bible

OLD TESTAMENT

Gen.	Jg.	1 Chr.	Ps.	Lam.	Ob.	Hag.
Exod.	Ru.	2 Chr.	Prov.	Ezek.	Jon.	Zech.
Lev.	1 Sam.	Ezr.	Ec.	Dan.	Mic.	Mal.
Num.	2 Sam.	Neh.	Ca.	Hos.	Nah.	
Dt.	1 Kg.	Est.	Isa.	Jl	Hab.	
Jos.	2 Kg.	Job	Jer.	Am.	Zeph.	

APOCRYPHA

1 Esd.	Tob.	Ad. Est.	Sir.	S 3 Ch.	Bel	1 Mac.
2 Esd.	Jdt.	Wis.	Bar.	Sus.	Man.	2 Mac.
			Ep. Jer.			

NEW TESTAMENT

Mt.	Ac.	Gal.	1 Th.	Tit.	1 Pet.	3 Jn
Mk	Rom.	Eph.	2 Th.	Phm.	2 Pet.	Jude
Lk.	1 C.	Phil.	1 Tim.	Heb.	1 Jn	Rev.
Jn	2 C.	Col.	2 Tim.	Jas	2 Jn	

A

ABANA: One of the two rivers of **Damascus** (2 Kg. 5:12); mod.
Nahr Baradā, which rises in the **Anti-Lebanon** and flows through
the city. The alternative name, **Amana (2)**, is found in RSVm.

ABARIM: Hill country in **Moab**, E. of the **Jordan**, overlooking
the **Dead Sea** and the Jordan valley. Here the Israelites encamped
(Num. 33:47f.). From one of its heights, **Mount Nebo**, Moses
viewed the Promised Land (Num. 27:12; Dt. 32:49). It is mentioned
in Jer. 22:20 with **Lebanon** and **Bashan**. *See* Iye-abarim.

ABDON: A Levitical city in **Asher (1)** (Jos. 21:30; 1 Chr. 6:74)
called **Ebron** in Jos. 19:28.; mod. *Khirbet 'Abdeh*, E. of **Achzib**.

ABEL: An abbreviation of **Abel-beth-maacah** in 2 Sam. 20:18.

ABEL-BETH-MAACAH (or ABEL OF BETH-MAACAH):
A city in N. **Israel** where Sheba took refuge and was killed (2 Sam.
20:14ff.). It was captured by Ben-hadad (1 Kg. 15:20; called
Abel-maim in 2 Chr. 16:4) and by Tiglath-pileser (2 Kg. 15:29). It
is mod. *Tell Âbil*, W. of **Dan (2)**.

ABEL-KERAMIM (*'meadow of the vineyards'*): A place which
marked the limit of Jephthah's pursuit of the Ammonites (Jg. 11:33);
perhaps mod. *Na'ûr*.

ABEL-MAIM (*'meadow of waters'*): An alternative name for
Abel-beth-maacah (2 Chr. 16:4).

ABEL-MEHOLAH (*'meadow of dancing'*): A place which marked
the limit of Gideon's pursuit of the Midianites (Jg. 7:22), and the
birthplace of Adriel, Saul's son-in-law (1 Sam. 18:19) and of
Elisha (1 Kg. 19:16). In Solomon's time it was in the administrative
district of **Taanach, Megiddo**, and **Beth-shean** (1 Kg. 4:12). It is
identified with mod. *Tell Abū Sifri* or *Tell Maqlûb*.

ABEL-MIZRAIM ('*meadow of Egypt*'): The place where Jacob was mourned (Gen. 50:11; there is a play on words, '*ābhīl* meaning 'meadow' and '*ēbhel* 'mourning'). It was beyond Jordan, but the site is unknown. *See* **Atad**.

ABEL OF BETH-MAACAH: *See* Abel-beth-maacah.

ABEL-SHITTIM ('*meadow of acacias*'): A place in the plains of **Moab**, where the Israelites encamped before crossing the **Jordan** (Num. 33:49). It is also called **Shittim** (Jos. 3:1), and here the Israelites sinned with Moabite women (Num. 25:1ff.), and from here the spies were sent to **Jericho** (Jos. 2:1). It is identified with mod. *Tell el-Ḥammâm*, S. of *Wâdī Kefrein*.

ABILENE: A district in the **Anti-Lebanon**, which formed the tetrarchy of Lysanias (Lk. 3:1). Its chief city was Abila, mod. *Sûq Wâdī Baradā*.

ABRON: A brook of unknown location mentioned in Jdt. 2:24; possibly the *Khābûr* is meant.

ABRONAH: A place where the Israelites encamped before reaching **Ezion-geber** (Num. 33:34f.); probably mod. *'Ain ed-Defîyeh*.

ACCAD: A city in the land of **Shinar**, or **Babylonia** (Gen. 10:10), identified with *Agade*. It was the capital of Sargon I, the founder of the first Semitic empire. It gave its name to the whole of northern Babylonia and to the Semitic language which became current in Babylonia and **Assyria**. Its site is not certainly known.

ACCO: A maritime city N. of **Carmel** and within the borders of **Asher**, which successfully resisted the Israelites (Jg. 1:31). In NT times it was called **Ptolemais**. It is mod. *Tell el-Fukhkhâr*, and its name is preserved in *'Akkâ*, less than a mile away.

ACHAIA: The name was once used for a district in SE. Thessaly and the N. coast of the Peloponnese, but after the Roman conquest of Greece in 146 B.C. it was used for the whole of **Greece and Macedonia**. In 27 B.C., however, Macedonia became a separate province and Achaia comprised the whole of the southern part of the mainland and some of the islands. It was a senatorial province under a proconsul. This arrangement was changed by Tiberius in A.D. 15, but restored by Claudius in A.D. 44. The proconsul who had his seat in Corinth, was Seneca's brother, Gallio, when Paul was in the city (Ac. 18:12), and Paul was accused before him in vain by the Jews (Ac. 18:12ff.). Paul's first converts in Achaia were the household of Stephanas (1 C. 16:15), and 2 Corinthians was addressed to the Christians of the whole province (2 C. 1:1), who contributed readily to the collection for the saints of Jerusalem (Rom. 15:26; 2 C. 9:2), but from whom Paul accepted nothing (2 C. 11:9), and to whom the Thessalonians set an example (1 Th. 1:7f.).

ACHOR ('*trouble*'): A valley near Jericho, on the border of Judah and Benjamin (Jos. 15:7), where Achan was stoned (Jos. 7:24, 26). In prophetic vision this desolate region was to become a place of pasturage (Isa. 65:10) and a symbol of hope (Hos. 2:15). It is possibly mod. *el-Buqei'ah*.

ACHSHAPH: A Canaanite city whose king joined a coalition against Joshua (Jos. 11:1) and was defeated (Jos. 12:20). It was afterwards assigned to Asher (Jos. 19:25). Its identification is uncertain, but possibly it is mod. *Tell Kîsân*, SE. of Acco.

ACHZIB: 1. A town in Judah, near Keilah (Jos. 15:44); perhaps the same as Chezib (Gen. 38:5). In Mic. 1:14 it is punningly said that Achzib ('*akhzîbh*) will be a 'deceitful thing' ('*akhzâbh*). It is probably mod. *Tell el-Beiḍā*.
   2. A town in Asher (1) (Jos. 19:29), which successfully resisted the Israelites (Jg. 1:31); mod. *Ez-Zîb*.

ACRABA: A place near Chusi (Jdt. 7:18); probably mod. '*Akrabeh*.

ADADAH: A place in the S. of Judah (Jos. 15:22), for which Ararah (= Aroer (3)) should probably be read; mod. *Khirbe* '*Ar'ârah*.

ADAM: A place near Zarethan, beside the Jordan, where the waters were cut off for the Israelites to cross (Jos. 3:16); mod. *ell ed-Dâmiyeh*. A cryptic reference in Hos. 6:7 (RSV) is to a place of transgression of the covenant. In I Kg. 7:46 we should perhaps read 'at the ford of Adamah' for 'in the clay ground', and connect with the same place (note that it was near Zarethan).

ADAMAH: 1. A fortified city of **Naphtali** (Jos. 19:36); its site is unknown, but possibly mod. *Abū esh-Shebaʿ*.

2. *See* **Adam**.

ADAMI-NEKEB: A place on the boundary of **Naphtali** (Jos. 19:33); mod. *Khirbet ed-Dâmiyeh*, SW. of **Tiberias**.

ADASA: A place near **Beth-horon**, where Judas defeated and killed Nicanor (1 Mac. 7:40, 45); mod. *Khirbet ʿAddâseh*.

ADDAN: A place from which some returning exiles, who were unable to prove their descent, came (Ezr. 2:59; 1 Esd. 5:36); called **Addon** in Neh. 7:61. Its location is unknown.

ADDAR: A place on the boundary of **Judah** (Jos. 15:3), here distinct from **Hezron**; but in Num. 34:4 they are combined as **Hazar-addar**. It is possibly mod. *Khirbet el-Qudeirât*, near **Kadesh**.

ADDON: A place from which some returning exiles, who were unable to prove their descent, came (Neh. 7:61); called **Addan** in Ezr. 2:59; I Esd. 5:36. Its location is unknown.

ADIDA: A place in the **Shephelah** fortified by Simon (1 Mac. 12:38), where Simon encamped (1 Mac. 13:13); probably the same as **Hadid**, mod. *el-Ḥadîtheh*.

ADITHAIM: A town of **Judah** in the lowland (Jos. 15:36); its location is unknown.

ADMAH: A city near **Sodom** (Gen. 10:19), one of the **Cities of the Valley**. It was allied with Sodom and **Gomorrah** against Chedorlaomer and his allies (Gen. 14:2, 8). Its destruction with Sodom is not stated in Gen. 19, but is stated in Dt. 29:23 (cf. Hos. 11:8). Its site is unknown, but it may be submerged under the **Dead Sea**.

ADORA: A city named in Trypho's campaign against Simon (1 Mac. 13:20); called **Adoraim** in 2 Chr. 11:9.

ADORAIM: A city of **Judah** fortified by Rehoboam (2 Chr. 11:9); mod. *Dûrā*. It is called **Adora** in 1 Mac. 13:20.

ADRAMYTTIUM: A seaport of Mysia, in Asia Minor. When Paul was sent as a prisoner to Rome, he embarked in a ship belonging to this port (Ac. 27:2), which took him as far as Myra (Ac. 27:5). It is mod. *Edremit*.

ADRIA: The Adriatic Sea, across which the ship in which Paul was being taken to Rome drifted between Crete and Malta (Ac. 27:27).

ADULLAM: A city of Judah in the lowland (Jos. 15:35), and earlier a Canaanite royal city (Jos. 12:15). Judah's friend Hirah was from this place (Gen. 38:1, 12, 20). In a cave near here David took refuge and was joined by others (1 Sam. 22:1f.; 2 Sam. 23:13; 1 Chr. 11:15), and Micah predicted that the glory of Israel should seek refuge there (Mic. 1:15). It was fortified by Rehoboam (2 Chr. 11:7), and was resettled by returning Jews after the exile (Neh. 11:30). Its site is marked by *Tell esh-Sheikh-Madhkûr*, near *'Îd el-Mâ*, which preserves the ancient name.

ADUMMIM, THE ASCENT OF: On the road between Jericho and Jerusalem (Jos. 15:7, 18:17); mod. *Tal'at ed-Damm*. Tradition locates the inn of Lk. 10:34 here.

AENON (*'springs'*): A place where John the Baptist baptized, near Salim (Jn 3:23). Tradition variously locates it, but its site is unknown.

AESORA: A Samaritan town mentioned only in Jdt. 4:4. Its site is unknown.

AHAVA: A river (Ezr. 8:21,31) and a place (Ezr. 8:15) in Babylonia, where Ezra encamped with the returning exiles; called Theras in 1 Esd. 8:41, 61. Its location is unknown.

AHLAB: A town in Asher (1), which successfully resisted the Israelites (Jg. 1:31); perhaps the same as Helbah (Jg. 1:31), and to be identified with Mahalab.

AI (*'ruin'*): 1. A place E. of Bethel (1) (Gen. 12:8), between which and Bethel Abraham twice encamped (Gen. 12:8, 13:3). Joshua's spies regarded it as insignificant (Jos. 7:2), but its successful resistance (Jos. 7:4f.) led to the discovery of the crime of Achan. It was then destroyed by an ambush (Jos. 8:1ff.). It is identified with mod. *et-Tell*, about two miles from Bethel (cf. Jos. 12:9). Modern excavations provide evidence of a flourishing city in the third millennium B.C., which was destroyed about 2000 B.C. and not rebuilt for some 800 years. Some scholars hold that the place was temporarily reoccupied in Joshua's time, some that an older story has been attached to the name of Joshua, and some that the Israelite conquest of Bethel (unrecorded in Joshua, but alluded to in Jg. 1:22ff.) has been recorded of Ai (cf. also Jos. 10:1f.). Families stemming from Ai were among the returning exiles (Ezr. 2:28; Neh. 7:32). It is perhaps called **Aija** in Neh. 11:32, and perhaps **Aiath** in Isa. 10:28.

2. A place, apparently in **Ammon**, mentioned in Jer. 49:3. But it is probable that the text is corrupt. JB has 'The destroyer is on the march' for 'Ai is laid waste'.

AIATH: A place mentioned as in the path of the Assyrian invader (Isa. 28:10). This may be the same as **Ai** (1), or a neighbouring site, mod. *Khirbet Ḥayyân. See* **Avvim, Ayyah.**

AIJA: A place in the neighbourhood of **Bethel** (1) occupied by Benjaminites after the exile (Neh. 11:32). It may be the same as **Ai** (1), or a nearby site, mod. *Khirbet Ḥayyân.*

AIJALON (*'place of deer'*) (1): 1. An ancient Amorite city, assigned to **Dan** (1) (Jos. 19:42), which successfully resisted the Israelites until the Joseph tribes subdued it (Jg. 1:35f.). It became a Levitical city (Jos. 21:24), and later an Ephraimite city of refuge (1 Chr. 6:69). Beriah and Shama, Benjaminites who defeated the men of **Gath,** came from Aijalon (1 Chr. 8:13). It was fortified by Rehoboam (2 Chr. 11:10), and captured by the Philistines in the time of Ahaz (2 Chr. 28:18). Its site is mod. *Yâlō. See* **Elon-beth-hanam.**

2. A place in **Zebulun,** where Elon was buried (Jg. 12:12). Here we should perhaps read **Elon** (2) for Aijalon with LXX[B] (so JB). It is mod. *Khirbet el-Lôn,* or *Tell el-Buṭmeh,* two neighbouring sites of which one may preserve the sound and the other the meaning of *'ēlôn* ('terebinth').

AIJALON, VALLEY OF: An important pass, taking its name from **Aijalon** (1), mentioned with **Gibeon,** which lay to the E., in the poem relating to Joshua's victory over an Amorite alliance (Jos.

10:12). In the same valley Saul won a victory over the Philistines (1 Sam. 14:31).

AIN ('*spring*'): 1. A place near Riblah (Num. 34:11). Its site is unknown.

2. A town of Judah (Jos. 15:32; 1 Chr. 4:32). But in these passages Ain and Rimmon should be combined to give En-rimmon (so JB in the former).

3. A Levitical city in the S. (Jos. 21:16). But we should probably read Ashan (so JB) with 1 Chr. 6:59; mod. *Khirbet 'Asan*, near Beersheba.

AKELDAMA ('*field of blood*'): A field bought by Judas Iscariot (Ac. 1:18f.), or by the priests with the money Judas had received for betraying Jesus (Mt. 27:3ff.). Here Judas died (Ac. 1:18). Tradition has variously located the site.

AKRABATTENE: The district of Idumea near Akrabbim (1 Mac. 5:3), where Judas defeated the Idumeans.

AKRABBIM, ASCENT OF ('*ascent of scorpions*'): A pass S. of the Dead Sea, marking the boundary of Judah (Num. 34:4; Jos. 15:3) and of the Amorite predecessors of the Israelites (Jg. 1:36); mod. *Naqb eş-Şafā*.

ALEMA: A city of Gilead (1) (1 Mac. 5:26); possibly the same as Helam (2 Sam. 10:16f.), mod. *'Almā*.

ALEMETH: A Levitical city in Benjamin (1 Chr. 6:60), mod. *Khirbet 'Almît*; called Almon in Jos. 21:18.

ALEXANDRIA: A city in Egypt founded by Alexander the Great in 332 B.C. It became the capital of Egypt, and for more than a century the Jews were ruled by its monarchs. It had a considerable Jewish population, and here the earliest Greek translation of the OT was made (the Pentateuch probably from the time of Ptolemy Philadelphus in the third century B.C.). Alexandrian Jews visited Jerusalem, and with these and others Stephen disputed (Ac. 6:9). Apollos was a native of this city (Ac. 18:24), and it was on a ship from Alexandria that Paul was taken as a prisoner from Myra (Ac. 27:6) to Malta, and on another from Malta (Ac. 28:11) to

7

Puteoli. It early became a strong centre of Christianity, and a famous catechetical school and many of the early Fathers were here.

ALLAMMELECH: A town of **Asher** (1) (Jos. 19:26), of unknown location.

ALLON-BACUTH ('*oak of weeping*'): The place near **Bethel** (1) where Rebekah's nurse, Deborah, was buried (Gen. 35:8); its site is unknown. *See* **Bochim**.

ALMON: A Levitical city in **Benjamin** (Jos. 21:18), mod. *Khirbet 'Almît*; called **Alemeth** in 1 Chr. 6:60.

ALMON-DIBLATHAIM: A station in the Wilderness wanderings (Num. 33:46f.), perhaps mod. *Khirbet Deleilât esh-Sherqiyah*, or *Deleilât el-Gharbîyeh* (these form a twin site, N. of **Dibon**, (1)); probably the same as **Beth-diblathaim** (Jer. 48:22).

ALUSH: A station in the Wilderness wanderings, after **Dophkah** (Num. 33:13f.); possibly mod. *Wâdî el-'Eshsh*.

AMAD: A town of **Asher** (1) (Jos. 19:26), of unknown location.

AMAM: A town of **Judah**, in the S. (Jos. 15:26), of unknown location.

AMANA: 1. A mountain mentioned with **Lebanon** and **Hermon** (Ca. 4:8); mod. *Jebel Zebedâni*.
  2. An alternative name for the river **Abana** (2 Kg. 5:12, RSVm.).

AMAW: The name of a country (Num. 22:5) in which **Pethor** was situated and to which Balak sent messengers to call Balaam to his aid. AV and RV, following MT, misunderstood, as also did the ancient versions. The name is known from inscriptions as that of a region W. of the **Euphrates**.

AMMAH: A hill near **Giah** on the way to the wilderness of **Gibeon** (2 Sam. 2:24), of unknown location.

AMMON: The name of a people and of their country, E. of the **Jordan**, its capital being **Rabbah** (1), mod. *'Ammân*. Here the

Ammonites displaced the Zamzummim (Dt. 2:20). The Jabbok formed the general boundary of Ammon (Dt. 3:16; Jos. 12:2, 13:10), but it was not a firm and unchanging boundary. At the time of the Israelite entry into the Land of Promise they did not attack Ammon (Num. 21:24; Dt. 2:37), but in the period of the Judges Ammon aided Eglon in subjecting Israel (Jg. 3:13), and attacked Gilead (1) in the time of Jephthah (Jg. 10:7f., 11:4ff.), and even crossed the Jordan (Jg. 10:9), but were defeated by Jephthah (Jg. 11:30–12:6). Later, Ammon besieged Jabesh-gilead (1 Sam. 11:1ff.), which was delivered by Saul (1 Sam. 11:5ff.). In the time of David the king of Ammon, Hanun, foolishly insulted David's messengers (2 Sam. 10:1ff.; 1 Chr. 19:1ff.) and was conquered in the war he had provoked (2 Sam. 10:6–11:1, 12:26ff.; 1 Chr. 20:1ff.). At the time of Absalom's rebellion Ammon was loyal to David (2 Sam. 17:27ff.), and an Ammonite was one of David's heroes (2 Sam. 23:37; 1 Chr. 11:39). Solomon married an Ammonite woman, whose son succeeded him (1 Kg. 14:21, 31; 2 Chr. 12:13). In the reign of Jehoshaphat, Ammon, which had regained independence, invaded Judah with her Moabite and Edomite allies (2 Chr. 20:1, 10), but the allies attacked and destroyed one another (2 Chr. 20:22f.). Amos denounced the inhumanity of Ammon in an unrecorded attack on Gilead (Am. 1:13–15). Uzziah subjected Ammon (2 Chr. 26:8), and Jotham defeated it in war (2 Chr. 27:5). When Jehoiakim rebelled against Nebuchadrezzar, Ammon harassed Judah (2 Kg. 24:2), and Jeremiah says Ammon had dispossessed Gad (Jer. 49:1) and threatens reprisals (Jer. 49:2ff.; cf. Zeph. 2:8f.). Under Zedekiah Judah and Ammon became allies (Jer. 27:3), and when Jerusalem fell, many from Judah fled to Ammon (Jer. 40:11f.). Ezekiel pictures the king of Babylon drawing lots to decide whether to attack Judah or Ammon first (Ezek. 21:18ff.). Gedaliah, who was appointed governor by Nebuchadrezzar (Jer. 40:11), was murdered by Ishmael, who had been sent for this purpose by the king of Ammon (Jer. 40:14–41:3). In Nehemiah's time Ammon helped Sanballat against the Jews (Neh. 2:10, 19, 4:3, 7f.), and Nehemiah retaliated by prohibiting intermarriage with Ammonites (Neh. 13:23ff.). Hostility between Ammon and the Jews continued in the Maccabean age, and Jason fled for refuge to Ammon (2 Mac. 4:26). Judas is said to have defeated the Ammonites (1 Mac. 5:6ff.), but by this time Ammon had been absorbed by the Nabateans and it was now part of an Arab kingdom. In the legendary story of Judith, Ammon figures as supporting Holofernes (Jdt. 5:2, 5, 6:5, 7:17).

9

AMPHIPOLIS: A town on the river *Strymon*, in **Macedonia**, and raised by the Romans to the rank of principal town of the first district of Macedonia. It stood on the Via Egnatia, along which Paul went from **Philippi** to **Thessalonica** (Ac. 17:1), but he does not seem to have stopped there.

ANAB (*'grape'*): A town of **Judah**, in the hill country (Jos. 15:20), taken from the Anakim (Jos. 11:21); mod. *Khirbet 'Anâb.*

ANAHARATH: A town of **Issachar** (Jos. 19:16); possibly mod. *En-Na'ûrah.*

ANATHOTH: A Levitical city in **Benjamin** (Jos. 21:18; 1 Chr. 6:60), to which Abiathar went when dismissed from **Jerusalem** (1 Kg. 2:26f.), and from which one of David's heroes (2 Sam. 23:27; 1 Chr. 11:28, 27:12) and another of his followers (1 Chr. 12:3) came, and from which also Jeremiah came (Jer. 1:1, 11:21, 23, 29:27). During the siege of Jerusalem, Jeremiah bought from his cousin a plot of land there (Jer. 32:7ff.). It is mentioned as in the path of the invading Assyrians (Isa. 10:30). It was resettled after the exile (Ezr. 2:23; Neh. 7:27, 11:32; 1 Esd. 5:18). The name is derived from that of the Canaanite goddess Anath. It is identified with mod. *Râs el-Kharrûbeh*, near *'Anâta.*

ANEM: A Levitical city in **Issachar** (1 Chr. 6:73); perhaps an error here, as it corresponds to **En-gannim** in Jos. 21:29. It is possibly mod. *Khirbet 'Anîn*, near the **Jordan**, or *Khirbet Umm el-Ghanem*, at the foot of **Mount Tabor**. But En-gannim is usually identified with *Jenîn.*

ANER: 1. A city of refuge in **Manasseh** (1 Chr. 6:70), of unknown location.

2. In Gen. 14:13, 24 Aner appears as a person, beside **Mamre** and **Eshcol**. As the others are place names, it is possible that Aner is also, and that the men of these three localities joined Abraham in his rescue of Lot.

ANIM: A town of **Judah**, in the hill country (Jos. 15:50); possibly mod. *Ghuwein et-Taḥtā.*

ANTI-LEBANON: The eastern mountain range, roughly parallel to the **Lebanon**, in N. **Syria**, mod. *Jebel esh-Sherqi*, separated from the Lebanon by a valley now called *el-Beqa'*. It is explicitly named only in Jdt. 1:7, but LXX has 'Anti-Lebanon' for MT 'Lebanon' in Dt. 1:7, 3:25, 11:24; Jos. 1:4, 9:1, and the Anti-Lebanon is meant by 'all Lebanon, toward the sunrising, from **Baal-gad** below Mount **Hermon** to the entrance of **Hamath**' (Jos. 13:5), The 'tower of Lebanon, overlooking **Damascus**' (Ca. 7:4) is probably Hermon, which lies at the S. end of the Anti-Lebanon, separated from it by the *Wâdî Baradâ*.

ANTIOCH: 1. A Syrian city on the *Orontes*, founded by Seleucus Nicator (312–280 B.C.), and the seat of government of **Syria** under the Seleucids (the 'kings of the north' in Dan. 11) and the Romans. It became notorious for its depraved morals. Its site is mod. *Anṭâkiyeh*. It is not referred to by name in the OT, but is mentioned sometimes in 1 & 2 Mac. Antiochus Epiphanes gave Jason, who bought the high priest-hood, authority to enrol the men of **Jerusalem** as citizens of Antioch (2 Mac. 4:9), and near Antioch the rightful high priest, Onias, was murdered (2 Mac. 4:33f.). From Jerusalem Antiochus removed to Antioch the wealth he plundered from the Temple (2 Mac. 5:21). When the Maccabean rising took place, Antiochus left the city for the east, after sending Lysias to crush the rising (1 Mac. 3:37), and Lysias enlisted mercenaries there (1 Mac. 4:35). Nicanor fled thither after his defeat (2 Mac. 8:35). Roman envoys wrote to the Jews saying they were on their way to Antioch (2 Mac. 11:36). After the death of Antiochus Epiphanes, Philip, the late king's friend, revolted in Antioch (2 Mac. 13:23), and Lysias made peace with the Jews (1 Mac. 6:63) and marched on the city (2 Mac. 13:26). The usurper Alexander Balas returned to Antioch when Demetrius II came from **Crete** (1 Mac. 10:68), and here Ptolemy VI made his ill-starred assumption of the crown of **Asia** (1 Mac. 11:13). Jonathan sent troops to Antioch to aid Demetrius II (1 Mac. 11:44). The upstart Trypho later gained control of the city (1 Mac. 11:56). In the NT we learn that a proselyte from Antioch, Nicolaus, was among the early converts to Christianity in Jerusalem, and he became one of the Seven (Ac. 6:5). The gospel soon reached Antioch (Ac. 11:19f.), and here the disciples were first called Christians (Ac. 11:26). Barnabas was sent to Antioch (Ac. 11:22) and soon fetched Paul from **Tarsus** (Ac. 11:25f.). To Antioch the prophet Agabus came (Ac. 11:27f.). The Church here sent Barnabas and Paul on their first missionary journey (Ac. 13:1ff.), and to this city they returned (Ac. 14:26). After the Council of Jerusalem Judas and Silas were sent to Antioch (Ac. 15:22ff.). On his return from his second missionary journey Paul came to Antioch (Ac. 18:22), and here, at a time which cannot with certainty be determined, he came into conflict with Peter on relations with Gentile Christians (Gal. 2:11ff.).

2. A Roman colony called Antioch of **Pisidia**, which was not strictly in Pisidia, but near Pisidia and ethnically in **Phrygia** and administratively in **Galatia**. It was visited by Paul and Barnabas on their first missionary journey (Ac. 13:14ff.), but they left when the Jews stirred up persecution (Ac. 13:50f.). Jews from Antioch stirred up fresh trouble in **Lystra** (Ac. 14:19). To Antioch they returned (Ac. 14:21) on their way back to **Antioch** (1). Paul refers to his sufferings on this journey in 2 Tim. 3:11. It is mod. *Yahaç*.

ANTIPATRIS: A town founded by Herod the Great on the site of **Aphek** (1), and named after his father. After his arrest in **Jerusalem**, Paul was escorted by 470 soldiers (Ac. 23:23) here by night (Ac. 23:31) on the way to **Caesarea**. It is mod. *Râs el-'Ain*.

APHAIREMA: A district added to **Judea** from **Samaria** (2) by Demetrius I (1 Mac.10:29, 38) and confirmed by Demetrius II 1 Mac. 11:34); called **Ephraim** (2) in 2 Sam. 13:23, Jn 11:54, **Ophrah** (1) in Jos. 18:23; 1 Sam. 13:17, and **Ephron** (1) in 2 Chr. 13:19 (**Ephrain** in RSVm). It is mod. *eṭ-Ṭaiyibeh*.

APHEK: 1. A Canaanite city which was conquered by Joshua (Jos. 12:18). Here the Philistines assembled their army against Israel for the battle in which the Ark was taken (1 Sam. 4:1) and again before the battle of **Gilboa** (1 Sam. 29:1). On its site **Antipatris** was founded. It is mod. *Râs el-'Ain*.

2. A town in **Asher** (1) (Jos. 19:30), which successfully resisted the Israelites (Jg. 1:31, where it is called **Aphik**); probably mod. *Tell Kurdâneh*.

3. A town on the border of the Amorites (Jos. 13:4); perhaps mod. *Afqa*, E. of **Byblos**.

4. A town E. of the **Jordan**, where Ahab defeated Benhadad (1 Kg. 20:26, 30) and where Elisha predicted that Joash would again be victorious (2 Kg. 13:17); perhaps mod. *Fîq*.

APHEKAH: A town in **Judah** (Jos. 15:53); perhaps *Khirbet Kâna'an*, S.W. of **Hebron**.

APHIK: A Canaanite town which resisted Asherite occupation (Jg. 1:31); called **Aphek (2)** in Jos. 19:30. It is probably mod. *Tell Kurdâneh*.

APOLLONIA: A town which stood on the **Via Egnatia**, between the rivers **Strymon** and **Axino**, through which Paul passed, apparently without stopping, when he went from **Philippi** to **Thessalonica** (Ac. 17:1); mod. *Pollina*.

APPIUS, FORUM OF: A market town where Paul was met by Christians from **Rome**, when he was being taken as prisoner to Rome (Ac. 28:15). It was on the **Appian Way** forty-three miles from Rome, near mod. *Foro Appio*.

AR (*'city'*): A town or region of **Moab** (Dt. 2:9, 29), S. of the **Arnon** (Num. 21:15), which was the N. boundary of Moab (Dt. 2:18). Isaiah prophesied its devastation (Isa. 15:1). It may be intended by 'city of Moab' in Num. 22:36. It is possibly mod. *el-Miṣnaʿ*.

ARAB: A town of **Judah** (Jos. 15:52); perhaps mod. *Khirbet er-Râbiyeh*, SSW. of **Hebron**.

ARABAH: The depression in which the **Jordan** from the **Sea of Galilee** and the **Dead Sea** (which is called the **Sea of Arabah**, Dt. 3:17, 4:49; Jos. 3:16, 12:3; 2 Kg. 14:25) lie (Dt. 3:17, 4:49, 11:30; Jos. 8:14, 11:2, 16, 12:1, 8, 18:18; 1 Sam. 23:24; 2 Sam. 2:29, 4:7; 2 Kg. 25:4; Jer. 39:4, 52:7; Ezek. 47:8), and which continues southwards to the *Gulf of ʿAqaba* (Dt. 2:8). Much of this area is arid country, and hence the word is sometimes translated 'wilderness' (Job 24:5), 'desert' (Isa. 33:9, 35:1, 6; Jer. 2:6, 5:6, 17:6, 50:12, 51:43) or 'steppe' (Job 39:6). In Isa. 40:3, 41:19, where it is rendered 'desert', it is used of the N. Arabian desert. The S. part of the Arabah, from the Dead Sea to the Gulf of *ʿAqaba*, was an important trade route, and copper was mined here. In some passages the word is used in the plural, and there it is rendered 'plains', especially of the 'plains of Moab' (Num. 22:1, 26:3, 63, 31:12, 33:48ff., 35:1, 36:13; Dt. 34:1, 8; Jos. 13:32) or the 'plains of **Jericho**' (Jos. 4:13, 5:10; 2 Kg. 25:5; Jer. 39:5, 52:8).

ARABAH, BROOK OF: Mentioned by Amos as the S. boundary of **Israel** (Am. 6:14). This may refer to the **Zered**.

ARABAH, SEA OF: *See* Arabah.

ARABIA: The largest peninsula in the world, mainly desert with scattered oases. In early times there was no single name for the whole peninsula, and its people are sometimes spoken of generally as 'the people of the east' (Job 1:3; Ps. 11:14; Jer. 49:28), but more often by the separate tribes. The word 'Arab' means 'nomad', and where it is found in the OT, it refers to the tribes of N. Arabia rather than to the inhabitants of the whole peninsula (2 Chr. 17:11, 21:16, 22:1, 26:7; Neh. 4:7). The 'kings of Arabia' (1 Kg. 10:15; 2 Chr. 9:14; Jer. 25:24) are the chiefs of these tribes, and in Isa. 21:13; Ezek. 27:21 Arabia means N. Arabia. In Ezek. 30:5 it may have a wider significance. In the Apocrypha Arabians means the people of N. Arabia (1 Mac. 5:39), or, more specifically, Zabadeans from the region of **Damascus** (1 Mac. 12:31) or Nabateans (2 Mac. 5:8, 12:10), and Arabia means N. Arabia (1 Mac. 11:16; Jdt. 2:25; 2 Esd. 15:29). In the NT, Paul says **Mount Sinai** is in Arabia (Gal. 4:25), and speaks of his own sojourn in Arabia (Gal. 1:17), probably some area E. of Damascus, while the Arabians in **Jerusalem** on the Day of Pentecost (Ac. 2:11) were Jews or proselytes from some Nabatean or other N. Arabian settlement. The S. part of the peninsula was not unknown to the Israelites, however. The Queen of **Sheba** (1 Kg. 10:1ff.) probably came from S. Arabia, and some of the names in Gen. 10:26–30; 1 Chr. 1:20–23 may point to that region (e.g. **Hazarmaveth, Ophir, Havilah,** 2).

ARAD: A Canaanite city in the Negeb (Num. 21:1, 33:40), which fought against Israel and was defeated (Num. 21:3). Its king was defeated by Joshua (Jos. 12:14). Near here there was a settlement of the Kenites (Jg. 1:16). It is probably mod. *Tell 'Arâd*. It is perhaps the same as **Eder** (Jos. 15:21).

ARADUS: A city to which the Roman consul wrote announcing the Roman friendship for the Jews (1 Mac. 15:23). This is the same as **Arvad** (Ezek. 27:8, 11), mod. *Erwâd*.

ARAH: *See* **Mearah**.

ARAM: This word is used most frequently for Aramean peoples who spread from **Arabia** into the surrounding lands, and especially into N. **Mesopotamia** and **Syria**, where they established a number of states. Their language became widely used, especially under Persian rule, and it became the common speech of **Palestine** in NT times. The eponymous ancestor of these peoples was represented as a son of Shem (Gen. 10:22; 1 Chr. 1:17). As a geographical term, Aram is used of the home of Balaam (Num. 23:7), which was near the **Euphrates** (Num. 22:5; cf. Dt. 23:4), of the Aram of **Damascus** (2 Sam. 8:6; cf. Zech. 9:1, where it seems to cover other N. Syrian states), and of **Geshur** in Aram (2 Sam. 15:8). In Hos. 12:12 Jacob is said to have fled to Aram, but Gen. 28:2 specifies **Paddan-aram**, which was an Aramean district in Mesopotamia, called **Aram-naharaim** (cf. Ps. 60 heading) in Gen. 24:10 (where RSV has Mesopotamia, as in Dt. 23:4; Jg. 3:8; 1 Chr. 19:6). Other states named are **Aram-zobah** (Ps. 60 heading; also 2 Sam. 10:6, 8, where RSV has 'the Syrians of Zobah'), **Aram Beth-rehob** (2 Sam. 10:6, where RSV has 'the Syrians of Beth-rehob; cf. 10:8), and **Aram-maacah** (1 Chr. 19:6). The Aramean kingdom which figures most in the OT is that which had its capital in Damascus, which is usually called Syria in RSV.

ARAM-MAACAH: The name of the state of Maacah found in 1 Chr. 19:6.

ARAM-NAHARAIM: A Mesopotamian state mentioned in RSV only in Ps. 60 heading, where David's war with it is referred to. This may be an allusion to what is referred to in 1 Chr. 19:6, where the Hebrew has Aram-naharaim, but where RSV has **Mesopotamia** (as also in Gen. 24:10; Dt. 23:4, Jg. 3:8).

ARAM-ZOBAH: An Aramean state in **Syria**, mentioned in Ps. 60 heading. Elsewhere it is called **Zobah**.

ARARAH: *See* **Adadah**.

ARARAT: A country in the N. part of mod. **Armenia**, known from Assyrian inscriptions as *Urarṭu*. The Ark is said to have come to rest on the mountains of Ararat (Gen. 8:4), and the assassins of Sennacherib escaped to Ararat (2 Kg. 19:37; Isa. 37:38; Tob. 1:21). Elsewhere it is mentioned only in Jer. 51:27. Vulg. has **Armenia** in Gen. 8:4, and so LXX in Isa. 37:38.

ARAUNAH, THRESHING FLOOR OF: A site David bought to erect an altar on when the plague ended (2 Sam. 24:18), for the price of 50 shekels of silver (2 Sam. 24:24). 1 Chr. 21:25 gives the price as 600 shekels of gold, and says it was paid to Ornan (1 Chr. 21:15). The Temple of Solomon included this threshing floor in its site (2 Chr. 3:1).

ARBATTA: A Palestinian district from which Simon rescued some Jews (1 Mac. 5:23); possibly the same as **Arubboth**, mod. *'Arrâbeh*.

ARBELA: A district in which lay **Mesaloth**, where Bacchides encamped (1 Mac. 9:2). According to Josephus, Arbela was in **Galilee**, and it may be mod. *Khirbet Irbid*, overlooking *Wâdī Ḥamâm*, W. of **Lake Gennesaret**.

ARDAT: The name of a field of unknown location (2 Esd. 9:26).

AREOPAGUS (*'hill of Ares'* or *'Mars'*); A rocky hill at **Athens**, on which a court or council met. Paul was brought here (Ac. 17:19), and delivered a speech (Ac. 17:22ff.), which brought him ridicule from most of the members (Ac. 17:32), but one convert, named Dionysius (Ac. 17:34).

ARGOB: A region of the kingdom of **Og**, in **Bashan**, containing sixty fortified cities (Dt. 3:4f., 1 Kg. 4:13), and which was allotted to half the tribe of Manasseh (Dt. 3:13f.). Its location is variously proposed as **Trachonitis**, mod. *el-Lejā*, or the western slopes of *Jebel ed-Drûz*. In MT of 2 Kg. 14:25 Argob and **Arieh** appear to be personal names (so AV and RV), but RSV omits them as probably misplaced from verse 29.

ARIEH: *See* **Argob**. As a place name Arieh is unknown, but many scholars think it is a corruption of **Havvoth-jair**.

ARIEL: A name for **Jerusalem** (Isa. 29:1f., 7). It probably means *'altar hearth'* (cf. Ezek. 43:15f.) and it is found on the Moabite Stone. It is then used for Jerusalem since the Temple with its altar was there (cf. Isa. 31:9). In 2 Sam. 23:20; 1 Chr. 11:22 the meaning may also be *'altar hearth'*.

ARIMATHEA: The place from which Joseph, a member of the Sanhedrin, who asked Pilate for the body of Jesus, came (Mt. 27:57; Mk 15:43; Lk. 23:51; Jn 19:38); perhaps the same as **Ramathaim-zophim**, mod. *Rentis*. *See* **Ramah** (4).

ARMAGEDDON: The place where the great eschatological battle is to be fought (Rev. 16:16). The name is connected by many with Megiddo, where battles were anciently fought (Jg. 5:19; 2 Kg. 23:19), and where Hadad-rimmon was mourned (Zech. 12:11). RV has Har-Magedon, or 'mountain of Megiddo', but there is no reference elsewhere to a mountain of Megiddo.

ARMENIA: *See* Ararat.

ARNON: A river flowing into the Dead Sea from the E., which formed the N. boundary of Moab (Num. 21:13; Jg. 11:18) and the S. boundary of the Amorites (Num. 21:13) and of the kingdom of Sihon and later of the Israelites (Dt. 3:8, 16; Jos. 13:16). It is a swift stream and it flows through a deep gorge as it nears the Dead Sea. Mesha states on the Moabite Stone that he built a road by the Arnon.

AROER (? *'juniper'*): 1. A town on the N. bank of the Arnon (Dt. 2:36; Jos. 12:2, 13:9, 16; Jg. 11:26; 2 Kg. 10:33), taken by the Israelites from Sihon (Dt. 2:36, 4:48) and assigned to Reuben (Dt. 3:12; cf. 1 Chr. 5:8), but fortified by Gad (Num. 32:34). Here the census of David began (2 Sam. 24:5). When Hazael overran Transjordan, he occupied Aroer (2 Kg. 10:33. Mesha records on the Moabite Stone that he occupied and fortified it, and in the time of Jeremiah it appears still to have been Moabite (Jer. 48:19). Its site is mod. *'Arâ'ir.*

2. A town in Gad, E. of Rabbah (Jos. 13:35), and in the neighbourhood of Minnith (Jg. 11:33); its location is unknown.

3. A town in Judah (1 Sam. 30:28); perhaps called Adadah (for which Ararah should be read) in Jos. 15:22. It is mod. *Khirbet 'Ar'ârah.*

4. In Isa. 17:2 RSVm mentions an Aroer belonging to Damascus, which is unknown; but RSV and JB follow LXX in reading 'her cities will be deserted for ever', instead of 'the cities of Aroer shall be forsaken'.

ARPAD: A Syrian city, N. of Aleppo, always mentioned with Hamath as cities conquered by Assyria (2 Kg. 18:34, 19:13; Isa. 10:9, 36:19, 37:13; Jer. 49:23); mod. *Tell Erfâd.*

ARUBBOTH: A town in Solomon's third administrative district, near Socoh (3) and Hepher (1 Kg. 4:10); possibly the same as Arbatta, mod. *Arrâbeh.*

ARUMAH: A place where Abimelech retired when **Shechem** revolted (Jg. 9:31, 41); perhaps mod. *Khirbet el-'Ormah.*

ARVAD: A Phoenician city on an island N. of **Gebal** (Byblos). Its people are reckoned as Canaanites in Gen. 10:18 and 1 Chr. 1:16. Ezekiel refers to them as supplying rowers (Ezek. 27:8) and defenders (Ezek. 27:11) for **Tyre.** It is called **Aradus** in 1 Mac. 15:23. It is mod. *Erwâd.*

ARZARETH: A distant region whence the ten exiled northern tribes are to return (2 Esd. 13:45). It probably stands for *'ereṣ 'aḥereth,* i.e. 'another land' (cf. RSVm).

ASARAMEL: Apparently a place name on the memorial pillar for Simon (1 Mac. 14:28), but it probably stands for *śar 'am 'ēl,* 'the prince of the people of God' (a title for Simon), as in RSVm.

ASCALON: A coastal city of **Palestine,** whose people feared Holofernes (Jdt. 2:28); the same as **Ashkelon,** mod. *Khirbet 'Asqalân.*

ASHAN: A town of **Simeon** (Jos. 19:7; 1 Chr. 4:32), appointed a city of refuge (1 Chr. 6:69); called **Ain** in Jos. 21:16, and **Bor-ashan** in 1 Sam. 30:30. Since the tribe of Simeon was early absorbed in Judah, Ashan is also found located in **Judah** (Jos. 15:42). It is perhaps mod. *Khirber 'Asan.*

ASHDOD: A city reckoned to **Judah** (Jos. 15:46f.), but in which Anakim remained (Jos. 11:22) until it became one of the five Philistine cities (Jos. 13:3). When the Ark was captured, it was brought to the temple of Dagon here (1 Sam. 5:1ff.), and when it was returned, Ashdod sent a guilt offering (1 Sam. 6:17). Uzziah destroyed its walls (2 Chr. 26:6), and Sargon captured it (Isa. 20:1). Several prophets predicted disaster for it (Am. 1:8; Jer. 25:20; Zeph. 2:4; Zech. 9:6). It opposed Nehemiah (Neh. 4:7), and in his day many Jews married women of Ashdod (Neh. 13:23), and their children spoke the language of Ashdod (Neh. 13:24). In the Apocrypha and the NT it is called **Azotus.** It is mod. *Esdûd.*

ASHER: 1. The territory occupied by the tribe of Asher. Its ideal limits are stated in Jos. 19:25–30.

2. A town in Manasseh (Jos. 17:7), unless the meaning is that the territory of Manasseh stretched from the border of Asher (1).

3. In Tob. 1:2 Asher stands for Hazor (1), mod. *Tell el-Qedaḥ*.

ASHKELON: A city on the coast of **Palestine** said to have been taken by Judah (Jg. 1:18), but which was actually one of the five Philistine cities (Jos. 13:3). Samson killed thirty men from the city (Jg. 14:19), and when the Ark was returned to **Israel**, there was a guilt offering for Ashkelon (1 Sam. 6:17). In David's lament for Saul, Israel's disaster was thought of as good news for the foe (2 Sam. 1:20). Several prophets prophesied against the city (Am. 1:8; Jer. 25:30, 47:5, 7; Zeph. 2:4, 7; Zech. 9:5). It is called **Ascalon** in Jdt. 2:28 and **Askalon** in 1 Mac. 10:86, 11:60, 12:33). It is mod. *Khirbet 'Asqalân*.

ASHKENAZ: The country (Jer. 51:27), apparently near **Armenia**, inhabited by a people mentioned in Gen. 10:3; 1 Chr. 1:6, probably to be identified with the Scythians.

ASHNAH: 1. A town in **Judah** (Jos. 15:33); perhaps mod. *'Aslin*.

2. A town in **Judah** (Jos. 15:43); perhaps mod. *Idhnâ*.

ASHTAROTH: The city of Og, king of **Bashan** (Dt. 1:4; Jos. 9:10, 12:4, 13:12), which was assigned to E. **Manasseh** (Jos. 13:31) and became a Levitical city (1 Chr. 6:71; called **Be-eshterah** in Jos. 21:27). The name is a plural of the name of the Canaanite goddess, Ashtoreth, as Anathoth is the plural of Anath. (Ashtaroth is used for localized cults of the goddess in Jg. 2:13, 10:6; 1 Sam. 7:3f., 12:10, 31:10.) **Ashteroth-karnaim** (Gen. 14:5) is perhaps to be identified with Ashtaroth, and the site identified as *Tell 'Ashtarah*.

ASHTEROTH-KARNAIM: The place where Chedorlaomer defeated the Rephaim (Gen. 14:5). It is either the same as **Ashtaroth**, or very near it, and possibly the same as **Karnaim** (Am. 6:13) and **Carnaim** (1 Mac. 5:26, 43f.; 2 Mac. 12:21, 26).

ASIA: In the books of Maccabees this is used for the Seleucid dominions (1 Mac. 6:6, 11:13, 12:29, 13:32; 2 Mac. 3:3, 10:24). In 133 B.C., on the death of Attalus III, the Romans formed a province of Asia in the western part of Asia Minor, and this was enlarged in 116 B.C. by the addition of **Phrygia**. In Ac. 2:9f. Phrygia is distinguished from Asia, and so the narrower usage is implied, and this may be true throughout Acts (Ac. 6:9, 16:6, 19:10, 22, 26f., 20:4, 16, 18, 21:27, 24:18, 27:2), though this is not certain. All of Paul's references to Asia could be to the narrower region (Rom. 16:5; 1 C. 16:19; 2 C. 1:8; 2 Tim. 1:15) and the seven churches of Asia (Rev. 1:4) all are in the area covered by the narrower usage. In 1 Pet. 1:1 the wider usage may be intended.

ASKALON: The form of the name of **Ashkelon** found in 1 Mac. Jonathan encamped against the city, which surrendered to him (1 Mac. 10:86), and he was received there with honour (1 Mac. 11: 60). Later Simon marched to Askalon (1 Mac. 12:33). Herod the Great is said by Justin Martyr to have been born there.

ASPHAR: A pool in the **Wilderness of Tekoa** near which Jonathan and Simon encamped (1 Mac. 9:33). An identification with mod. *Bîr Selhûb* has been suggested.

ASSEMBLY, MOUNT OF: A mythical mountain 'in the far north', where the gods were thought to dwell, referred to in Isa. 14:13; cf. also Ps. 82:1, 6; Ezek. 28:16. Ps. 48:2 declares that **Zion** is the true mountain in the far north, since it is the dwelling place of the Lord.

ASSHUR: A city situated on the W. side of the **Tigris**, which was the capital of **Assyria**, to which it gave its name, until the seventh century B.C. (Ezek. 27:23); mod. *Qal'at Sherqât*. In Gen. 2:14 we should read **Asshur** for 'Assyria' (so JB).

ASSOS: A seaport of **Mysia**, where Paul embarked after going by land from **Troas** (Ac. 20:13f.); mod. *Berhamköy*.

ASSYRIA: A country through which flowed the river **Tigris** (Gen. 2:14, where **Asshur** should be read for 'Assyria') in its upper reaches, which became the imperial power figuring frequently in Israelite history. The city of **Nineveh**, which replaced Asshur as capital, is said to have been founded by Nimrod (Gen. 10:11). The eponymous ancestor of the Assyrians is represented as a son of Shem (Gen. 10:22; 1 Chr. 1:17). It was not until the ninth century B.C. that Israel began to feel the pressure of the now powerful and warlike Assyrian empire. In 853 B.C. a coalition of small states, which included a large contingent under Ahab, resisted Shalmaneser III at *Karkar*, and Ahab's sparing of Benhadad (1 Kg. 20:34) may have been due to the Assyrian threat. In 842 B.C. Jehu paid tribute to Shalmaneser. Both of these events are recorded in Assyrian inscriptions, but not in the OT, where the first Assyrian king to be named is Tiglath-pileser III (or Pul) (2 Kg. 15:19; 1 Chr. 5:26), who subjected Menahem to tribute (2 Kg. 15:19) and deported northern Israelites (2 Kg. 15:29ff.), and to whom Ahaz sent tribute (2 Kg. 16:7ff.; 2 Chr. 28:16ff.), despite the warning of Isaiah (Isa. 7:3ff.). Hoshea rebelled against Shalmaneser V, who besieged **Samaria** (1) (2 Kg. 17:3f., 18:9); this fell to Sargon, whose attack on **Ashdod** is mentioned in Isa. 20:1. When Samaria fell and numbers of people were deported, the northern kingdom came to an end. Hezekiah rebelled against Sargon's successor, Sennacherib (2 Kg. 18:7), whose forces invaded **Judah** (2 Kg. 18:13; Isa. 36:1) and reduced Hezekiah to submission (2 Kg. 18:14ff.), but **Jerusalem** was miraculously delivered (2 Kg. 19; Isa. 37). Sennacherib was murdered some years later (2 Kg. 19:37; Isa. 37:38). His successor, Esarhaddon, brought some foreign peoples to occupy Samaria (Ezr. 4:2; 1 Esd. 5:69). Esarhaddon's successor, Ashurbanipal, is mentioned as Osnappar, who also transferred foreigners to Samaria (Ezr. 4:10). He is also referred to, but not by name, as having taken Manasseh away in fetters (2 Chr. 33:10). When the Assyrian empire was collapsing, **Egypt** gave it support (2 Kg. 23:29), but too late to be effective. Nineveh fell in 612 B.C., and two years later **Haran**, to which the seat of government was moved, fell, and Assyria finally collapsed. The prophets of the eighth and seventh centuries (Amos, Hosea, Isaiah, Micah, Jeremiah and Zephaniah) issued many warnings against resistance to Assyria, though with no tenderness for the enemy (Isa. 10:5ff.), and the book of Nahum is a sustained song of triumph over the destruction of Nineveh. In the Apocrypha, Tobit is said to be descended from a captive of Shalmaneser (Tob. 1:2), and the legendary book of Judith is about Holofernes, who is said to have been the general of Nebuchadnezzar, wrongly called king of Assyria (Jdt. 1:1).

ATAD: A threshing-floor E. of the **Jordan**, where Joseph mourned for his father (Gen. 50:10f.); it was renamed **Abel-mizraim**. Its site is unknown.

ATAROTH: 1. A place near **Dibon**, which the men of **Gad** rebuilt (Num. 32:3, 34); mod. *Khirbet 'Aṭṭarûs*. On the Moabite Stone, Mesha says the men of Gad had long dwelt in Ataroth.

2. A town on the boundary of **Ephraim** (1) and **Benjamin** (Jos. 16:2); called **Ataroth-addar** in Jos. 16:5, 18:13. It is possibly mod. *Khirbet 'Aṭṭâra*.

3. Another town on the boundary of **Ephraim** (1) (Jos. 16:7), probably mod. *Tell el-Mazar*.

ATAROTH-ADDAR: A town on the boundary of **Ephraim** (1) and **Benjamin** (Jos. 16:5, 18:13); called **Ataroth** in Jos. 16:2. It is possibly mod. *Khirbet 'Aṭṭâra*.

ATHACH: A town in S. **Judah** to which David sent gifts (1 Sam. 30:30); perhaps the same as **Ether** (2), mod. *Khirbet 'Attîr*.

ATHARIM: An unknown place, where the king of **Arad** attacked the Israelites (Num. 21:1).

ATHENS: The centre of Greek culture, where Paul preached (Ac. 17:15ff.) and where he argued in the market place (Ac. 17:17). He was brought before the council of the **Areopagus** (Ac. 17:19ff.), where he made his defence, winning one convert (Ac. 17:34) and making many scoffers (Ac. 17:32). Apparently Timothy joined him in Athens, but was sent back to **Thessalonica** (1 Th. 3:1), and later rejoined him in **Corinth** (Ac. 18:5).

ATROTH-BETH-JOAB: An unknown place near Bethlehem (1), personified as a descendant of Judah (1 Chr. 2:54).

ATROTH-SHOPHAN: An unknown place in **Gad** (Num. 32:35).

ATTALIA: A seaport of **Pamphylia**, from which Paul and Barnabas sailed when they returned to **Antioch** (1) from their first missionary journey (Ac. 14:25f.); mod. *Adalia*.

AVEN: A name which stands for **Beth-aven** (Hos. 4:15, 5:8, 10:5) in Hos. 10:8. **Bethel** (1) is intended (cf. the references to the 'calf'), but Bethel is distinguished from Beth-aven in Jos. 7:2. In the Hosea passages *'āwen* ('iniquity') is a derogatory substitute for *'el* ('God').

AVEN, VALLEY OF: A valley near **Damascus** (Am. 1:5); probably mod. *el-Beqa'*, between the **Lebanon** and the **Anti-Lebanon**.

AVITH: A place in Edom (Gen. 36:35; 1 Chr. 1:46); possibly mod. *Khirbet el-Jiththeh*.

AVVA: A place from which the Assyrians brought settlers to Samaria (1) (2 Kg. 17:24, 31); probably the same as Ivvah (2 Kg. 18:34, 19:13). It is possibly mod. *Tell Kefr ʿAyā*.

AVVIM: A town in Benjamin (Jos. 18:23); perhaps the same as Aiath.

AYYAH: A place in Ephraim (1) (1 Chr. 7:28); probably the same as Aiath.

AZEKAH: A town in Judah in the lowland (Jos. 15:35), overlooking the Valley of Elah (1 Sam. 17:1f.). Joshua pursued the defeated Canaanite kings to Azekah (Jos. 10:10f.). It was fortified by Rehoboam (2 Chr. 11:9), and it and Lachish held out against Nebuchadrezzar longer than any other city except Jerusalem (Jer. 34:7), but it seems to have fallen before Lachish, since reference is made in the Lachish letters to the cessation of the fire-signals from Azekah. After the exile it was resettled (Neh. 11:30). It is mod. *Tell Zakarîyeh*.

AZMAVETH: A place in Benjamin, from which some returning exiles traced their descent (Ezr. 2:24), and which was resettled (Neh. 12:29); called Beth-azmaveth in Neh. 7:28 and Beth-asmoth in 1 Esd. 5:18. It is probably mod. *Ḥizmeh*.

AZMON: A place in Judah (Num. 34:4f.; Jos. 15:4); possibly mod. *ʿAin el-Quseimeh*.

AZNOTH-TABOR: A place in Naphtali (Jos. 19:34), near Mount Tabor; possibly mod. *Umm Jebeil*.

AZOTUS: The Greek form of the name of Ashdod, found in the Apocrypha (Jdt. 2:28; 1 Mac. 4:15, 9:15) and in the NT. Judas (1 Mac. 5:68) and Jonathan (1 Mac. 10:83ff.) sacked the town and John Hyrcanus (1 Mac. 16:10) did the same. After his encounter with the Ethiopian eunuch, Philip, one of the Seven, went to Azotus and from there to Caesarea (Ac. 8:40).

B

BAAL: A place in **Simeon** (1 Chr. 4:33); called **Baalath-beer** in Jos. 19:8. Its site is unknown.

BAALAH: 1. A place in **Judah**, identified with **Kiriath-jearim** (Jos. 15:9f.; 1 Chr. 13:6); mod. *Tell el-Azhar*.

2. A place in S. **Judah** (Jos. 15:29); called **Balah** in Jos. 19:3 and **Bilhah** in 1 Chr. 4:29. It is possibly mod. *Tulûl el-Medhbah*.

BAALAH: On the border of **Judah**, between **Shikkeron** and **Jabneel** (Jos. 15:11); perhaps mod. *Mughâr*.

BAALATH: 1. A place in **Dan** (1) (Jos. 19:44). Its site is unknown.

2. A place fortified by Solomon (1 Kg. 9:18; 2 Chr. 8:6); possibly the same as 1.

BAALATH-BEER: A place in **Simeon**, identified with **Ramah of the Negeb** (Jos. 19:8); called **Baal** in 1 Chr. 4:33, and perhaps the same as **Bealoth** (1) in Jos. 15:24. Its site is unknown.

BAALE-JUDAH: A place from which the Ark was brought (2 Sam. 6:2), and so probably the same as **Kiriath-jearim**, mod. *Tell el-Azhar*. *See* **Baalah** (1).

BAAL-GAD (? *'Baal of good fortune'*): A place in the **Valley of Lebanon**, the N. limit of Joshua's conquest (Jos. 11:17, 12:7, 13:5); perhaps mod. *Ḥāṣbeiyah*.

BAAL-HAMON (*'Baal of abundance'*): The site of Solomon's vineyard (Ca. 8:11), of unknown location.

BAAL-HAZOR (? *'possessor of a court'*): A place where Amnon was killed (2 Sam. 13:23ff.); probably mod. *Jebel el 'Aṣûr*.

BAAL-HERMON (*'Baal of Hermon'*): A place on the slopes of Mount **Hermon** (Jg. 3:3), in E. **Manasseh** (1 Chr. 5:23). Its location is unknown.

BAAL-MEON (*'Baal of habitation'*): A town in Reuben (Num. 32:38), occupied by the family of Bela (1 Chr. 5:8); mentioned as Moabite in Ezek. 25:9. It is called Beth-baal-meon in Jos. 13:17, Beth-meon in Jer. 48:23, and Beon in Num. 32:3. It is mod. *Ma'în*. On the Moabite Stone Baal-meon and Beth-baal-meon are found, and the town was Moabite then (ninth century B.C.).

BAAL-PEOR (*'Baal of Peor'*): A place where Israel suffered punishment for defection from God (Dt. 4:3; Hos. 9:10); probably the same as Beth-peor, mod. *Khirbet esh-Sheikh-Jâyil*. In Num. 25:3 'the Baal of Peor' is the god worshipped here (so Num. 25:5, 31:16; Ps. 106:28), called simply Peor in Num. 25:18.

BAAL-PERAZIM (*'Baal of breaches'*): A place where David defeated the Philistines (2 Sam. 5:20; 1 Chr. 14:11); cf. Mount Perazim (Isa. 28:21). It is probably mod. *Sheikh Bedr* or *Râs en-Nâdir*.

BAAL-SHALISHAH: A place from which a man brought firstfruits to Elisha, with which he fed 100 men (2 Kg. 4:42ff.); probably mod. *Kefr Thilth*. See Shalishah.

BAAL-TAMAR (*'Baal of the palm'*): A place from which Gibeah was attacked (Jg. 20:33). Its site is unknown.

BAAL-ZEPHON (*'Baal of the north'*): A place in Egypt, near which the Israelites crossed the Red Sea (Exod. 14:2, 9; Num. 33:7). The god after whom the place was named figures in the *Râs Shamrā* texts, and was later known as Zeus Kasios and worshipped on Mt. Casius, near *Râs Shamrā*. Hence the location of Egyptian Baal-zephon at Greco-Roman *Casium* (mod. *Râs Kasiun*) has been suggested. But other locations have also been proposed.

BABEL: A city of Nimrod's kingdom (Gen. 10:10), where the Tower of Babel was built (Gen. 11:4ff.); the same as Babylon. By the 'Tower of Babel' was probably meant the temple of Marduk in the city.

BABYLON, BABYLONIA: Babylon was a very ancient city which became the capital of the dynasty of which Hammurabi was the sixth ruler, and the name of which stands frequently in the OT for the lower Mesopotamian country of Babylonia. This comprised Sumer and Accad, two areas originally ethnically and linguistically distinct. For much of the OT period it was controlled by **Assyria**, but became independent again under Nabopolassar, who founded the Neo-Babylonian (or Chaldean) empire, which absorbed the western part of the Assyrian empire and conquered **Palestine**, giving place later to the Persian empire. There are very many references to the city or country in the Bible. For its founding and Tower, see **Babel**. After the fall of **Samaria** (1) the king of Assyria brought people from Babylon to settle in Samaria (2 Kg. 17:24, 30), and in the reign of Hezekiah Merodach-baladan, who led an abortive rebellion against Assyria and temporarily made himself king of Babylon, sent an embassy to **Judah** to foment rebellion there (2 Kg. 20:12ff.; Isa. 39:1ff.). Manasseh is said to have been taken in fetters to Babylon by the king of Assyria (2 Chr. 23:10ff.). When the Assyrian empire was collapsing and Babylon became independent under Nabopolassar, the king's son, Nebuchadrezzar (often called Nebuchadnezzar), led the army against the remnants of Assyrian power and their ally Egypt, and defeated them at **Carchemish** (Jer. 46:2; 2 Chr. 35:20), thus bringing Palestine under his control in the time of Jehoiakim (2 Kg. 24:1). When Jehoiakim rebelled, Babylon moved against him, but before the army reached **Jerusalem**, Jehoiachin had succeeded to the throne. He swiftly surrendered and was taken prisoner to Babylon along with many of the people (2 Kg. 24:1–16; 2 Chr. 36:6–10), amongst them Ezekiel (Ezek. 1:2). When later Zedekiah rebelled (2 Kg. 24:20; 2 Chr. 36:13), the Babylonians came again and after a long siege destroyed Jerusalem and took large numbers into exile, and the kingdom of Judah came to an end (2 Kg. 25:1–21; 2 Chr. 36:11–21). Jeremiah, who had frequently declaimed against the folly of resisting Babylon (Jer. 20:4ff., 25:8ff., 27:4ff., 32:1ff.), and who was arrested as a traitor (Jer. 37:11ff.), was offered the chance to go to Babylon, but chose to remain (Jer. 40:2ff.). He wrote a letter to the exiles in Babylon (Jer. 29:1ff.) and the book of Baruch (Bar. 1:1) and the Letter of Jeremiah (6:1) are said to have been sent to Babylon. Ezekiel in Babylonia had also predicted the fall of Jerusalem (Ezek. 12:10ff., 17:12ff., 21:24ff., 24:1ff.). He also predicted disaster for **Tyre** (Ezek. 26:7ff.) and for **Egypt** (Ezek. 29:18ff., 30:10ff., 24ff., 32:11ff.; cf. Jer. 46:13ff.) at the hands of the Babylonians. The successor of Nebuchadrezzar, Evil-merodach, freed Jehoiachin from prison (2 Kg. 25:27ff., Jer. 52:31ff.), but after a short reign was succeeded by Neriglissar (perhaps the same as the officer Nergal-sharezer of Jer. 39:3, 13f.). After a few years Nabonidus usurped the throne of Babylon, but through most of his reign left the administration of the state in the hands of his son Belshazzar, who is wrongly called king (Dan. 5:1, 8:1) and son of Nebuchadnezzar (Dan. 5:11) in Daniel. This reign saw the rise of Cyrus, and the Jews in Babylonia eagerly looked forward to the fall of Babylon. From this time probably date Isa. 13:1–14:23; Jer. 50f., and Isa. 43:14ff., 47:1ff., 48:14ff., and all the encouraging hopes of deliverance that abound in Isa. 40ff., hopes that were fulfilled after Cyrus had destroyed the Babylonian empire. The Persian kings retained Babylon as one of their royal cities, and so Cyrus (Ezr. 5:13) and Artaxerxes (Neh. 13:6) are called kings of Babylon. Similarly Babylon belonged to the kingdom of the Seleucids and it is recorded that Antiochus Epiphanes went there (1 Mac. 6:4). In the NT Babylon sometimes refers to this same city (Mt. 1:11, 12, 17; Ac. 7:43), but in the book of Revelation it is a symbol for **Rome** (Rev. 14:8, 16:19, 17:5, 18:2, 10, 21), and so probably in 1 Pet. 5:13. The Apocalypse of Ezra is represented as received in a vision in Babylon (2 Esd. 3:1), and here again it is possible that Rome is meant.

BACA, VALLEY OF: An allegorical name (from a root meaning 'weep') found in Ps. 84:6.

BAHARUM: A place from which Azmaveth came (1 Chr. 11:33); called **Bahurim** in 2 Sam. 23:31.

BAHURIM: A place in **Benjamin**, to which Paltiel accompanied Michal (2 Sam. 31:16). Here Shimei lived (2 Sam. 16:5; 1 Kg. 2:8), and from this place Azmaveth came (2 Sam. 23:31; called **Baharum** in 1 Chr. 11:33). Here Jonathan and Ahimaaz hid in a well (2 Sam. 17:18). It is probably mod. *Râs et-Tmîm. See* **Horonaim** (2).

BALAH: A place in **Simeon** (Jos. 19:3); called **Bilhah** in 1 Chr. 4:29, and **Baalah** (2) in **Judah**, which early absorbed Simeon, in Jos. 15:29. It is probably mod. *Tulûl el-Medhbaḥ.*

BALAMON: A place near **Dothan** (Jdt. 8:3); probably the same as **Belmain** (Jdt. 4:4) and **Balbaim** (Jdt. 7:3). *See* **Belmain**.

BALBAIM: *See* **Balamon**.

BAMOTH ('*high places*'): A station in the Wilderness wanderings (Num. 21:19f.); probably the same as **Bamoth-baal**.

BAMOTH-BAAL ('*high places of Baal*'): A town in **Reuben** (Jos. 13:17). Here Balaam was brought (Num. 22:41). It is possibly mod. *Khirbet el-Quweiqîyeh.*

BASHAN: A district E. of the **Sea of Galilee**, formerly the king-dom of Og (Num. 21:33, 32:33; Dt. 1:4, 3:1ff., 4:47 +), conquered by Israel and assigned to **Manasseh** (Jos. 13:30, 17:5, 22:7), though later part is said to be in **Gad** (1 Chr. 5:11, 16). It contained the Levitical cities of **Golan** and **Be-eshterah** (Jos. 21:27; cf. 1 Chr. 6:71), the former being also a city of refuge (Dt. 4:43; Jos. 20:8). It belonged to Solomon's sixth district (I Kg. 4:13) and in the reign of Jehu was annexed by Hazael (2 Kg. 10:33). It was famous for its mountains (Ps. 68:15; cf. Jer. 22:20), oak trees (Isa. 2:13; Ezek. 27:6; Zech. 11:2), lions (Dt. 33:22), flocks and herds (Dt. 32:14; Ps. 22:12; Ezek. 38:19; Am. 4:1), its pastures and foliage (Jer. 50:19; Isa. 33:9; Neh. 1:4).

BASKAMA: A town in **Gilead** (1), where Jonathan was buried (1 Mac. 13:23); possibly mod. *el-Jummeizeh.*

BATH-RABBIM: A gate in **Heshbon** (Ca. 7:4).

BEALOTH: 1. A place in **Judah** (Jos. 15:24); possibly the same as **Baalath-beer** (Jos. 19:8, which is assigned to **Simeon**, which was early absorbed in Judah). Its site is unknown.
2. A place in Solomon's ninth district (1 Kg. 4:16), of unknown location.

BEAUTIFUL GATE: A gate of the Temple mentioned in Ac. 3:2, 10 as the scene of the healing of the lame man by Peter and John. It is probable that this was the gate of Corinthian bronze which Josephus describes as outside the sanctuary, leading into the Court of the Women.

BECTILETH: A plain between **Nineveh** and Upper **Cilicia** (Jdt. 2:21), of unknown location.

BEER ('*well*'); 1. A stopping-place in the Wilderness wanderings, between the **Arnon** and the **Jordan** (Num. 21:16); perhaps the same as **Beer-elim** (Isa. 15:8). Its location is unknown.

2. The place to which Jotham escaped (Jg. 9:21), possibly mod. *Khirbet el-Bîreh*.

BEER-ELIM (? '*well of leaders*', or '*well of terebinths*'): A town of Moab (Isa. 15:8), of unknown location; possibly the same as **Beer** (1) (Num. 21:16).

BEER-LAHAI-ROI ('*well of the living one who sees me*'): A well where Hagar was met by an angel (Gen. 16:7ff.). Here Isaac met Rebekah (Gen. 24:62ff.), and here he dwelt after Abraham died (Gen. 25:11).

BEEROTH ('*wells*'): A Gibeonite town (Jos. 9:17), within the borders of **Benjamin** (Jos. 18:25; 2 Sam. 4:2). From it came the murderer of Ish-bosheth (2 Sam. 4:2) and Joab's armour-bearer (2 Sam. 23:37). At an unknown time its people fled to **Gittaim** (2 Sam. 4:3). Some of the returning exiles traced their descent from here (Ezr. 2:25; Neh. 7:29; 1 Esd. 5:19). It is perhaps mod. *el-Bîreh*.

BEEROTH BENE-JAAKAN ('*wells of the sons of Jaakan*'): A stopping-place in the Wilderness wanderings (Dt. 10:6); called **Bene-Jaakan** in Num. 33:31f. It is possibly mod. *Birein*.

BEERSHEBA ('*well of the oath*', or '*well of the seven*'): An important city of the **Negeb**. It was visited by Abraham (Gen. 21:31), who planted a tree there (Gen. 21:33). From here Hagar and her child were sent away (Gen. 21:14), and near here an angel came to her (Gen. 21:17). Isaac came here (Gen. 26:23), and experienced a theophany (Gen. 26:24); he built an altar (Gen. 26:25), and dug a well (Gen. 26:32f.). Jacob set out from Beersheba to seek a wife (Gen. 28:10) and later experienced a theophany here (Gen. 46:1ff.). It was reckoned to **Simeon** (Jos. 19:2) but later to **Judah** (Jos. 15:28) which early absorbed Simeon. Samuel's sons were judges here (1 Sam. 8:2). When Elijah fled from Jezebel he came here (1 Kg. 19:3), and near here experienced a theophany (1 Kg. 19:5). The mother of Joash was from Beersheba (2 Kg. 12:1). It was regarded as the southern boundary of the land (cf. 'from **Dan** (2) to Beersheba', Jg. 20:1 +). Its shrine was long an important one and it was visited by people from N. **Israel** (cf. Am. 5:5, 8:14). After the exile it was resettled (Neh. 11:27, 30). It is mod. *Tell es-Seba'*.

BE-ESHTERAH: A Levitical city in E. **Manasseh** (Jos. 21:27); called **Ashtaroth** in 1 Chr. 6:71. It is probably mod. *Tell 'Ashtarah.*

BELA: Alternative name of **Zoar** (Gen. 14:2, 8), one of the **Cities of the Valley.**

BELMAIN: A place mentioned in Jdt. 4:4; called **Balbaim** in Jdt. 7:3, and **Balamon** in Jdt. 8:3. It was near **Dothan** (Jdt. 7:3, 8:3), but its location is uncertain. It has been suggested that it is the same as **Ibleam** or **Bileam.**

BENE-BERAK: A place in **Dan** (1) (Jos. 19:45); mod. *Ibn Ibrâq.*

BENE-JAAKAN: A stopping-place in the Wilderness wanderings (Num. 33:31f.); called **Beeroth Bene-Jaakan** in Dt. 10:6; possibly mod. *Birein.*

BENJAMIN: The territory occupied by the tribe of Benjamin. Its ideal limits are stated in Jos. 18:11–28.

BENJAMIN GATE: A gate in **Jerusalem**, mentioned in Jer. 17:19, 20:2, 38:7, where Jeremiah was arrested as he was leaving the city (Jer. 37:13). It is mentioned in Zech. 14:10 as belonging to the stretch of the wall which went to the **Corner Gate.** It is possibly the same as the **Muster Gate.**

BEON: A town in **Reuben** (Num. 32:3); called **Baal-meon** in Num. 32:38, **Beth-baal-meon** in Jos. 13:17, and **Beth-meon** in Jer. 48:23. It is mod. *Ma'în.*

BERACAH, VALLEY OF (*'valley of blessing'*): A valley where Jehoshaphat gave thanks for victory (2 Chr. 20:26); probably mod. *Wâdî el-'Arrub*, near *Khirbet Bereikût.*

BEREA: A place to which Bacchides marched against Judas (1 Mac. 9:4). Some MSS have *Beērzath*, which is perhaps **Birzaith**, about 15 miles N. of **Jerusalem**, where Josephus says Judas pitched his last camp. Mod. *Bîr ez-Zeit.*

BERED: An unidentified place near **Beer-lahai-roi** (Gen. 16:14).

BEROEA: 1. A town in **Macedonia** in which Paul preached (Ac. 17:10ff.). The Jews here examined the Scriptures and many believed. Sopater was a native of the city (Ac. 20:4). It is mod. *Verria*.

2. The place where Menelaus was killed (2 Mac. 13:4ff.). It is the Greek name of *Aleppo*; mod. *Ḥaleb*.

BEROTHAH: A place on the northern boundary of Ezekiel's ideal restoration of the kingdom (Ezek. 47:17), between **Damascus** and **Hamath**; perhaps the same as **Berothai** (2 Sam. 8:8); mod. *Bereitân*.

BEROTHAI: A city of **Syria**, belonging to **Zobah**, which David took (2 Sam. 8:8); called **Cun** in 1 Chr. 18:8. It is perhaps the same as **Berothah** (Ezek. 47:17); possibly mod. *Bereitân*.

BESOR, BROOK: A stream S. or SW. of **Ziklag** (2 Sam. 30:9f., 21); perhaps mod. *Wâdî Ghazzeh*.

BETAH: A city belonging to **Zobah** which David took (2 Sam. 8:8); called **Tibhath** in 1 Chr. 18:8. Its site is unknown.

BETEN: A place in **Asher** (1) (Jos. 19:25); possibly mod. *Abṭûn*.

BETH-ANOTH ('*house of Anath*'): A town in **Naphtali** (Jos. 19:38), whose inhabitants successfully resisted the Israelites (Jg. 1:33); possibly mod. *el-Ba'neh*.

BETH-ANOTH ('*house of Anath*'): A place in **Judah** (Jos. 15:59); perhaps the same as **Bethany** (3) (Jdt. 1:9). It is possibly mod. *Khirbet Beit 'Ainûn*, N. of **Hebron**.

BETHANY: 1. A village less than two miles from **Jerusalem** on the Mount of Olives, on the way to **Jericho** (Jn 11:18), close to **Bethphage** (Mk 11:1; Lk. 19:29. Here Martha and Mary and Lazarus lived (Jn 11:1), and here Lazarus was restored to life (Jn 11:43f.). Jesus lodged in Bethany when He came to the Passover (Mt. 21:17; Mk 11:11f.). In Bethany He was entertained by Simon the Leper, when His feet were anointed (Mt. 26:6ff.; Mk 14:3ff.; Jn 12:1ff.). At Bethany the Ascension took place (Lk. 24:50); it is mod. *el- 'Azariyeh*.

2. The place where John baptized (Jn 1:28); possibly the same as Beth-barah (Jg. 7:24). Its site is unknown.

3. A place apparently S. of Jerusalem (Jdt. 1:9); possibly the same as Beth-anoth (Jos. 15:59); perhaps mod. *Khirbet Beit 'Ainûn*.

BETH-ARABAH: A place in the wilderness of Judah (Jos. 15:6, 61; 18:18, 22), possibly mod. *'Ain el-Gharabeh*.

BETH-ARBEL: A place said to have been destroyed by Shalman in battle (Hos. 10:14); perhaps *Irbid* in Gilead (1).

BETH-ASHBEA: An else unknown place, occupied by Judahite linen workers (1 Chr. 4:21).

BETH-ASMOTH: A place in Benjamin, from which some returning exiles traced their descent (1 Esd. 5:18); called Azmaveth in Ezr. 2:24; Neh. 12:29, and Beth-azmaveth in Neh. 7:28. It is probably mod. *Ḥizmeh*.

BETH-AVEN (*'house of iniquity'*): A place near Ai (1) (Jos. 7:2), in the wilderness (Jos. 18:2), and W. of Michmash (1 Sam. 13:5). It is mentioned in Hos. 5:8, and called Aven in Hos. 10:8. In the latter and in Hos. 4:15 **Bethel** (1) is meant, and *'āwen* ('iniquity') is a derogatory substitute for *'ēl* ('God'). In fact, though Beth-aven was near Bethel, it was distinct from it (Jos. 7:2).

BETH-AZMAVETH: A place in Benjamin, from which some returning exiles traced their descent (Neh. 7:28); called Azmaveth in Ezr. 2:24; Neh. 12:29, and Beth-asmoth in 1 Esd. 5:18. It is probably mod. *Ḥizmeh*.

BETH-BAAL-MEON: A town in Reuben (Jos. 13:17); called Baal-meon in Num. 32:38, Beth-meon in Jer. 48:23, and Beon in Num. 32:3. It is mod. *Ma'în*.

BETH-BARAH: An unlocated place in the Jordan valley, occupied by Gideon (Jg. 7:24).

BETH-BASI: A place in the wilderness occupied by Jonathan and Simon and attacked by Bacchides (1 Mac. 6:62ff.); it is mod. *Khirbet Beit Baṣṣā*.

BETH-BIRI: A place in **Simeon** (1 Chr. 4:21); called **Beth-lebaoth** in Jos. 19:6. Its location is unknown.

BETH-CAR (*'house of a lamb'*): A place to which Israel pursued the Philistines (1 Sam. 7:11); its location is unknown.

BETH-DAGON (*'house of Dagon'*): 1. A place in **Judah** in the lowland (Jos. 15:41); perhaps mod. *Khirbet Dajûn.*
  2. A place on the border of **Asher** (1) (Jos. 16:27); possibly mod. *Jelâmet el-Aṭîqah.*
  3. The name of the temple of Dagon in **Azotus**, burned by Jonathan (1 Mac. 10:83f.).

BETH-DIBLATHAIM (*'house of two fig-cakes'*): A place in **Moab** (Jer. 48:22), mentioned on the Moabite Stone; probably the same as **Almon-diblathaim** (Num. 33:46f.). It is perhaps mod. *Khirbet Deleilât esh-Sherqîyeh* or *Deleilât el-Gharbîyeh*, which form a twin site.

BETH-EDEN: A region associated with **Damascus** (Am. 1:5), referred to as *Bit Adini* in Assyrian inscriptions; probably the same as **Eden** (2 Kg. 19:12; Isa. 37:12; Ezek. 27:23).

BETH-EKED (*'house of shearing'*): A place between **Jezreel** and **Samaria** (1), where Jehu slew the kinsmen of Ahaziah (2 Kg. 10:12ff.); perhaps mod. *Beit Qâd*, near *Jenîn.*

BETHEL (*'house of God'*): 1. A city W. of Ai (1) (Gen. 12:18), originally called **Luz** (Gen. 28:19; 35:6; Jos. 18:13; Jg. 1:23). Abraham twice encamped between Bethel and Ai (Gen. 12:8, 13:3), and here Jacob dreamed (Gen. 28:11ff.) and later experienced another theophany (Gen. 35:6ff.). Its conquest is not recorded in Joshua, but in Jg. 1:22ff. the house of Joseph is said to have conquered it. It was assigned to Joseph according to Jos. 16:1, but to **Benjamin** according to Jos. 18:22. An important shrine stood here (Jg. 20:18, 26; 21:2; 1 Sam. 10:3), and when the kingdom was divided, this became a royal shrine for the north in which one of the bull calves was put (1 Kg. 12:29), and to which the man of God from Judah (1 Kg. 13:1ff.), and later Amos (Am. 7:10ff.) came to prophesy. Samuel judged Israel here (1 Sam. 7:16), and in the time of Elijah there were prophets here (2 Kg. 2:2f.). The worship of Bethel is frequently condemned (2 Kg. 10:29; 17:16; 2 Chr. 11:15, 13:8f.; Am. 3:14;

4:4; 5:5f.; Hos. 4:15, here called **Bethaven**), and in the reform of Josiah the shrine and its altar were destroyed (2 Kg. 23:15ff.). One of the priests taken into exile by **Assyria** and sent back was at Bethel (2 Kg. 17:28), and after the exile some who returned traced their descent from here (Ezr. 2:28; Neh. 7:32; 1 Esd. 5:21) and it was resettled (Neh. 11:31). It was fortified by Bacchides (1 Mac. 9:50). It is called Beth-aven in Jos. 7:2, 18:12; 1 Sam. 13:5; Hos. 5:8, and **Aven** in Hos. 10:8. It is mod. *Beitîn*.

2. A place in S. **Judah** to which David sent spoil (1 Sam. 30:27); the same as **Bethul** (Jos. 19:4), **Bethuel** (1 Chr. 4:30), and **Chesil** (Jos. 15:30). It is possibly mod. *Khirbet er-Râs*.

BETH-EMEK (*'house of the valley'*): A place in **Asher** (1) (Jos. 19:27); perhaps mod. *Tell Mîmâs*.

BETHER: A place in the hill country of **Judah** (Jos. 15:59, in an addition in LXX and JB, not in MT and RSV).

BETHESDA: A pool in **Jerusalem**, where Jesus healed an invalid man (Jn 5:2 RSVm and NEB). The better attested reading is **Beth-zatha** (so RSV and JB).

BETH-EZEL: A place in **Judah** (Mic. 1:11); perhaps mod. *Deir el-ʿAṣal*, near **Debir**.

BETH-GABER (*? 'house of the wall'*): A place in **Judah**, near **Bethlehem** (1) and **Kiriath-jearim** (1 Chr. 2:52), of unknown location; possibly the same as **Geder** (Jos. 12:13).

BETH-GAMUL (*'house of reward'*): A place in **Moab** (Jer. 48:23); mod. *Khirbet Jumeil*.

BETH-GILGAL: A place resettled after the exile (Neh. 12:29); perhaps the same as **Gilgal** (1) or **Gilgal** (5).

BETH-HACCHEREM (*'place of the vineyard'*): A town in **Judah** (Jer. 6:1), the chief town of a district (Neh. 3:14); probably mod. *Khirbet Sâliḥ*.

BETH-HAGGAN (*'house of the garden'*): A place towards which Ahaziah was going when he was murdered (2 Kg. 9:27); probably the same as **En-gannim** (2) (Jos. 19:21, 21:29); mod. *Jenîn*.

BETH-HANAN: *See* Elon-beth-hanan.

BETH-HARAM: A place in **Gad** in the **Jordan** valley (Jos. 13:27), called **Beth-haran** in Num. 32:36; mod. *Tell Iktanû*.

BETH-HARAN: *See* Beth-haram.

BETH-HOGLAH (*'house of the partridge'*): A place in **Benjamin** (Jos. 18:21), on the border between Benjamin and **Judah** (Jos. 15:6, 18:19); mod. *'Ain Ḥajlah*.

BETH-HORON: The name of two neighbouring places, Upper Beth-horon (mod. *Beit 'Ûr el-Foqā*) and Lower Beth-horon (mod. *Beit 'Ûr'et-Taḥtâ*), near which Joshua defeated the Canaanite kings (Jos. 10:10ff.). They were allotted to **Ephraim** (1) (Jos. 16:3, 5; 1 Chr. 7:34) and were not far from the border of **Benjamin** (Jos. 18:13f.), and one was a Levitical city (Jos. 21:22). Both were fortified by Solomon (1 Kg. 9:17; 2 Chr. 8:5). Beth-horon was attacked with much slaughter by Ephraimites in the time of Amaziah, when it seems to have been reckoned to **Judah** (2 Chr. 25:13). Here Judas defeated Seron (1 Mac. 3:13ff.) and Nicanor (1 Mac. 7:39ff.), but it was occupied and fortified by Bacchides (1 Mac. 9:50). The Jews are said to have occupied Beth-horon against the approach of Holofernes (Jdt. 4:4f.).

BETH-JESHIMOTH (*'house of the desert'*): A place within the kingdom of Sihon (Jos. 12:3), where the Israelites encamped in the plains of **Moab** (Num. 33:49). It was allotted to **Reuben** (Jos. 13:20), but was later in Moabite hands (Ezek. 25:9). It is perhaps mod. *Tell el-'Azeimeh*.

BETH-LE-APHRAH (*'house of dust'*): Apparently a Philistine town (Mic. 1:10), of unknown location. There is a play on words in the Micah passage.

BETH-LEBAOTH (*'house of lions'*): A place in **Simeon** (Jos. 19:6); called **Beth-biri** in 1 Chr. 4:31. It is probably the same as **Lebaoth** (Jos. 15:32). Its location is unknown.

BETHLEHEM (*'house of bread'*) 1. A city in **Judah** (Jg. 17:7, 19:1; Ru. 1:1; 1 Sam. 17:12), some of whose people were called Ephrathites (Ru. 1:2; 1 Sam. 17:12; *see* **Ephrath**). From Bethlehem came

Micah's Levite (Jg. 17:7ff.) and the concubine of another Levite (Jg. 19:1), whose mishandling in **Gibeah** led to internecine war in Israel (Jg. 19f.). Elimelech was from Bethlehem (Ru. 1:1f.), which is the scene of most of the book of Ruth, leading to the birth of David's grandfather (Ru. 4:17). In Bethlehem David was anointed by Samuel (1 Sam. 16:1ff.). From Bethlehem, too, came Asahel, who was buried here (2 Sam. 2:32); also Elhanan (2 Sam. 21:19, 23:24). Moving is the story of David's desiring water from the well of Bethlehem and its sequel (2 Sam. 23:14ff.; 1 Chr. 11:16ff.). Rehoboam fortified Bethlehem (2 Chr. 11:6). Some of the returning exiles traced their descent from Bethlehem (Ezr. 2:21; Neh. 7:26; 1 Esd. 5:17). Micah predicted the rise of the expected Davidic Messiah from Bethlehem (Mic. 5:2; cf. Jn 7:42), and Mt. 2:5f. cites this, and sees in the birth of Jesus the fulfilment of the hope. Both accounts of the birth of Jesus (Mt. 2:1ff.; Lk. 2:4ff.) place it in Bethlehem. It still retains its name. mod. *Beit Laḥm*, about 5 miles S. of **Jerusalem**.

2. A town in **Zebulun** (Jos. 19:15), form which Ibzan came (Jg. 12:8) and where he was buried (Jg. 12:10). It is mod. *Beit Laḥm*, about 7 miles NW. of **Nazareth**.

BETH-MAACAH (*'house of Maacah'*): *See* **Abel-beth-Maacah**.

BETH-MARCABOTH (*'house of chariots'*): A place in **Simeon** (Jos. 19:5; 1 Chr. 4:31); probably the same as **Madmannah** (Jos. 15:31) in **Judah**, which early absorbed Simeon. It is perhaps mod. *Umm Deimneh*.

BETH-MEON (*'house of habitation'*): A Moabite city (Jer. 48:23), formerly in **Reuben**. *See* **Baal-meon**.

BETH-MILLO: A place near **Shechem** (Jg. 9:6, 20), of unknown location. It was perhaps the **Tower of Shechem** (Jg. 9:46f.), which may have been a fortress within the city, or near it.

BETH-NIMRAH (*'house of the leopard'*): A place in **Gad** (Jos. 13:27; Num. 32:36); called **Nimrah** in Num. 32:3. It is mod. *Tell el-Beleibil*, near *Tell Nimrîn*.

BETH-PAZZEZ: A place in **Issachar** (Jos. 19:21), of unknown location.

BETH-PELET (*'house of refuge'*): A place in Judah (Jos. 15:27), resettled after the exile (Neh. 11:26). Helez, one of David's heroes, was from here (2 Sam. 23:26; but cf. 1 Chr. 11:27, which describes him as a Pelonite, instead of a Paltite). Its location is unknown.

BETH-PEOR (*'house of Peor'*): A place in Reuben (Jos. 13:20); called Peor in Jos. 22:17). Near here the Israelites encamped (Dt. 3:29, 4:46), and here Moses was buried (Dt. 34:6). It is probably the same as Baal-peor, mod. *Khirbet esh-Sheikh-Jâyil.*

BETH-PHAGE: A village close to Bethany (1) (Mk 11:1; Lk. 19:29) on the Mount of Olives, from which Jesus sent two disciples to bring the ass on which He made His entry into Jerusalem (Mt. 21:1ff,; Mk 11:1ff.; Lk. 19:29ff.). It is mod. *Kefr et-Ṭûr.*

BETH-RAPHA (*'house of a giant'*): An unidentified place (or possibly a clan name) in Judah (1 Chr. 4:12).

BETH-REHOB: A region near Laish (Jg. 18:28), with a Syrian or Aramean population, which was allied with the Ammonites against David (2 Sam. 10:6). It is called Rehob (1) in 2 Sam. 10:8, and it is the same as Rehob in Num. 13:21, where it marks the northern limit of the journey of the spies. Its exact site is unknown, but it was in the neighbourhood of *Bâniyâs.*

BETHSAIDA (*'house of the fisherman'*): A place on the shore of the Sea of Galilee, from which Philip, Andrew and Peter came (Jn. 1:44; 12:21). Jesus went here after feeding the five thousand Mk 6:45; Lk. 9:10), and here He healed a blind man (Mk 8:22ff.). He denounced it together with Chorazin for its unreceptivity of His message (Mt. 11:21; Lk. 10:13). It is mod. *Khirbet el-'Araj*, at the N.E. end of the Sea of Galilee. Near by is *et-Tell*, where stood Bethsaida Julias, which Herod Philip built.

BETH-SHAN, BETH-SHEAN (the former spelling in 1 and 2 Sam., the latter elsewhere): This Canaanite stronghold stood within the boundaries of Issachar, but was assigned to Manasseh (Jos. 17:11); its inhabitants, however, successfully resisted them (Jos. 17:12, 16; Jg. 1:27). The Philistines hung the bodies of Saul and his sons on its walls (1 Sam. 31:10), from which they were rescued and buried by the people of Jabesh-gilead (1 Sam. 31:11ff.; cf. 2 Sam. 21:12). The city was in Solomon's fifth district (1 Kg. 4:12). Near Beth-shan Judas crossed the Jordan (1 Mac. 5:52) and Trypho came with an army against Jonathan. who was treacherously killed (1 Mac. 12: 39ff.). Elsewhere in the Apocrypha Beth-shan is called by its Greek name of **Scythopolis** (2 Mac. 12:29f.; Jdt. 3:10). It is mod. *Tell el-Husn*, near *Beisân*.

BETH-SHEMESH (*'house of the sun'*): 1. A town in **Judah** (Jos. 15:10), assigned to the priests (Jos. 21:16; 1 Chr. 6:59). When the Ark returned from the Philistines, it came to Beth-shemesh (1 Sam. 6:12ff.), but some of the people were punished for sacrilege (1 Sam. 6:19ff.). It was in Solomon's second district (1 Kg. 4:9). Amaziah was defeated in battle here (2 Kg. 14:11ff.; 2 Chr. 21:20ff.), and in the time of Ahaz it was captured by the Philistines (2:20ff.), It is called **Ir-shemesh** in Jos. 19:41. *See also* **Har-heres**. It is mod. *Tell er-Rumeileh*, near *'Ain Shems*.

 2. A place in **Issachar** (Jos. 19:22); probably mod. *el-'Abeidiyeh*.

 3. A place within the borders of **Naphtali** (Jos. 19:38), whose inhabitants successfully resisted the Israelites (Jg. 1:33); possibly mod. *Ḥâris*.

BETH-SHITTAH (*'house of the acacia'*): A place to which the Midianites fled when attacked by Gideon (Jg. 7:22); possibly mod. *Shaṭṭah*.

BETH-TAPPUAH (*'house of apples'*): A place in the hill country of **Judah** (Jos. 15:53); mod. *Taffuḥ*.

BETH-TOGARMAH: a place in 'the uttermost parts of the north' (Ezek. 38:6), which traded with **Tyre** in horses and mules (Ezek. 27:14). It was possibly in Asia Minor.

BETHUEL: A place in **Simeon** (1 Chr. 4:30); called **Bethul** in Jos. 19:4, **Chesil** in Jos. 15:30, where it is assigned to **Judah**, which early absorbed Simeon, and **Bethel** (2) in 1 Sam. 30:27. It is possibly mod. *Khirbet er-Râs*.

BETHUL: *See* **Bethuel**.

BETHULIA: The place where Judith lived (Jdt. 8:1ff.), which was attacked by Holofernes (Jdt. 6:10, 7:1 +). It is impossible to identify it with certainty, though many theories have been proposed.

BETH-ZAITH: A place where Bacchides encamped (I Mac. 7:19); perhaps mod. *Beit Zeitā*.

BETH-ZATHA: A pool in Jerusalem, where Jesus healed an invalid man (Jn 5:2, RSV and JB; RSVm and NEB follow the reading **Bethesda**).

BETH-ZECHARIAH: A place where Judas encamped (1 Mac. 6:32f.), and where he was defeated (1 Mac. 6:33ff.); mod. *Khirbet Beit Skāriā*.

BETH-ZUR (*'house of the rock'*): A city in the hill country of Judah (Jos. 15:58). It was fortified by Rehoboam (2 Chr. 11:7), and was the chief town of a district after the exile (Neh. 3:16). It is frequently mentioned in 1 and 2 Maccabees. Lysias camped here (1 Mac. 4:29) and garrisoned it (1 Mac. 4:61), and Bacchides fortified it (1 Mac. 9:52). Simon fought against it (1 Mac. 11:65) and ruled over it (1 Mac. 14:7) and fortified it (1 Mac. 14:33). It is mentioned further in 1 Mac. 6:7, 26, 31, 49f., 10:14; 2 Mac. 13:19, 22. It is mod. *Khirbet eṭ-Ṭubeiqah*.

BETOMASTHAIM: An else unknown place mentioned in Jdt. 15:4.

BETONIM: A place in Gad (Jos. 13:26); mod. *Khirbet Baṭneh*.

BEULAH (*'married'*): An allegorical name for the land of Israel (Isa. 62:4, RSVm; RSV 'married').

BEZEK: 1. A place where Judah and Simeon fought against Adoni-bezek (Jg. 1:4f.); mod. *Khirbet Bezqā*, near Gezer.
  2. A place where Saul mustered his army before relieving Jabeshgilead (1 Sam. 11:8); probably mod. *Khirbet Ibziq*, about 12 miles NE. of Shechem.

BEZER: A city of refuge in Reuben (Dt. 4:43; Jos. 20:8), and a Levitical city (Jos. 21:36; 1 Chr. 6:78). It is mentioned on the Moabite Stone. It is perhaps the same as Bozrah (2) and is possibly mod. *Umm el-'Amad*, NE. of Medeba.

BILEAM: A Levitical city in Manasseh (1 Chr. 6:70); it corresponds to **Gath-rimmon** in Jos. 21:25 (perhaps erroneously

39

repeated from verse 24). It is the same as **Ibleam** (Jos. 17:11; Jg. 1:27; 2 Kg. 9:27).

BIRZAITH: 1. Apparently an individual in 1 Chr. 7:31; but possibly a place in **Asher** (1), perhaps mod. *Bir Zeit*.
  2. *See* **Berea**.

BITHYNIA: A Roman province in N.W. Asia Minor, bordering on the Black Sea. Paul and Silas were prevented by the Spirit from preaching there (Ac. 16:7). By the time 1 Pet. was written churches had been founded there (1 Pet. 1:1).

BIZIOTHIAH: A place in **Judah** (Jos. 15:28). But LXX has 'and her villages', which is probably correct (cf. Neh. 11:27).

BOCHIM ('*weepers*'): An unknown place where an angel rebuked the Israelites (Jg. 2:1, 5). Some would identify it with **Allon-bacuth**, near **Bethel** (1).

BOHAN, STONE OF: A stone marking the division between **Judah** and **Benjamin** (Jos. 15:6, 18:17); possibly mod. *Ḥajar el-Aṣbaḥ*.

BOR-ASHAN: A place to which David sent spoils (1 Sam. 30:30); probably the same as **Ashan** (Jos. 15:42, 19:7; 1 Chr. 4:32), perhaps mod. *Khirbet 'Asan*.

BOSOR: A place in **Gilead** (1) (1 Mac. 5:26, 28, 36); mod. *Buṣr el-Ḥarîrî*.

BOZEZ: A crag overlooking the **Michmash** gorge, opposite **Seneh** (1 Sam. 14:4).

BOZKATH: A place in **Judah** near **Lachish** (Jos. 15:39). Josiah's mother came from here (2 Kg. 22:1). Its location is unknown.

BOZRAH ('*fortress*'): 1. A city in **Edom** (Gen. 36:33; 1 Chr. 1:44). It nowhere figures in the history, but is frequently mentioned in prophecy (Isa. 34:6, 63:1; Jer. 49:13, 22; Am. 1:12). It must have been an important stronghold; probably mod. *Buṣeirah*, 25 miles SE. of the **Dead Sea**.
  2. A city in **Moab** against which Jeremiah prophesied (Jer.

48:24); perhaps the same as **Bezer**, at that time in Moabite occupation. It is possibly mod. *Umm el-ʿAmad*, NE. of **Medeba**.

3. A city E. of the **Sea of Galilee** (1 Mac. 5:26, 28); mod. *Buṣra Eski-Sham*.

C

CABBON: A place in **Judah** (Jos. 15:40); possibly mod. *Khirbet Hebrah*.

CABUL: A place in **Asher** (1) (Jos. 19:27), which, with the surrounding district, was ceded by Solomon to **Tyre** (1 Kg. 9:13); probably mod. *Kabul*, E. of **Acco**.

CAESAREA: A city on the coast of **Palestine**, rebuilt by Herod the Great, and, after Archelaus was banished, the residence of the Roman procurators of Palestine. Philip preached from **Azotus** to Caesarea (Ac. 8:40), and after his first visit to **Jerusalem** after his conversion Paul sailed from Caesarea for **Tarsus** (Ac. 9:30). Cornelius sent from this city for Peter and was converted (Ac. 10:1ff., 11:11). On his return from his second and third missionary journeys, Paul landed at Caesarea (Ac. 18:22, 21:8). Here Philip still lived, and here Agabus prophesied Paul's arrest (Ac. 21:8ff.). Paul was imprisoned here for two years (Ac. 23:24, 33, 24:27). It was here Paul made his defence before Felix (Ac. 24) and before Festus (Ac. 25) and Agrippa (Ac. 26). From here Paul sailed as a prisoner bound for **Rome** (Ac. 27:1). It is mod. *Qaisâriyeh*.

CAESAREA PHILIPPI: A place (then called **Paneas**) near which Antiochus III defeated **Egypt** and brought **Palestine** under Seleucid rule. It was rebuilt by Herod's son, Philip, who renamed it after Caesar Augustus and himself. It was near here that Peter made his great confession of faith (Mt. 16:13ff.; Mk 8:27). It is mod. *Bāniyās*.

CALAH: A city in **Assyria**, said to have been built by Nimrod (Gen. 10:11f.). It was one of the chief cities of Assyria, mod. *Nimrûd*.

CALNEH: A city linked with **Hamath** (Am. 6:2); probably the same as **Calno** (Isa. 10:9). It is probably mod. *Kullān Köy*.

CALNO: *See* **Calneh**

CALVARY: *See* **Golgotha**.

CANA: A village in **Galilee**, where Jesus turned water into wine (Jn 2:1ff.) and later healed with a word a child who lay ill at **Capernaum** (Jn 4:46ff.). Nathanael came from here (Jn 21:2). It is mod. *Khirbet Qâna*.

CANAAN: The name frequently given to the Land of Promise (Gen. 11:31, 12:5, 17:8 +). It is sometimes used in a restricted sense of the territory W. of the **Jordan** (Num. 33:51, 34:2ff.; Jos. 22:32), or of the kingdom of **Tyre** (Isa. 23:11), or even of the land of the Philistines (Zeph. 2:5); but in Dt. 34:1ff (cf. 32:49) it includes territory on both sides of the Jordan. The name means 'purple' (cf. the Greek name of **Phoenicia**) and is derived from the purple dye it exported. The Canaanites, whose eponymous ancestor is said to have been Canaan, the son of Ham (Gen. 10:6, 15ff.), were one of the two principal elements of the pre-Israelite population (the Amorites being the other), though there were several others. They were merchants (cf. Ezek. 27:12ff.); the Hebrew word for 'Canaanite' means also 'merchant', and is sometimes so translated.

CANNEH: A town which traded with **Tyre** (Ezek. 27:23), of unknown location.

CAPERNAUM: A city on the shore of the **Sea of Galilee**, which Jesus counted as his dwelling-place during His ministry (Mt. 4:13; Mk 2:1; cf. Jn 2:12). It was here He taught in the synagogue (Mk 1:21; Lk. 4:31; Jn 6:59), healed the centurion's servant (Mt. 8:5ff.; Lk. 7:2ff.; cf. Jn 4:46ff.) and performed other miracles (Mk 1:23–2:12; Lk. 4:23, 33ff.), taught His disciples (Mk 9:33), and provided the Temple tax (Mt. 17:24). He denounced the unbelief of its people (Mt. 11:23; Lk. 10:15). Peter and Andrew lived here (Mk 1:29; Lk. 4:38). It is mod. *Tell Ḥûm*.

CAREM: *See* **Karem**.

CAPHARSALAMA: A place where Nicanor was defeated by Judas (1 Mac. 7:31); possibly mod. *Khirbet Selmah*.

CAPHTOR: The place from which the Philistines came (Am. 9:7; Jer. 47:4), and the 'Caphtorim who came from Caphtor' (Dt. 2:23) are the Philistines (cf. **Gaza**, one of the Philistine cities). Caphtor means **Crete**, but the Philistines were not of Cretan origin. They came into **Palestine** after the fall of the Minoan empire of Crete as part of the movement of Mediterranean peoples associated with that fall.

CAPPADOCIA: A Roman province in E. Asia Minor, formed A.D. 17. In 1 Mac. 15:22 the Roman consul wrote to Ariathes, who was king of Cappadocia, declaring the friendship of the Romans for the Jews, and Jews from Cappadocia were in **Jerusalem** at Pentecost (Ac. 2:9). 1 Peter was addressed to Christians in Cappadocia (1 Pet. 1:1).

CARCHEMISH: An important city on the **Euphrates** in N. **Syria**, which was once the capital of a Hittite kingdom. It was captured by the Assyrians (Isa. 10:9), and when the Assyrian empire was collapsing, **Egypt** came to its aid, and after the final end of the Assyrian power a battle was fought here in 605 B.C. (Jer. 46:2; 2 Chr. 36:20; 1 Esd. 1:25; cf. 2 Kg. 23:29), in which Nebuchadrezzar was victorious. It is mod. *Jerablus*.

CARIA: A region in Asia Minor to which the Roman consul wrote announcing Roman friendship for the Jews (1 Mac. 15:23).

CARMEL: A place in **Judah** (Jos. 15:55), where Saul set up a monument to commemorate his victory over the Amalekites (1 Sam. 15:12). Here too lived Nabal (1 Sam. 25:2ff.), and it was the home of one of David's heroes (2 Sam. 23:35; 1 Chr. 11:37). It is mod. *el-Kermel*. See **Racal**.

CARMEL, MOUNT: A mountain on the coast of **Palestine**, with a ridge running inland. On the ridge stood **Jokneam** (Jos. 12:22), whose king Joshua conquered. The territory of **Asher** (1) reached to Carmel (Jos. 19:26), and on this mount Elijah had his contest with the prophets of Baal (1 Kg. 18:19ff.). Elisha too resided here (2 Kg. 2:25, 4:25). It was well wooded (Isa. 33:9), so that a lady's head could be compared with it (Ca. 7:5); and it made a good hiding place (Am. 9:3). It had rich pasture land (Jer. 50:19; Am. 1:2; Mic. 7:14) and was renowned for its beauty (Isa. 35:2). It is mod. *Jebel Mâr Elyâs*.

CARNAIM: A place E. of the Jordan attacked and burned by Judas (1 Mac. 5:26, 43f.; 2 Mac. 12:26). It was difficult of access (2 Mac. 12:21). It is mod. *Sheikh Sa'ad*. It is perhaps the same as **Ashteroth-karnaim** and **Karnaim**.

CASIPHIA: An unidentified place in **Babylonia** (Ezr. 8:17), from which some Temple servants came.

CASPIN: An unknown place in **Gilead** (2 Mac. 12:13), near a large lake; probably the same as **Chaspho** (1 Mac. 5:26, 36).

CAUDA: An island off **Crete**, where the ship on which Paul was a prisoner found some temporary relief from the storm, but threw their cargo overboard (Ac. 27:16ff.); mod. *Gaudho*.

CENCHREAE: The southern harbour of **Corinth**, where Paul sailed for **Ephesus**, after cutting his hair (Ac. 18:18f.). Phoebe was a deaconess of the church here (Rom. 16:1). It is mod. *Kechries*.

CHALDEA: A district in the S.E. of **Babylonia**, from which Merodach-baladan came (2 Kg. 20:12; Isa. 39:1); later Nabopolassar came from here and established the Neo-Bayloninan or Chaldean empire with **Babylon** as its capital. Hence Chaldea is sometimes used for Babylonia (Isa. 48:20; Jer. 50:10; 51:1, 24, 35; Ezek. 11:24, 16:29, 23:15f.), and Chaldeans for Babylonians very frequently.

CHAPHENATHA: An unknown place near **Jerusalem** which Jonathan repaired (1 Mac. 12:17).

CHARAX: An unknown place where some Jews lived (2 Mac. 12:17).

CHASPHO: An unknown place in **Gilead** (1 Mac. 5:26, 36); probably the same as **Caspin** (2 Mac. 12:13), which was near a large lake (2 Mac. 12:16).

CHEBAR: A river in **Babylonia**, on which **Tel-abid** stood, where Ezekiel and a colony of the Jewish exiles lived (Ezek. 1:1, 3; 3:15, 23; 10:15, 20, 22; 43:2); probably the great canal near *Nippur*.

CHELOUS: A place mentioned in Jdt. 1:9; possibly mod. *el-Khalaṣah*, SW. of **Beersheba**.

CHEPHAR-AMMONI (*'village of the Ammonite'*): A village in Benjamin (Jos. 18:24); possibly mod. *Khirbet Kefr 'Ânah*.

CHEPHIRAH: A city within Benjamin (Jos. 18:26) that joined the Gibeonite alliance and made peace with the Israelites (Jos. 9:17). Some who returned from exile traced their descent from here (Ezr. 2:25; Neh. 7:29; 1 Esd. 5:19). It is mod. *Tell Kephîreh*, SW. of Gibeon.

CHERITH: The brook by which Elijah lived (1 Kg. 17:3, 5). It was E. of the Jordan; mod. *Wâdi Yâbis*.

CHERUB: A place in Babylonia from which came some exiles who could not prove their descent (Ezr. 2:59; Neh. 7:61; 1 Esd. 5:36).

CHESALON: A place in Judah, near Kiriath-jearim, and identified with Mount Jearim (Jos. 15:10); mod. *Keslah*.

CHESIL: A place in Judah (Jos. 15:30); called Bethul in Jos. 19:4 and Bethuel in 1 Chr. 4:30. It is the same as Bethel (2); possibly mod. *Khirbet er-Râs*.

CHESULLOTH: A place in Issachar (Jos. 19:18); probably the same as Chisloth-tabor (Jos. 19:12). It is mod. *Iksâl*, SE. of Nazareth.

CHEZIB: A place where Shua bore Shelah (Gen. 38:5); perhaps the same as Achzib (1) (Jos. 15:44). It is probably mod. *Tell el-Beiḍā*.

CHIDON: The name of the threshing-floor where Uzzah died, or its owner (1 Chr. 13:9); called Nacon in 2 Sam. 6:6.

CHILMAD: An unknown place which traded with Tyre (Ezek. 27:23).

CHINNERETH: A city in Naphtali (Dt. 3:17; Jos. 19:35), which gave its name to the Sea of Chinnereth (Num. 34:11; Jos. 13:27); spelt Chinneroth in Jos. 11:2, 12:3; 1 Kg. 15:20. It is mod. *Tell el-'Oreimeh*.

CHINNERETH, SEA OF: One of the names of the **Sea of Galilee** (Num. 34:11; Jos. 13:27). *See* **Chinnereth.**

CHINNEROTH: *See* **Chinnereth.**

CHINNEROTH, SEA OF A name for the **Sea of Galilee** (Jos. 12:3). *See* **Chinnereth.**

CHIOS: An Aegean island, mentioned in the account of Paul's return from his third missionary journey (Ac. 20:15).

CHISLOTH-TABOR: A place on the border of **Zebulun** and **Issachar** (Jos. 19:12); probably the same as **Chesulloth** (Jos. 19:18). It is mod. *Iksâl*, SE. of **Nazareth.**

CHITLISH: A place in **Judah** (Jos. 15:40); possibly mod. *Khirbet el-Maqhaz*, SW. of **Lachish.**

CHOBA: A district mentioned only in Jdt. 4:4; 15:4f.; of uncertain location, but possibly the same as **Hobah** (Gen. 14:15).

CHORAZIN: A city of **Galilee** condemned for its unbelief by Jesus (Mt. 11:21; Lk. 10:13) but the Gospels contain no account of His preaching there; mod. *Khirbet Kerâzeh.*

CHUSI: A place near **Acraba** (Jdt. 7:18); perhaps mod. *Kurzah.*

CILICIA: A region in S.E. Asia Minor, part of which formed a a Roman province with **Tarsus** as capital (Ac. 21:39, 22:3), and which was administratively linked with **Syria** (cf. Gal. 1:21; Ac. 15:23, 41). It is associated with **Asia** in Ac. 6:9.

CNIDUS: A coastal city of **Caria**, to which the Roman consul wrote announcing the Roman friendship for the Jews (1 Mac. 15:23). The ship in which Paul was carried as a prisoner arrived with difficulty off Cnidus (Ac. 27:7). It was on mod. *Cap Krio.*

COELESYRIA: Originally the great valley between the **Lebanon** and the **Anti-Lebanon**, mod. *el-Beqa'* (*See* **Valley of Lebanon**). But it is often used loosely and more widely. In 1 Esd. 2:17, 24:27, 'Coelesyria and **Phoenicia**' corresponds to 'the province beyond the River' in Ezr. 4:11, 16, 20 (note that in 1 Esd. 2:25 **Syria** replaces

Coelesyria, and in 1 Esd. 4:48 Lebanon appears to be separate from it; cf. also I Esd. 6:29, 7:1). In 2 Mac. 3:58 (cf. 2 Mac. 4:4, 10:11; and 1 Mac. 10:69, where Coelesyria alone is used) Coelesyria and Phoenicia denote a province under Seleucid rule that included Jerusalem (v. 6).

COLOSSAE: A city in **Phrygia**, to which Paul wrote one of his letters (Col. 1:2). The apostle never visited it (Col. 2:1), but it may have been evangelized by Epaphras (Col. 4:12f.) or by Timothy (Col. 1:1). Since Onesimus was one of the bearers of Paul's letter (Col. 4:9) and Onesimus was being sent to Philemon (Phm. 10ff.), it is generally believed that Philemon lived there. It was near mod. *Khonai.*

CORINTH: The capital of the Roman province of **Achaia**, on the isthmus. Paul came to it from **Athens** (Ac. 18:1) and stayed there a year and a half (Ac. 18:11), preaching first to Jews and then in the house of Titius Justus (Ac. 18:2–7). He was brought by the Jews before Gallio, who dismissed the case (Ac. 18:12ff.). The date of Paul's work in Corinth can be dated by an inscription from *Delphi,* which shows that Gallio became proconsul in A.D. 51 or 52. Another inscription mentions an Erastus, possibly the city treasurer (Rom. 16:23). Paul appears to have paid another 'painful visit' to Corinth, of which we have no account (2 Cor. 2:1). Two letters to the Corinthians stand in the NT, but Paul himself refers to four. Here Paul met Aquila and Priscilla (Ac. 18:2), and they left with him. In **Ephesus** they met Apollos, who later went to Corinth (Ac. 19:1), where the church in course of time became split into Paul and Apollos factions (1 C. 3:4).

CORNER GATE: A gate in the wall of **Jerusalem,** four hundred cubits from the **Ephraim Gate** (2 Kg. 14:13; 2 Chr. 25:23). This stretch of wall was broken down by Jehoash. Uzziah built a tower here (2 Chr. 26:9). Jeremiah spoke of the time when the wall should be rebuilt from the **Tower of Hananel** to the Corner Gate (Jer. 31:38). It is mentioned also in Zech. 14:10.

CORRUPTION, MOUNT OF: A mountain E. of **Jerusalem,** where Solomon built high places for his foreign wives and which Josiah defiled (1 Kg. 11:7f.; 2 Kg. 23:13f.). It must have been some spot on the **Mount of Olives.**

47

COS: An island off **Caria,** to which the Roman consul wrote announcing Roman friendship for the Jews (1 Mac. 15:23). It is mentioned in the account of Paul's return from his third missionary journey (Ac. 23:1).

COZEBA: A place in **Judah** (1 Chr. 4:22); possibly the same as **Achzib** (1), (Jos. 15:44) and **Chezib** (Gen. 38:5), or alternatively mod. *Khirbet ed-Dibb,* NW. of **Hebron.**

CRAFTSMEN, VALLEY OF: *See* **Ge-harash.**

CRETE: A large island S. of **Greece,** once the centre of the Minoan culture. Its people had a poor reputation in a later age (Tit. 1:12). Demetrius II came from Crete to claim the Seleucid throne (1 Mac. 10:67). The Roman consul wrote to **Gortyna,** a city on the island, announcing Roman friendship for the Jews (1 Mac. 15:23), from which it would appear that there were Jews on the island in the second century B.C. There were Jews from Crete in **Jerusalem** at Pentecost (Ac. 2:11). The ship on which Paul was a prisoner sailed along the coast of Crete (Ac. 27:7ff.). We do not know how the gospel came to the island, but Titus was in charge of the church there (Tit. 1:5). *See* **Caphtor.**

CUN: A town in **Syria** which David despoiled (1 Chr. 18:8); replacing **Berothai** of 2 Sam. 8:8. It is possibly mod. *Râs Ba'albek.*

CUSH: A name used for **Ethiopia** (Gen. 10:6; 1 Chr. 1:8, where it stands beside other geographical names) and for the source of some tribes occupying S. Arabian districts (Gen. 10:7; 1 Chr. 1:9). Moses married a Cushite woman (Num. 12:1), and Joab sent a Cushite messenger to David (2 Sam. 18:21ff.). In most of its occurrences in the OT it is translated 'Ethiopia'.

CUSHAN: A tribe, or the territory it occupied, near **Midian** (Hab. 3:7).

CUTH, CUTHAH: A city from which Sargon brought colonists to **Samaria** (1) (2 Kg. 17:24, 30); mod. *Tell Ibrāhīm.*

CYAMON: A place 'which faces **Esdraelon**' (Jdt. 7:3); probably the same as **Jokneam,** mod. *Tell Qeimûn.*

CYPRUS: A large island in the **Mediterranean**. It is referred to four times in the OT (Isa. 23:1, 12; Jer. 2:10; Ezek. 27:6), where it renders *Kittîm* (which in Dan. 11:29 stands for the Romans and in 1 Mac. 1:1 for **Greece**). The Roman consul wrote to Cyprus announcing Roman friendship for the Jews (1 Mac. 15:23), and a contingent of troops from Cyprus were in the Seleucid army (2 Mac. 4:29), while Antiochus V abandoned the island (2 Mac. 10:13), Nicanor was a governor of the island (2 Mac. 12:2). Barnabas was a native of Cyprus (Ac. 4:36), and the gospel was carried there after the martyrdom of Stephen (Ac. 11:19f.). Paul and Barnabas began the first missionary journey of Paul here (Ac. 13:4), landing at **Salamis** (Ac. 13:5) and proceeding to **Paphos** (Ac. 13:6), where they converted the proconsul (Ac. 13:12). After Paul and Barnabas separated, the latter again proceeded to Cyprus (Ac. 15:39). Mnason was from Cyprus (Ac. 21:16).

CYRENE: A city of **Libya** in N. Africa. Simon, who bore the cross of Jesus, was from there (Mt. 27:32; Mk 15:21; Lk. 23:26), and some Jews from there were present in **Jerusalem** at Pentecost (Ac.2:10). In Ac. 6:9 we read of a synagogue of Cyrenians in Jerusalem. Some Christians of Cyrenian origin carried the gospel to **Antioch** (Ac. 11:20), and among the leaders of the church there was Lucius of Cyrene (Ac. 13:1).

D

DABBESHETH ('*hump*'): A place in **Zebulun** (Jos. 19:11); perhaps mod. *Tell esh-Shammâm*.

DABERATH: A place in **Zebulun** (Jos. 19:12) or **Issachar** (Jos. 21:28), probably on the border between them; a Levitical city (Jos. 21:28; 1 Chr. 6:72). It is perhaps the same as **Rabbith** (Jos. 19:20). It is probably mod. *Dabûriyeh*, at the foot of **Mount Tabor**.

DALMANUTHA: A place on the W. shore of the **Sea of Galilee** (Mk 8:10), corresponding to **Magadan** in Mt. 15:39. Its location is unknown.

DALMATIA: A district of the E. coast of the Adriatic Sea, where Titus preached (1 Tim. 4:10).

DAMASCUS: An ancient city of **Syria**, mentioned in Gen. 14:15. Abraham's steward came from there (Gen. 15:2). It is next mentioned as conquered by David (2 Sam. 8:5f.; 1 Chr. 18:5f.) and then as becoming independent under Rezon in Solomon's time (1 Kg. 11:23ff.). Asa appealed for help to Damascus (1 Kg. 15:18ff.; 2 Chr. 16:2ff.), and Elijah was told to anoint Hazael to be its king (1 Kg. 19:15ff.). Benhadad agreed to let Ahab establish bazaars in Damascus (1 Kg. 20:34). From Damascus came Naaman (2 Kg. 5), and later Elisha visited the city (2 Kg. 8:7ff.). In the reign of Joash the spoil of **Jerusalem** was carried there (2 Chr. 24:23), and again in the time of Ahaz captives from **Judah** were taken to Damascus (2 Chr. 28:5). Jeroboam II temporarily recovered control of it (2 Kg. 14:28), but a few years later it fell to the Assyrians (2 Kg. 16:9), as predicted by Isaiah (Isa. 8:4). Ahaz met Tiglathpileser here (2 Kg. 16:10). Prophecies against Damascus stand in Am. 1:3ff.; Isa. 17:1ff.; Jer. 49:23ff. There are references to Damascus in the book of Judith (Jdt. 1:7, 12, 2:27, 15:5). Jonathan marched to the city (1 Mac. 11:62, 12:62). The Church early reached Damascus, and Paul was on a persecuting errand there when he was converted (Ac. 9:1ff., 22:5ff., 26:12ff.). The Jews there sought to kill him, but he escaped over the wall (Ac. 9:23ff.). At that time Damascus was ruled by the Nabatean king, Aretas IV, whose governor aided the Jews (2 C. 11:32). Paul went into **Arabia**, but returned to Damascus (Gal. 1:17).

DAN: 1. The territory occupied by the tribe of Dan. Its ideal limits are stated in Jos. 19:40–46. But the tribe failed to establish itself here (Jg. 1:34, 18:1), and migrated to the north (Jg. 18). See 2.

2. A city, formerly called **Laish** (Jg. 18:7, 29), or **Leshem** (Jos. 19:47), mentioned in Gen. 14:14. When the tribe of Dan was under pressure (Jg. 1:34f.), it migrated to the north and fell on this city and occupied it, bringing with them Micah's priest and image (Jg. 18). When Jeroboam I divided the kingdom, he set up in the shrine of Dan one of his bull calves (1 Kg. 12:29), and this continued after the purge of Jehu (1 Kg. 10:29), but was condemned by Amos (Am. 8:5). Dan was conquered by Benhadad (1 Kg. 15:20; 2 Chr. 16:4). It was the most northerly city of Israel (cf. 'from Dan to **Beersheba**', Jg. 20:1 +); mod. *Tell el-Qâḍi*.

DAN-JAAN: A place mentioned in RSVm (as in AV, RV) in the account of David's census (2 Sam. 24:6). But RSV and JB have **Dan** (2), following LXX.

DANNAH: A place in **Judah**, S.W. of **Hebron** (Jos. 15:49); its location is unknown.

DAPHNE: A place famous for its temple, its right of asylum, its fountain, and its shameless morals. Onias took refuge here (2 Mac. 4:33), but was treacherously induced to leave it and then murdered (2 Mac. 4:34). It is mod. *Beit el-Mâ*, 5 miles from **Antioch** (1).

DATHEMA: A stronghold in **Gilead** (1 Mac. 5:9); perhaps mod. *Tell Ḥamad*.

DAVID, CITY OF: *See* **Jerusalem.**

DEAD SEA: The lowest stretch of water in the world, into which the **Jordan** flows. It has no outlet, and its waters are so salt that no fish can live in them; hence its name. It is never so called in the Bible, however, where it is named the **Salt Sea** (Gen. 14:3; Num. 34:3 +), the **Sea of the Arabah** (Dt. 3:17, 4:49), or the **Eastern Sea** (Ezek. 47:18). 2 Esd. 5:7 calls it the **Sea of Sodom.** The **Valley of Siddim** was S. of the Dead Sea, and the cities of **Sodom** and **Gomorrah**, which it contained, may be submerged beneath the waters of the S. end of the Sea.

DEBIR: 1. A city in the hill country of **Judah** (Jos. 15:49), for-formerly called **Kiriath-sepher** (Jos. 15:15f.; Jg. 1:11f.; **Kiriath-sannah** in Jos. 15:49), and inhabited by Anakim (Jos. 11:21). It was conquered by Joshua (Jos. 10:38f., 11:21, 12:13) or Othniel (Jos. 15:17; Jg. 1:13). It became a Levitical city (Jos. 21:15; 1 Chr. 6:58). It is mod. *Tell Beit Mirsim*.

2. A place on the N. border of **Judah** (Jos. 17:7); perhaps mod. *Ṭûghret ed-Debr*.

3. An unidentified place in **Gad** (Jos. 13:26), with an alternative reading **Lidebir** (so RSVm; probably the same as **Lo-debar.**

DECAPOLIS: A loose federation of ten cities, which others joined from time to time. Pliny lists them as **Scythopolis** (**Bethshan**), **Pella, Gadara, Dion, Hippos, Philadelphia** (2), **Gerasa, Kanatha** (*see* **Kenath**), **Damascus, Raphana,** of which the first only was W. of the **Jordan**. The people from this region flocked to hear Jesus (Mt. 4:25; Mk 5:20, 7:31).

DEDAN: A people in N. **Arabia**, descended from Cush (Gen. 10:7) or from Abraham (Gen. 25:3), occupying a region called by their name (Jer. 25:23, 49:8), which must have been near **Edom** (Ezek. 25:13). The caravans of Dedan are mentioned in Isa. 21:13, and in Ezek. 27:20 their trade with Tyre is referred to. Dedan is probably the oasis of *el-'Ulâ*.

DELOS: A small Aegean island to which the Roman consul wrote announcing Roman friendship for the Jews (1 Mac. 15:23).

DERBE: A city in the Roman province of **Galatia**, but in the ethnic area of **Lycaonia** (Ac. 14:6). Paul came here from **Lystra** on his first missionary journey (Ac. 14:20) and made many disciples. He then returned via Lystra and **Iconium** (Ac. 14:21). On his second missionary journey he came from **Cilicia** to Derbe and then to Lystra (Ac. 16:1). One of Paul's helpers, Gaius, was from Derbe (Ac. 20:4). It is mod. *Kerti Hüyük*.

DESSAU: An unknown village where the Jews fought Nicanor (2 Mac. 14:16).

DIBON: 1. A city E. of the **Dead Sea** and N. of the **Arnon**. It was captured from Moab by Sihon (Num. 21:26ff.) and from Sihon by the Israelites (Jos. 13:9f.). It was allotted to **Reuben** (Jos. 13:17), but is said to have been rebuilt by the Gadites (Num. 32:34), and its alternative name is **Dibon-gad** (Num. 33:45f.). The Moabite Stone was found here, and on it Mesha records how he captured the city, it is referred to as Moabite in Isa. 15:2; Jer. 48:18, 22. It is mod. *Dhîbān*. In Isa. 15:9 RSV and JB have Dibon where MT has **Dimon** (so AV, RV). A Dead Sea Scroll reading agrees with RSV. but not all editors prefer this, and Dimon is perhaps the same as **Madmen**.

2. A place in **Judah** to which some exiles returned (Neh. 11:25), Perhaps the same as **Dimonah** (Jos. 15:22). Its location is unknown.

DIBON-GAD: *See* **Dibon** (1).

DILEAN: A place in **Judah** (Jos. 15:38); perhaps mod. *Tell ne-Nejîleh*.

DIMNAH: A Levitical city in Zebulun (Jos. 21:35); probably the same as **Rimmon** (3) (Jos. 19:13), mod. *Rummâneh.*

DIMON: *See* **Dibon** (1).

DIMONAH: A place in S. Judah (Jos. 15:11); perhaps the same as **Dibon** (2) (Neh. 11:25). Its location is unknown.

DINHABAH: The city of Bela in **Edom** (Gen. 36:32; 1 Chr. 1:43), of unknown location.

DIVINERS' OAK: A spot near **Shechem** (Jg. 9:37).

DIZAHAB: A place beyond the **Jordan** in the **Arabah** (Dt. 1:1), where Moses delivered his farewell address. Its location is unknown. *See* **Me-zahab.**

DOK: A stronghold where Simon was treacherously murdered (1 Mac. 16:15); mod. *Jebel Qarantal,* at the foot of which is the spring of *'Ain Dûq,* about 4 miles NW. of **Jericho.**

DOPHKAH: A stopping-place in the Wilderness wanderings (Num. 33:12f.); perhaps mod. *Serābît el-Khâdim.*

DOR: A Canaanite city which joined the alliance against the Israelites, and whose king was defeated (Jos. 12:33); but the city successfully resisted the Israelites (Jos. 17:12; Jg. 1:27). It was assigned to **Manasseh,** though it lay within the borders of **Issachar** or **Asher** (1) (Jos. 17:11). In 1 Chr. 7:29 it is reckoned to **Ephraim** (1). It was in Solomon's fourth district (1 Kg. 4:11). Trypho fled to Dor (1 Mac. 15:11), which was twice besieged by Antiochus VII (1 Mac. 15:13, 25). It is called **Naphath-dor** in Jos. 12:23; 1 Kg. 4:11, and **Naphoth-dor** in Jos. 11:2. It is probably mod *el-Burj,* near *eṭ-Ṭanṭûrah.*

DOTHAN: A city N. of **Shechem,** to which Joseph went to his brothers (Gen. 37:7), and whence he was taken to Egypt (Gen. 37:28). Here Elisha was when the Syrians surrounded the city, and it was miraculously delivered (2 Kg. 6:13ff.). In the story of Judith, Holofernes camped near Dothan (Jdt. 3:9f., 7:18), which was not far from **Bethulia** (Jdt. 4:6, 7:3, 18, 8:3). It is mod. *Tell Dôthā.*

DUMAH: 1. An Ishmaelite region (Gen. 25:14; 1 Chr. 1:30); mod. *Dûmat el-Jendel*, now called *el-Jôf.*

2. A place in the highlands of **Judah** (Jos. 15:52); mod. ed-*Dômeh*, SW. of **Hebron**.

3. In Isa. 21:11, Dumah stands for **Edom** (cf. Seir in the next line), and this should perhaps be read (so JB).

DUNG GATE: A gate of **Jerusalem** leading to the **Valley of Hinnom**, repaired in Nehemiah's time (Neh. 2:13, 3:13f., 12:31).

DURA, PLAIN OF: A plain in which Nebuchadnezzar's image was set up (Dan. 3:1). It was near **Babylon**, but of uncertain location.

E

EASTERN SEA: The name by which the **Dead Sea** is described in Ezek. 47:18, Jl 2:20; Zech. 14:8, in contrast to the **Western Sea**, or **Mediterranean**.

EAST GATE: A gate of the Temple in **Jerusalem** (Ezek. 10:19, 11:1; cf. 2 Chr. 31:14). In the time of Nehemiah, Shemaiah was the keeper of this gate (Neh. 3:29).

EBAL, MOUNT: A mountain near **Shechem**, facing **Mount Gerizim** described as the mountain of curse (Dt. 11:29), on which stones containing the Law were to be set up (Dt. 27:4), and on which six tribes were to be stationed when the curses on evil-doers were pronounced (Dt. 27:13). Here Joshua built an altar and sacrificed, and erected a copy of the Law on stones (Jos. 8:39ff.). It is mod. **Jebel** *Eslâmîyeh.*

EBEN-EZER ('*stone of help*'): 1. The scene of two battles with the Philistines, in the second of which the Ark was captured (1 Sam. 4:1ff., 5:1); probably mod. *Mejdel Yâbā.*

2. A stone which Samuel erected between **Mizpah** (3) and **Jeshanah** to commemorate a victory over the Philistines (1 Sam. 7:12).

EBEZ: A place in Issachar (Jos. 19:20), of unknown location.

EBRON: A city in Asher (1) (Jos. 19:28); called **Abdon** in Jos. 21:30; 1 Chr. 6:74, where it is described as a Levitical city. It is mod. *Khirbet 'Abdeh*, E. of **Achzib**.

ECBATANA: The captial of **Media**, where the decree of Cyrus was found in the archives (Ezr. 6:2). Tobit journeyed to Ecbatana (Tob. 3:7, 6:5, 7:1), and there married Sarah (Tob. 7:8ff.). Later he returned (Tob. 14:12) and died there (Tob. 14:14). In Jdt. 1:1f. Arphaxad is said to have ruled here and to have fortified it, and it is said to have been plundered by Nebuchadnezzar (Jdt. 1:13ff.). To Ecbatana Antiochus IV retreated from **Persia** (2 Mac. 9:3). It is mod. *Hamadân*.

EDEN: A place which engaged in trade with **Tyre** (Ezek. 27:23). Its people are said to have been conquered by the Assyrians in **Telassar** (2 Kg. 19:12; Isa. 27:12). It is probably the same as **Beth-eden** (Am. 1:5).

EDEN, GARDEN OF: A garden planted by God in which the first human couple were set (Gen. 2:7ff.), and from which they were ejected after their disobedience (Gen. 3:24). Reference is made to it in Isa. 51:3; Ezek. 28:13, 31:9, 16, 18; 36:35, Jl 2:3. It is impossible to define its geographical position from Gen. 2:10ff.

EDER: A place in S. **Judah** (Jos. 15:21); perhaps the same as **Arad** (Num. 21:1, 33:40), probably mod. *Tell 'Arâd*.

EDER, TOWER OF: A point near the place where Jacob pitched his tent (Gen. 35:21). It stood between **Bethlehem** (1) and **Hebron** (cf. verses 19, 27).

EDOM: The region occupied by the Edomites (Gen. 32:3, 36:16), which was around **Mount Seir** (Gen. 32:3; cf. Jg. 5:4), with **Mount Hor** on its border (Num. 33:37), but sometimes extended much further (cf. 1 Kg. 9:26, **Eloth**). Edom refused to let Moses and the Israelites pass through (Num. 20:14ff.; Jg. 11:17), but became Israel's neighbours (Jos. 15:1). In Saul's time Edom was conquered (1 Sam. 14:47), but in David's reign it needed to be done again (2 Sam. 8:12), and garrisons were put there (2 Sam. 8:14; 1 Chr. 18:13); but in Solomon's reign Edom recovered independence

(1 Kg. 11:14ff.). In the reign of Jehoshaphat Edom again became dependent on Judah (1 Kg. 22:47ff.), and marched with Jehoshaphat and Israel against Moab (2 Kg. 3:9ff.); but in the next reign it again recovered independence (2 Kg. 8:20ff.). Amaziah defeated Edom in battle (2 Kg. 14:7, 10), and appears to have brought it once more to dependence; but in the reign of Ahaz it once more broke free (2 Kg. 16:6). Prophecies against Edom are found in Isa. 11:14, 34:5ff.; Jer. 9:26, 25:21, 27:3, 49:7ff.; Am. 1:11f.; Ob. 1ff. At the time of the exile, Edom took advantage of Judah's sorrows and aroused bitter and lasting resentment (Ps. 137:7; Lam. 4:21f.; Ezek. 25:12ff., 35:1ff.; Isa. 63:1ff.). In the Hellenistic period the Nabateans overran Edom, and many Edomites were pressed into S. Judah and their country became known as **Idumea**, which included **Hebron** (1 Mac. 5:65).

EDREI: 1. The city of Og, king of **Bashan** (Dt. 1:4, 3:10; Jos. 12:4, 13:12), where he was defeated (Num. 21:33; Dt. 3:1); mod. *Der'â*. It was allotted to **Manasseh** (Jos. 13:31).

2. A place in **Naphtali** (Jos. 19:37); possibly mod. *Tell Khureibeh*.

EGLAIM: A place in **Moab** (Isa. 15:8), of unknown location.

EGLATH-SHELISHIYAH: An unknown place in **Moab** (Isa. 15:5; Jer. 48:34).

EGLON: A city which joined the alliance against Joshua (Jos. 10:3ff.). It was destroyed (Jos. 10:34) and its king conquered (Jos. 12:12). It lay within **Judah** (Jos. 15:39), and is probably mod. *Tell el-Ḥesi*.

EGYPT: A country through which flows the **Nile**, on which its whole life depends, and which is mentioned several hundred times in the Bible. Its people are reckoned to the family of Ham (Gen. 10:6; 1 Chr. 1:8). Abraham went into Egypt to avoid famine, and Sarah narrowly escaped dishonour (Gen. 12:10ff.); Ishmael married a wife from Egypt (Gen. 21:21). Joseph was carried as a slave into Egypt (Gen. 37:28); after vicissitudes of fortune (Gen. 39f.) he rose to high office (Gen. 41), and brought his whole family into Egypt (Gen. 46). At some time after his death (Gen. 50:26) the Israelites were reduced to slave labour and oppressed (Exod. 1:8ff.), until Moses was sent to bring them out (Exod. 3:7ff.). Following the plagues of Egypt (Exod. 5ff.), culminating in the death of the first-born (Exod. 12:29ff.), the Israelites were miraculously delivered from the Egyptian pursuers (Exod. 14:5ff.). The memory of the Exodus from Egypt was deeply stamped upon Israel, and is referred to continually throughout the OT. The names of the Pharaohs of all these incidents are unrecorded. Egypt next figures in Israel's history when Hadad fled from **Edom** to Egypt in David's reign to return later in Solomon's (1 Kg. 11:14ff.) and when Solomon married Pharaoh's daughter (1 Kg. 3:1), who received **Gezer** as a dowry (1 Kg. 9:16). But before the end of Solomon's reign Shishak, the first king of a new dynasty, gave asylum to Jeroboam (1 Kg. 11:40). After Jeroboam returned and the kingdom was divided, Shishak invaded **Palestine** and despoiled **Jerusalem** (1 Kg. 14:25ff.). He also ravaged northern **Israel**, though this is not recorded in the Bible. When **Assyria** was extending her power into Israel, Egypt intrigued against her with promises of support (2 Kg. 17:17; cf. Hos. 7:11), and similarly promised support to **Judah** in Hezekiah's time (2 Kg. 18:21; Isa. 36:6ff.; cf. Isa. 30:1ff.; 31:1ff.). When Assyria was collapsing, Pharaoh Neco of Egypt came to her aid and defeated Josiah, who had resisted him (2 Kg. 23:29f.); but he was himself defeated by Nebuchradrezzar at **Carchemish** (Jer. 46:2; 2 Chr. 36:20). When Zedekiah rebelled against **Babylon**, Pharaoh Hophra was encouraging him (Jer. 37:3ff.; Ezek. 17:15ff.), but gave no effective aid. After the murder of Gedaliah, Jeremiah was carried into Egypt (Jer. 43:6). In the prophets there are many references to Egypt and her intrigues (Isa. 19:1ff.; Jer. 25:19, 43:10ff.; 46:1ff.; Ezek. 29:1ff., 30:1ff., 31ff.). After the death of Alexander the Great, Egypt came under the rule of the Ptolemies (the 'kings of the south' in Dan. 11), and for more than a century Palestine was under their rule, until Antiochus III wrested it from them (Dan. 11:11ff.). Antiochus IV twice invaded Egypt (1 Mac. 1:16ff.; 2 Mac. 5:1ff.). Alexander Balas married the daughter of Ptolemy VI (1 Mac. 10:51ff.), who tried to bring the Seleucid kingdom under Egyptian control (1 Mac. 11:1ff.). In the NT we read that Jesus was carried into Egypt for safety (Mt. 2:13), that Jews from Egypt were in Jerusalem at Pentecost (Ac. 2:10), and that Apollos was from **Alexandria** (Ac. 18:24).

EGYPT, BROOK OF: The boundary between **Palestine** and Egypt (Num. 34:5; Jos. 15:4, 47; 1 Kg. 8:65; 2 Kg. 24:7; 2 Chr. 7:8; Isa. 27:12; Ezek. 47:19, 48:28); mod. *Wâdî el-'Arîsh*.

EGYPT, RIVER OF: The southern limit of the land promised to Abraham (Gen. 15:18). Although the word used here is 'river' and not 'wady', the reference must be to mod. *Wâdī el-'Arîsh*. Cf. also Jdt. 1:9. *See* **Egypt, Brook of.**

EKRON: The most northerly of the five Philistine cities (Jos. 13:3). It is reckoned to **Judah** (Jos. 15:11, 45f.) or to **Dan** (Jos. 19:43), but in fact was held by neither. It was unconquered by Joshua (Jos. 13:3), but is said to have been conquered by Judah (Jg. 1:18). Yet it nowhere figures save as Philistine. It was certainly Philistine when the Ark was in Philistine hands (1 Sam. 5:16, 6:17), and from Ekron it was sent back to **Israel** (1 Sam. 6:10). It is said to have been taken by Israel in the days of Samuel (1 Sam. 7:14), but was certainly Philistine in the days of Saul (1 Sam. 17:52). Ahaziah sent to Ekron to consult its god Baal-zebub (2 Kg. 1:2ff.). Prophecies against Ekron stand in Jer. 25:20; Am. 1:8; Zeph. 2:4; Zech. 9:5, 7. Alexander Balas gave it to Jonathan (1 Mac. 10:89). It is probably mod. *Khirbet el-Muqanna'*.

ELAH, VALLEY OF: The valley where David slew Goliath (1 Sam. 17:2, 19); mod. *Wâdī es-Sanṭ*.

ELAM: A country E. of **Babylonia**, whose king Chedorlaomer, is represented as the head of the coalition which Abraham routed (Gen. 14:1, 5, 9). Some Elamites were transferred to settle in **Samaria** (1) (Ezr. 4:9). It figures in the prophecies (Isa. 21:2ff., 22:6; Jer. 25:25, 49:34ff.; Ezek. 32:34). Its capital was **Susa**, which became one of the Persian royal cities (Neh. 1:1; Est. 1:2; Dan. 8:2). In the Apocrypha it is called **Elymais** (Tob. 2:10; 1 Mac. 6:1). Some Jews were early found there (Isa. 11:11), and Jews from there were in **Jerusalem** at Pentecost (Ac. 2:9), In 1 Esd. 5:22 'the other Elam' (RSV) corresponds to **Lod, Hadid** in Ezr. 2:33; Neh. 7:37.

ELASA: The scene of the battle in which Judas was defeated and died (1 Mac. 9:5ff.); perhaps mod. *Khirbet Il'asa*.

ELATH: A place on the Gulf of *'Aqaba*, mentioned in the account of the Wilderness wanderings (Dt. 2:8). Solomon built a merchant fleet here (called **Eloth**, 1 Kg. 9:26; 2 Chr. 8:17), but access to the port was lost (2 Kg. 8:20). It was recovered under Amaziah (2 Kg.

14:22), and rebuilt by Uzziah (again called Eloth, 2 Chr. 26:2), but lost again by Ahaz (2 Kg. 16:6). It was near mod. *'Aqaba*.

EL-BETHEL: Jacob's name for the place of his vision (Gen. 35:7).

ELEALEH: A place in Moab, conquered and allotted to Reuben (Num. 32:3, 37), but later in Moabite hands (Isa. 15:4, 16:9; Jer. 48:34); mod. *el-'Al*, N. of Heshbon.

ELEUTHERUS, RIVER: A river flowing from the Lebanon to the Mediterranean, and the boundary between Syria and Phoenicia (1 Mac. 11:7; 12:30); mod. *Nahr el-Kebîr*.

ELIM: A stopping-place in the Wilderness wanderings (Exod. 15:27, 16:1; Num. 33:9f.); probably mod. *Wâdî Gharandel*.

ELISHAH: The 'son' of Javan (Gen. 10:4; 1 Chr. 1:7), representing a geographical district. It is the source of blue and purple dyes for Tyre (Ezek. 27:7), and is probably a part of Cyprus.

ELKOSH: The home of Nahum (Nah. 1:1), of unknown location.

ELLASAR: The territory ruled by Arioch (Gen. 14:1, 9); commonly, but improbably, identified with the Babylonian city, *Larsa*.

ELON (*'terebinth'*): 1. An unidentified place in Dan (1) (Jos. 19:42).
2. LXX^B reads Elon in Jg. 12:12 (so JB), where AV, RV and RSV have Aijalon (2).

ELON-BETH-HANAN: One of Solomon's store cities, in his second district (1 Kg. 4:9); perhaps the same as Aijalon (1) + Beth-hanan, a neighbouring city (JB reads 'Aijalon as far as Beth-hanan').

ELOTH: The alternative spelling of Elath, found in 1 Kg. 9:26; 2 Chr. 8:17, 26:2.

EL-PARAN: *See* Paran.

ELTEKEH: A city in Dan, near Ekron and Gibbethon (Jos. 19:44); it was a Levitical city (Jos. 21:23). Its location is unknown.

ELTEKON: A place in Judah (Jos. 15:59); perhaps mod. *Khirbet ed-Deir*.

ELTOLAD: A place assigned to Simeon (Jos. 19:4), but later to Judah (Jos. 15:30), which early absorbed Simeon; called Tolad in 1 Chr. 4:29. Its site is unknown.

ELYMAIS: The Greek name for Elam, found in Tob. 2:10; 1 Mac. 6:1.

EMEK-KEZIZ: An unknown place in Benjamin (Jos. 18:21).

EMMAUS: The village to which Jesus went with Cleopas and his companion (Lk. 24:13ff.). This is said to be 60 stadia (about 7 miles) from Jerusalem, but one important MS has 160 stadia, and the site is commonly identified with *Amwâs*, about 20 miles from Jerusalem. In that case it is the same as Emmaus 'in the plain', where Judas and Gorgias fought (1 Mac. 3:40, 57, 4:3ff.), which was fortified by Bacchides (1 Mac. 9:50).

ENAIM: An unidentified place where Tamar sat (Gen. 38:14, 21), near Timnah; perhaps the same as Enam.

ENAM: A place in Judah (Jos. 15:34); perhaps the same as Enaim. Its location is unknown.

EN-DOR: A place within the boundaries of Issachar allotted to W. Manasseh (Jos. 17:11). Here lived the medium whom Saul consulted (1 Sam. 28:7ff.). According to Ps. 83:10, it was the scene of the destruction of Sisera. It is probably mod. *Endôr*.

EN-EGLAIM (*'spring of two calves'*): A place near En-gedi on the shore of the Dead Sea (Ezek. 47:10). It is probably mod. *'Ain Feshkha*, near *Qumrân*, where many Dead Sea Scrolls have been found.

EN-GANNIM (*'spring of gardens'*): 1. A place in Judah (Jos. 15:34); possibly mod. *Beit Jemâl*.
    2. A city in Issachar (Jos. 19:21), allotted as a Levitical city (Jos. 21:29); corresponding to Anem (perhaps in error) in 1 Chr. 6:73. It is perhaps the same as Beth-haggan (2 Kg. 9:27), and probably mod. *Jenîn*.

EN-GEDI (*'spring of the kid'*): A place in Judah (Jos. 15:62), where David took refuge (1 Sam. 23:29, 24:1). Moab and Ammon came here against Jehoshaphat (2 Chr. 20:2). Ezekiel describes it as a place for the spreading of nets (Ezek. 47:10). Its vineyards are referred to in Ca. 1:14. It is equated with Hazazon-tamar in 2 Chr. 20:2, but this may be a gloss. It is mod. *Tell el-Jurn*, near *'Ain Jidi*.

EN-HADDAH: A place in Issachar (Jos. 19:21); possibly mod. *el-Ḥadetheh*.

EN-HAKKORE (*'spring of the partridge'*): A fountain at Lehi (Jos. 15:19); it is unidentified.

EN-HAZOR (*'spring of Hazor'*): A town in Naphtali (Jos. 19:37); perhaps mod. *Khirbet Ḥaṣîreh*.

EN-MISHPAT (*'spring of judgment'*): An alternative name of Kadesh (Gen. 14:7).

EN-RIMMON (*'spring of pomegranate'*): A place in Simeon (Jos. 19:7), resettled after the exile (Neh. 11:29. In 1 Chr. 4:32) Ain (2) and Rimmon should be combined to read En-rimmon. So also in Jos. 15:32 (so JB), where it is assigned to Judah, which early absorbed Simeon. It is mod. *Khirbet Umm er-Ramāmîn*.

EN-ROGEL (*'spring of the fuller'*): A spring near Jerusalem, on the border between Judah (Jos. 15:7) and Benjamin (Jos. 18:16), where Jonathan and Ahimaaz were waiting for news of Absalom for David (2 Sam. 17:17), and where Adonijah was feasting when Solomon was proclaimed king (1 Kg. 1:9). It is usually identified with mod. *Bîr Ayyûb*.

EN-SHEMESH (*'spring of the sun'*): A spring near En-rogel (Jos. 15:7, 18:17); mod. *'Ain el-Ḥôḍ*.

EN-TAPPUAH (*'spring of Tappuah'*): A place in W. Manasseh (Jos. 17:7); probably the same as Tappuah (2) (Jos. 16:8, 17:8). It is probably mod. *Tell esh-Sheikh Abū Zarad*.

EPHES-DAMMIM: The scene of the battle in which Goliath was killed (1 Sam. 17:1); called Pas-dammim in 1 Chr. 11:13. Its site is unknown.

EPHESUS: The capital of the Roman province of **Asia**, where Paul paid a short visit on his way back from his second missionary journey (Ac. 18:19f.). Here Apollos met Aquila and Priscilla (Ac. 18:24), who perhaps first brought the gospel here; after Apollos had left, Paul came to Ephesus on his third missionary journey (Ac. 19:1) for a longer stay (Ac. 19:8ff.). Here there was a riot against Paul (Ac. 19:23ff.; cf. 1 C. 15:32), led by the devotees of the goddess Artemis, whose worship made Ephesus famous. Despite the opposition, Paul made many converts (1 C. 16:8f.). On his return from his third journey, after visiting **Greece**, Paul did not call at Ephesus (Ac. 20:13), but invited the elders of the church there to meet him at **Miletus** (Ac. 20:17). One of his letters is addressed to Ephesus, though some of the earliest MSS omit 'who are at Ephesus' in Eph. 1:1 (omitted from RSV and JB), and it is held by many that this letter was not addressed to any single church. The church at Ephesus was one of the seven to which John wrote (Rev. 1:11, 2:1ff.). Timothy ministered at Ephesus (1 Tim. 1:3; 2 Tim. 1:18), and also Tychicus (2 Tim. 4:12).

EPHRAIM: 1. The territory occupied by the tribe of **Ephraim**, which was one of the two divisions of the house of Joseph. Its ideal limits are stated in Jos. 16:5ff.

2. A town near **Baal-hazor** (2 Sam. 13:23); probably the same as **Ephron** (1) (2 Chr. 13:19). It is perhaps the town to which Jesus went after raising Lazarus (Jn 11:54). It is probably the same as Aphairema (1 Mac. 10:29, 38, 11:34), which was transferred from **Samaria** (2) to **Judea**. It is identified with mod. *eṭ-Ṭaiyibeh*.

EPHRAIM, FOREST OF: The scene of Absalom's defeat and death (2 Sam. 18:6ff.). It was E. of the **Jordan** (2 Sam. 17:22, 24, 26), near **Mahanaim**.

EPHRAIM GATE: A gate in the wall of **Jerusalem**, four hundred cubits from the **Corner Gate** (2 Kg. 14:13; 2 Chr. 25:23). This stretch of wall was broken down by Jehoash. Beside this gate there was an open square in Nehemiah's time (Neh. 8:16, 12:39).

EPHRAIM, HILL COUNTRY OF: The name for the part of the central highlands occupied by the *Ephraimites* (Jos. 17:15; 19:50; Jg. 2:9; 3:27; 1 Sam. 1:1 +). It formed Solomon's first district (1 Kg. 4:8).

EPHRAIN: *See* **Ephron** (1).

EPHRATH: 1. *See* **Ephrathah** (1).

2. The place where Rachel died (Gen. 35:16ff., 48:7). Elsewhere Rachel's death is located at **Ramah** (3) (Jer. 31:15; Mt. 2:18), which was 5 miles N. of **Jerusalem**; cf. 1 Sam. 10:2, which sets her tomb at Zelzah in **Benjamin**. It is therefore probable that the words 'that is Bethlehem' in Gen. 35:16, 48:7 are an erroneous gloss, confusing Ephrath with **Ephrathah** (1).

EPHRATHAH: 1. In 1 Chr. 4:4 Ephrathah is said to have founded **Bethlehem**, and in Ru. 4:11 Ephrathah stands parallel to Bethlehem as an alternative name. In Mic. 5:2 we find Bethlehem Ephrathah. Elimelech and his family (Ru. 1:2) and Jesse (1 Sam. 17:12) are called Ephrathites of Bethlehem.

2. In Ps. 132:6 Ephrathah is connected with the Ark when it was at *Kiriath-jearim*. 1 Chr. 2:50f. connects the founding of **Bethlehem** and Kiriath-jearim with two members of the same family, indicating some ancient link between these places.

EPHRON: 1. A town which Abijah took from Jeroboam I (2 Chr. 13:19); in RSVm **Ephrain**. It is probably the same as **Ephraim** (2) and **Ophrah** (1), mod. *eṭ-Ṭaiyibeh*.

2. A fortified city E. of the **Jordan** taken by Judas (1 Mac. 5:46ff.; 2 Mac. 12:27), of unknown location.

EPHRON, MOUNT: A district on the border of **Judah** in the neighbourhood of **Kiriath-jearim** (Jos. 15:9).

ERECH: A city of **Babylonia** (Gen. 10:10), citizens from which were transferred to **Samaria** (1) (Ezr. 4:9); mod. *Warka*.

ESCAPE, ROCK OF: A place in the wilderness of **Maon** (1) where Saul abandoned the pursuit of David to meet the Philistines (1 Sam. 23:28); possibly in mod. *Wâdī el- Malâqī*.

ESDRAELON, PLAIN OF: The Greek name for the W. part of the **Valley of Jezreel** (Esdraelon may be derived from Jezreel), found in Jdt. 1:8, 3:9, 4:6, 7:3; mod. *Merj Ibn 'Amir*.

ESEK (*'contention'*): A well dug by Isaac (Gen. 26:20); its location is unknown.

ESHAN: A place in **Judah** (Jos. 15:52); possibly mod. *Khirbet Sam'ah*.

ESHCOL, VALLEY OF (*'valley of bunch of grapes'*): A fruitful valley from which the spies brought back grapes (Num. 13:23f., 32:9; Dt. 1:24). Its location is unknown.

ESHTAOL: A city of Judah in the lowland (Jos. 15:33), at one time reckoned to **Dan** (1) (Jos. 19:41). Near here Samson began to feel the Spirit of the Lord (Jg. 13:25), and near here he was buried (Jg. 16:31). Some of the migrating Danites were from here (Jg. 18:2, 11). In 1 Chr. 2:53 the men of Eshtaol are reckoned as Calebites. It is perhaps mod. *Eshwa'*.

ESHTEMOA: A Levitical city in the hill country of **Judah** (Jos. 21:14; 1 Chr. 6:57). To it David sent spoils (1 Sam. 30:28). It is called **Eshtemoh** in Jos. 15:50. It is perhaps mod. *es-Semû'*.

ESHTEMOH: *See* **Eshtemoa.**

ETAM: 1. A place where Samson stayed (Jg. 15:8) and from which he was taken and handed over to the Philistines (Jg. 15:11ff.). Its location is unknown.
2. A place in **Judah**, mentioned in LXX (also JB) in Jos. 15:59, but not in MT or RSV. It was fortified by Rehoboam (2 Chr. 11:6); possibly mod. *Khirbet el-Khôkh*.
3. A place in **Simeon** (1 Chr. 4:32), of unknown location.

ETHAM: A stopping place in the Wilderness wanderings, on the edge of the wilderness (Exod. 13:20; Num. 33:6ff.); its site is unknown.

ETHER: 1. A place in **Judah** (Jos. 15:42); perhaps mod. *Khirbet el-'Ater*.
2. A place in **Simeon** (Jos. 19:7); perhaps the same as **Athach** (1 Sam. 30:30), mod. *Khirbet 'Attîr*.

ETHIOPIA: A country of **Egypt**, called *Kûsh* in Hebrew (*see* **Cush**). Ethiopians were in Shishak's army (2 Chr. 12:3) and Asa is said to have destroyed a large army of them (2 Chr. 16:8). In 2 Kg. 19:9 and Isa. 37:9 reference is made to Tirhakah, king of Ethiopia, who became Pharaoh of Egypt. Jews were early found in Ethiopia and their restoration was prophesied (Isa. 11:11). Other references to Ethiopia in prophecies stand in Isa. 18:1; 20:3ff., 43:3 (where

Ethiopia is promised as a ransom for Israel); 45:14 (where the wealth of Ethiopia is promised to the Jews); Jer. 46:9; Ezek. 29:10, 30:4f.; Neh. 3:9; Zeph. 3:10. Job 28:9 speaks of the topaz of Ethiopia. In the Psalter Ethiopia is twice mentioned (Ps. 68:31, 87:4), and in Est. 1:1, 8:9 it is the limit of the Persian empire. Jeremiah was rescued by an Ethiopian eunuch (Jer. 38:7ff.) and in the NT Philip converted another Ethiopian eunuch (Ac. 8:27ff.).

EUPHRATES: A river which rises in **Armenia** and is joined by the **Tigris** before reaching the Persian Gulf; mod. *Shatt el-Furât*. It is represented as one of the rivers of the **Garden of Eden** (Gen. 2:14). In the OT it is frequently called simply 'the River' (Num. 22:5; Jos. 24:3, 14; Ezr. 4:10ff.; Isa. 7:20; Mic. 7:12). It formed ideally the northern limit of the Promised Land (Gen. 15:18; Exod. 23:31; Dt. 1:7, 11:24; Jos. 1:4) and the kingdom of Solomon is said to have reached it (1 Kg. 1:24). Jacob crossed the Euphrates when he left Laban (Gen. 31:21). Pharaoh Neco marched to it to try to save **Assyria** (2 Kg. 23:29), but was defeated at the battle of **Carchemish** and the country W. of the Euphrates fell to **Babylon** (2 Kg. 24:7). Under the Persians the country W. of the Euphrates formed an administrative province (Ezr. 4:10 +) and under the Seleucid monarch, Antiochus IV, Lysias was left in charge of the same area (1 Mac. 3:32), while the king himself crossed the river to the E. (1 Mac. 3:37). Other references in the Apocrypha are in Jdt. 1:6, 2:24; Sir. 24:26. In the NT the river is referred to in Rev. 9:14, 16:12.

EZEM ('*bone*'): A place in **Simeon** (Jos. 19:3; 1 Chr. 4:29), later reckoned in **Judah** (Jos. 15:29), which early absorbed Simeon; possibly mod. *Umm el-'Azâm*, S.E. of **Beersheba**.

EZION-GEBER: A town on the coast of the Gulf of '*Aqaba*, near **Elath**. It was a stopping place in the Wilderness wanderings (Num. 33:35f.; cf. Dt. 2:8). Solomon used it as the port for his merchant fleet (1 Kg. 9:26ff.; 2 Chr. 8:17), and later Jehoshaphat experienced misfortune when he attempted the same thing (1 Kg. 22:48; 2 Chr. 20:36f.). It is mod. *Tell el-Kheleifeh*. A copper refinery, which was probably used by Solomon, has been discovered there.

F

FAIR HAVENS: A harbour on the S. coast of **Crete**, where the captain of the ship on which Paul was a prisoner was unwilling to remain (Ac. 27:8); mod. *Kali Limenes*.

FISH GATE: A gate of **Jerusalem** associated with the **Second Quarter** (Zeph. 1:10). It was strengthened by Manasseh (2 Chr. 33:14), and rebuilt in Nehemiah's time (Neh. 3:3). It is mentioned also in the account of the procession (Neh. 12:39). It was on the N. side of the city.

FOUNDATION, GATE OF THE: A gate in **Jerusalem** where one third of the guard at the enthronement of Joash was posted (2 Chr. 23:5), apparently a gate leading from the royal palace to the Temple. It is unmentioned in the parallel account in 2 Kg. 11:6, which mentions the **Gate Sur.** The Hebrew word *Sur* closely resembles the word for Foundation.

FOUNTAIN GATE: A gate of **Jerusalem** repaired in Nehemiah's time (Neh. 2:14, 3:15). It was near the **Stairs of the City of David** (Neh. 12:37) .It was either the same as the **Gate Between the Two Walls,** or near it.

FULLER'S FIELD: The place near **Jerusalem** where Isaiah met Ahaz (Isa. 7:3), and where Sennacherib's messengers stood to deliver their message (2 Kg. 18:17; Isa. 36:2). Its location is unknown.

G

GAASH, MOUNTAIN OF: A mountain in **Ephraim** (1), near **Timnath-serah,** where Joshua was buried (Jos. 24:30; Jg. 2:9).

GAASH, BROOKS OF: The birthplace of one of David's heroes (2 Sam. 23:30; 1 Chr. 11:32); probably in the neighbourhood of the **Mountain of Gaash.**

GABBATHA: The paved area where Pilate tried Jesus (Jn 19:13). The site favoured by tradition is near to the site of the Antonia, the Roman fortress N. of the Temple, and the pavement consists of large blocks of stone two feet thick and more than a yard square.

GAD: The territory occupied by the tribe of Gad. Its ideal limits are stated in Jos. 13:24–28.

GAD, VALLEY TOWARD: The starting place for David's census (2 Sam. 24:5). The reference is to the valley of the **Arnon.**

GADARA: One of the cities of the **Decapolis,** mentioned only in connection with the healing of the demoniac (Mt. 8:28, Matthew says two demoniacs). In the parallel Mk 5:1; Lk. 8:26, RSV and JB have Gerasenes, i.e. inhabitants of **Gerasa,** instead of Gadarenes. In all three places the MSS vary between Gadarenes, Gerasenes and Gergesenes, (i.e. inhabitants of **Gergesa**). Gadara is mod. *Umm Qeis.*

GALATIA: A region in Central Asia Minor inhabited by the descendants of invading Gauls. The name is also used for a Roman province which, in addition to this, included Paphlagonia and parts of **Pontus, Phrygia,** and **Lycaonia.** One of Paul's letters is addressed to the churches in Galatia (Gal. 1:2), which he had evidently visited. He refers to the directions he had given to these churches in 1 C. 16:1. On his second missionary journey Paul went through Phrygia and Galatia (Ac. 16:6) and again on his third journey (Ac. 18:23). Most British scholars hold that the reference is to the churches founded on his first missionary journey in **Derbe, Lystra, Iconium,** and **Antioch of Pisidia,** but many continental scholars continue to follow the older view that it was to churches in Galatia in the narrower sense (N. Galatia). In 2 Tim. 4:10 Crescens is said to have gone to Galatia, but there is a variant reading, **Gaul** (RSVm). I Peter is addressed to Galatia among other places (I Per. 1:1).

GALEED (*'cairn of witness'*): Jacob's name for the heap of stones made by Laban and himself (Gen. 31:47f.). It is of the same meaning as **Jegar-sahadutha.**

GALILEE (*'ring'*): The region N. of **Samaria** (2). Joshua conquered a king from this region (Jos. 12:23); and **Kedesh** (3), a city of refuge and a Levitical city, was within it (Jos. 20:7, 21:32; 1 Chr. 6:76). Solomon ceded twenty Galilean cities to Hiram (1 Kg. 9:11). Galilee was conquered and its people deported by Tiglath-pileser (2 Kg. 15:29). Nazareth, where Jesus was brought up, lay in Galilee (Mt. 2:22f., 21:11; Mk 1:9; Lk. 1:26), which was then ruled by Herod Antipas (Lk. 3:1). Much of the ministry of Jesus was exercised in Galilee (Mt. 4:23; Mk 1:39; Lk. 4:14f.), and **Capernaum** (Lk. 4:31), **Cana** (Jn 2:1), and **Bethsaida** (Jn 12:21) were all within its borders. Resurrection appearances were promised in Galilee (Mt. 26:32, 28:7, 10; Mk 14:28, 16:7) and were made (Mt. 28:16ff.; Jn 21). The Church early spread in Galilee (Ac. 9:31). In the Maccabean war, fighting took place in Galilee (1 Mac. 5:14ff., 11:63, 12:47ff.). Other references to Galilee in the Apocrypha stand in Tob. 1:2; Jdt. 1:8, 15:5; 1 Mac. 10:30.

GALILEE, SEA OF: A lake in the valley of the **Jordan**, also called the Sea of **Chinnereth** (Num. 24:11) or of **Chinneroth** (Jos. 12:3), Lake of **Gennesaret** (Lk. 5:1), or Sea of **Tiberias** (Jn 6:1, 21:1). It is mod. *Baḥr Ṭabarîyeh*. **Capernaum** and **Bethsaida** were on its shores. Four of the disciples of Jesus were fishermen in the Sea before Jesus called them (Mt. 4:18ff.; Mk 1:16ff.); Jesus taught from Peter's boat (Lk. 5:3), and from a fish caught in the Sea by Peter He paid the Temple tax (Mt. 17:24). Sudden storms arise in the Sea, and Jesus and His disciples were twice caught in them (Mt. 8:23ff., 14:22ff.; Mk 4:35ff., 6:45ff.; Lk. 8:22ff.; Jn 6:16ff.). We read of two miraculous draughts of fishes in the Sea (Lk. 5:4ff.; Jn 21:1ff.).

GALLIM (*'heaps'*): 1. A place near **Jerusalem** on the expected route of the Assyrian approach (Isa. 10:30). Palti, to whom Michal was given, came from here (1 Sam. 25:44). It is perhaps mod. *Khirbet Ka'kûl*.

2. A place in the hill country of **Judah** (Jos. 15:59, in an addition in LXX and JB, not in MT and RSV).

GAMAD: An unidentified place near **Tyre**, mentioned in Ezek. 27:11.

GAREB: A hill near **Jerusalem** (Jer. 31:39), of unknown location.

GATH (*'winepress'*): one of the Philistine cities (Jos. 13:3), formerly occupied by Anakim (Jos. 11:22). It is not mentioned as allotted to any Israelite tribe, but Samuel is said to have restored it to Israel (1 Sam. 7:14). Some Ephraimites were killed by Gittites (1 Chr. 7:21), and their death was later avenged (1 Chr. 8:13). When the Philistines captured the Ark, it was brought to Gath (1 Sam. 5:8f.); and when it was returned, Gath sent an offering (1 Sam. 6:17). Goliath came from Gath (1 Sam. 17:4; 2 Sam. 21:19), and other giants are said to have lived there (2 Sam. 21:22; 1 Chr. 20:8). When David fled from Saul, he came to Gath (1 Sam. 21:10ff., 27:2ff.), and its king assigned him the dependent town of Ziklag (1 Sam. 27:6), and six hundred men of Gath were among his soldiers at the time of Absalom's rebellion (2 Sam. 15:18). Shimei pursued his slaves to Gath, and lost his life in consequence (1 Kg. 2:39ff.). The Chronicler records that David took the city (1 Chr. 18:1), and that Rehoboam fortified it (2 Chr. 11:8). Hazael conquered it (2 Kg. 12:17), and later Uzziah conquered it for Judah (2 Chr. 26:6). Its site is not certainly identified.

GATH-HEPHER (*'winepress of digging'*): A place in Zebulun (Jos. 19:13), from which Jonah came (2 Kg. 14:25); perhaps mod. *Khirbet ez-Zurrâ'*.

GATH-RIMMON (*'winepress of the pomegranate'*): 1. A place in Dan (1) (Jos. 19:45) and a Levitical city (Jos. 21:24), but reckoned to Ephraim (1) in 1 Chr. 6:69. It is perhaps mod. *Tell Jerîsheh*.

2. A Levitical city of Manasseh (Jos. 21:25; replaced by Bileam in 1 Chr. 6:70. In Jos 21:25 it is perhaps erroneously repeated from verse 24, and we should read Ibleam (cf. JB).

GAUL: *See* Galatia.

GAZA: One of the Philistine cities (Jos. 13:3), formerly occupied by Canaanites (Gen. 10:19), Avvim (Dt. 2:23), or Anakim (Jos. 11:22 It was conquered by Joshua (Jos. 10:41) or by Judahites (Jg. 1:18), and allotted to Judah (Jos. 15:47), but in most of its occurrences in the Bible it is securely Philistine. It was the scene of some of Samson's exploits (Jg. 16:1ff.), and when he was captured and blinded he was brought as a prisoner here (Jg. 16:21ff.). When the Ark was returned by the Philistines Gaza sent an offering (1 Sam. 6:17). It was on the border of Solomon's kingdom (1 Kg. 4:24), and in a later age it was conquered by Hezekiah (2 Kg. 18:8) and also by Pharaoh Neco (Jer. 47:1). Prophecies against it are in Jer. 25:20; Am. 1:6f., Zeph. 2:4; Zech. 9:5. It was taken and sacked by Jonathan (1 Mac. 11:61f.). Philip was on the Jerusalem to Gaza road when he met the Ethiopian eunuch (Ac. 8:26). It is mod. *Ghazzeh*.

GAZARA: The form of the name **Gezer** found in Maccabees. Judas twice pursued his defeated enemies as far as here (1 Mac. 4:15, 7:45). It was fortified by Bacchides (1 Mac. 9:52), and later conquered and fortified by Simon (1 Mac. 13:43ff.; cf. 15:27ff.), who made his son John its commander (1 Mac. 13:53, 16:1). In 2 Mac. 10:32ff. its capture by Judas is recorded, but either this is a wrong attribution to him of Simon's exploit, or we should read **Jazer** instead of Gazara. *See* **Jazer**.

GEBA ('*hill*'): 1. A city in **Benjamin** (Jos. 18:24; cf. 1 Chr. 8:6), allocated as a Levitical city (Jos. 21:17; 1 Chr. 6:60). It was the northern limit of the kingdom of **Judah** (2 Kg. 23:8). In Jg. 20:33 and 1 Sam. 13:3 it is perhaps confused with the neighbouring **Gibeah**. In 2 Sam. 5:25 it is probably confused with **Gibeon** (so LXX; cf. 1 Chr. 14:16). Asa fortified Geba (1 Kg. 15:22; 2 Chr. 16:6), and Isaiah pictures it as on the route of the Assyrian approach (Isa. 10:29). Some who traced their descent from here returned from exile (Ezr. 2:26; Neh. 7:30; 1 Esd. 5:20), and it was resettled (Neh. 11:31). Some Temple singers lived here (Neh. 12:29). Its position is indicated in 1 Sam. 14:5 as near **Michmash**; mod. *Jeba'*.

2. A place near **Dothan**, where Holofernes encamped (Jdt. 3:10).

GEBAL: 1. A region in the S. which was allied with **Edom, Moab,** and others against **Israel** (Ps. 83:7). Its location is unknown.

2. A Phoenician city (Ezek. 27:9), included in the ideal limits of Israel (Jos. 13:5). It provided workmen who helped to build Solomon's Temple (1 Kg. 5:18). It was the Greek *Byblos*, mod. *Jebeil*.

GEBIM: An unlocated and else unknown place mentioned as on the route of the Assyrian advance (Isa. 10:31).

GEDER: A Canaanite city conquered by Joshua (Jos. 12:13), from which Baal-hanan came (1 Chr. 27:28). It is perhaps the same as **Beth-gader** (1 Chr. 2:51). Its location is unknown.

GEDERAH: 1, A place in the lowland of **Judah** (Jos. 15:36; 1 Chr. 4:23); perhaps mod. *Khirbet Jedîreh*.

2. A place in **Benjamin**, from which one of David's supporters came (1 Chr. 12:4); perhaps *Jedîreh*, near **Gibeon**.

GEDEROTH: A place in the lowland of **Judah** (Jos. 15:41), captured by the Philistines (2 Chr. 28:18); its location is unknown.

GEDEROTHAIM: A place in the lowland of **Judah**, mentioned as one of fourteen cities in Jos. 15:36. As there are fourteen cities without it, it is probably a dittograph of **Gederah**, which precedes it.

GEDOR: 1. A place in the hill country of **Judah** (Jos. 15:58); probably mod. *Khirbet Jedûr*.

2. A place in **Judah**, founded by Penuel (1 Chr. 4:4), of unknown location.

3. A place in **Judah**, founded by Jered. (1 Chr. 4:18), of unknown location. Possibly either 2 or 3 should be identified with 1.

4. A place in **Benjamin**, from which one of David's followers came (1 Chr. 12:7); of unknown location.

5. A district in **Simeon** taken from the Hamites (1 Chr. 4:39ff.). But LXX reads **Gerar**, and this is probably correct (so JB.)

GE-HARASH (*'valley of craftsmen'*): A Kenizzite town in **Judah** (1 Chr. 4:14). After the exile, Benjaminites settled in a **Valley of Craftsmen** (Neh. 11:35), which may be the same place. Its location is unknown.

GELILOTH (*'circles'*): A place opposite the **Ascent of Adummim** (Jos. 18:17); called **Gilgal** (5) in Jos. 15:7. It is possibly the same as **Beth-gilgal** (Neh. 12:29).

GENNESARET (*'garden of princes'*): The region on the NW. shore of the **Sea of Galilee** (Mt. 14:34; Mk 6:53).

GENNESARET, LAKE OF: Name of the **Sea of Galilee** found in Lk. 5:1; called the 'Waters of Gennesaret' in 1 Mac. 11:67.

GERAR: A city in the S. of **Palestine**, inhabited by Canaanites (Gen. 10:19), In the time of Abraham (Gen. 20:1ff.) and Isaac

(Gen. 26:1ff.) it was ruled over by Abimelech. Isaac encamped in a valley near it and dug wells there (Gen. 26:17ff). Asa pursued his enemies to Gerar, and plundered it (2 Chr. 14:13f.). It is mentioned in 2 Mac. 13:24. In 1 Chr. 4:39 we should read Gerar for **Gedor** (5). It is perhaps mod. *Tell Abū Hureirah.*

GERASA: One of the cities of the **Decapolis**, mentioned only in connection with the healing of the demoniac (Mk. 5:1; Lk. 8:26, 37), where the MSS vary between Gerasenes (i.e. inhabitants of Gerasa), Gadarenes and Gergesenes. In Mt. 8:28 the better attested reading is Gadarenes (*see* **Gadara**). Gerasa is mod. *Jerash,* N. of *'Amman.*

GERGESA: A place near the E. shore of the **Sea of Galilee**, according to Origen, Eusebius and Jerome, mentioned in some MSS in Mt. 8:28; Mk 5:1; Lk. 8:26, 37. *See* **Gerasa**. (In Jdt. 5:15 Gergesites means Girgashites (so JB reads); cf. Gen. 10:16, 15:21; Dt. 7:1 +.)

GERIZIM, MOUNT: A mountain near **Shechem**, facing **Mount Ebal**, described as the mountain of blessing (Dt. 11:29), on which six tribes were to be stationed when the blessings were pronounced (Dt. 27:12; cf. Jos. 8:33). from this mountain Jotham told his parable (Jg. 9:7). The Samaritans erected their temple on this mountain, and it was their rival to the **Jerusalem** Temple. It was destroyed by John Hyrcanus in 128 B.C., but the Samaritans continued to hold that this mountain was the only legitimate place for the Temple (Jn 4.20). It is mod. *Jebel eṭ-Ṭôr.*

GERUTH CHIMHAM ('*lodging place of Chimham*'): A place near **Bethlehem** where Johanan stayed (Jer. 41:17); perhaps named after Chimham (2 Sam. 19:37ff.). Its location is unknown.

GESHUR: The territory occupied by an Aramean tribe on the borders of **Bashan** (Dt. 3:14; Jos. 12:5, 13:11). Their territory was allotted to Manasseh, but they resisted the Israelites (Jos. 13:13), and David married the daughter of their king (2 Sam. 3:3; 1 Chr. 3:2). Absalom fled here for refuge (2 Sam. 13:37f., 14:23, 32, 15:8). Geshur encroached on Israelite territory in **Gilead** (1 Chr. 2:23). (The Geshurites of Jos. 13:2 and 1 Sam. 27:8 were people who lived near the Philistine cities.)

GETHSEMANE (*'oil press'*): A place on the **Mount of Olives**, not precisely identified, where Jesus went with His disciples (Mt. 26:36ff.; Mk 14:32ff.; cf. Lk. 22:39ff.; Jn 18:1ff.), and where He was seized by the authorities. It was here that He prayed His agonized prayer.

GEZER: A Canaanite city whose king was defeated by Joshua (Jos. 10:33, 12:12). It was allotted to **Ephraim** (1) (Jos. 16:3; Jg. 1:29; 1 Chr. 7:28), but the Canaanites successfully resisted (Jos. 16:10; Jg. 1:29). In David's time it was the scene of war with the Philistines (1 Chr. 20:4; cf. 2 Sam. 5:25; 1 Chr. 14:16). It was first conquered by Pharaoh, who gave it to Solomon with his daughter as a dowry (1 Kg. 9:16), and Solomon fortified it (1 Kg. 9:15, 17). It became a Levitical city (Jos. 21:21; 1 Chr. 6:67). In the Hellenistic age it was rebuilt and called **Gazara**. It is mod. *Tell Jezer*.

GIAH: An unidentified place mentioned in the account of Joab's pursuit of Abner (2 Sam. 2:24).

GIBBETHON (*'mound'*): A place in **Dan** (1) (Jos. 19:44), appointed as a Levitical city (Jos. 21:23). It became Philistine; Baasha assasinated Nadab when he was besieging it (1 Kg. 15:27), and Omri was again besieging it when Zimri assassinated Elah (1 Kg. 16:15ff.). It is probably mod. *Tell el-Melât*.

GIBEAH (*'hill'*): 1. A city in **Benjamin** (Jos. 18:28; Jg. 19:14). Here a Levite's concubine was abused (Jg. 19:12ff.), leading to war between the other Israelite tribes and Benjamin (Jg. 20f.), one result of which was the supply of brides from **Jabesh-gilead** for the Benjaminites (Jg. 21:8ff.). Hence, when Jabesh-gilead was in trouble, messengers were sent to Gibeah for aid (1 Sam. 11:4), which was given under the leadership of Saul (1 Sam. 11:5ff.), whose home was here (1 Sam. 10:26; Isa. 10:29). Here was a garrison of the Philistines (1 Sam. 10:5 (**Gebeath-elohim**); 13:3 (**Geba**, in error), and it was when he met prophets near here that Saul was first moved by the spirit of God (1 Sam. 10:10). Jonathan's forces at Gibeah defeated the Philistine garrison (1 Sam. 13:2ff.). Saul was in Gibeah (1 Sam. 14:2, 16) when Jonathan made his attack on the Philistines at **Michmash** from Geba (1 Sam. 13:16, 14:5ff.) and after his attack on the Amalekites he returned to Gibeah (1 Sam. 15:34). He was at Gibeah when Doeg told him of David's visit to Ahimelech (1 Sam. 22:6ff.), and to Gibeah the Ziphites went to betray David (1 Sam.

23:19ff., 26:1ff.). One of David's heroes was from Gibeah (2 Sam. 23:29; 1 Chr. 11:31), and two other supporters came from here (1 Chr. 12:3). Abijah's mother was also from Gibeah (2 Chr. 13:2). To Hosea Gibeah was a symbol of Israel's sinfulness (Hos. 9:9, 10:9). It is mod. *Tell el-Fûl*.

2. A place in the hill country of Judah (Jos. 15:57); perhaps mod. *el-Jeba'*.

3. An unidentified place in the hill country of **Ephraim** (1) where Joshua was buried (Jos. 24:33).

GIBEATH-ELOHIM (*'hill of God'*): A town in **Benjamin** in which the Philistines had their garrison (1 Sam. 10:5); called **Gibeah** (1) in 1 Sam. 10:10. In 1 Sam. 13:3 this garrison is located at **Geba**, where Gibeah should be read, with LXX and JB.

GIBEATH-HA-ARALOTH (*'hill of the foreskins'*): The place near **Gilgal** (1) where Joshua circumcised the Israelites (Jos. 5:3).

GIBEON (*'hill'*): A Hivite city (Jos. 9:7, 11:19), whose inhabitants by a ruse made a covenant with Joshua (Jos. 9:3ff.), and which was therefore attacked by an Amorite alliance (Jos. 10:1ff.), and delivered by Joshua (Jos. 10:6ff.). It was reckoned to **Benjamin** (Jos. 18:25) and made a priestly city (Jos. 21:17). Here the armies of David and Ishbosheth met in a battle in which Asahel was killed (2 Sam. 2:12ff., 3:30), and here Joab slew Amasa (2 Sam. 20:8ff.). At some unknown time Saul had violated the covenant with Gibeon, and put Gibeonites to death (2 Sam. 21:1f.); David atoned for this by killing all of Saul's surviving descendants except Mephibosheth (2 Sam. 21:3ff.). David defeated the Philistines here (1 Chr. 14:16; cf. 2 Sam. 5:25 (Geba)). An important shrine was here, and Solomon came to it and was promised wisdom (1 Kg. 3:4ff., 9:2; 1 Chr. 1:3ff.). The Chronicler locates the Tabernacle here (1 Chr. 21:29); he says Zadok was priest here (1 Chr. 16:39), but in 2 Samuel he appears as priest only in **Jerusalem**. Johanan overtook Ishmael and his captives at Gibeon (Jer. 41:12ff.). Men of Gibeon shared in rebuilding the walls of Jerusalem (Neh. 3:7). Jeiel (1 Chr. 8:29, 9:35), Ishmaiah (1 Chr. 12:4), and Hananiah (Jer. 28:1) were natives of Gibeon. It is mod. *el-Jib*.

GIDOM: An unidentified place to which the other tribes pursued the Benjaminites (Jg. 20:45).

GIHON (*'a gushing forth'*) 1. One of the four rivers of the **Garden of Eden** (Gen. 2:13; Sir. 24:27, where it is perhaps identified with the **Nile**.)

2. A spring near **Jerusalem**, where Solomon was anointed king (1 Kg. 1:33ff.). Hezekiah brought the waters into the city (2 Chr. 32:30; cf. 2 Kg. 20:20; Sir. 48:17), almost certainly by the **Siloam** tunnel. Manasseh built an outer wall of Jerusalem W. of it (2 Chr. 33:14). It is mod. *'Ain Sittî Maryam*.

GILBOA, MOUNT: A ridge of hills W. of **Beth-shan**, where Saul assembled his army (1 Sam. 28:4) for the battle with the Philistines, in which he was defeated and slain (1 Sam. 31:1ff.; 2 Sam. 1:6ff., 21, 21:12; 1 Chr. 10:1ff.). It is mod. *Jebel Fuqqûʿah*.

GILEAD: 1. The territory E. of the **Jordan**, occupied by members of the tribe of Manasseh (Num. 26:29f., 32:39ff.; Jos. 17:1; 1 Chr. 27; 21) or of Reuben and Gad (Num. 32:1ff., 25f., 29ff.; Jos. 13:25; 1 Chr. 5:14ff.). Half of Gilead was bounded by the **Jabbok** and the **Arnon** (Dt. 3:15f.; Jos. 12:2). In Jg. 5:17 Gilead stands for the tribe of **Gad**, but in 1 Sam. 13:7 Gad is distinguished from Gilead. Laban overtook Jacob in Gilead (Gen. 31:23ff.) and the Ishmaelites who took Joseph into **Egypt** were coming from here (Gen. 37:25). Gilead provided two of the Judges (Jg. 10:3ff., 11:1ff.), and engaged in war with **Ephraim** (Jg. 12:4ff.). After the death of Saul it was ruled over by Ishbosheth (2 Sam. 2:9), and here David's army fought with Absalom (2 Sam. 17:26). Gilead formed Solomon's twelfth administrative district (1 Kg. 4:19). Elijah was from **Tishbe** in Gilead (1 Kg. 17:1). Hazael annexed Gilead (2 Kg. 10:33; cf. 1 Chr. 2:23), and Tiglath-pileser conquered it and deported its people (2 Kg. 15:29). It was famous for its herds and flocks (Num. 22:1; Ca. 4:1; 6:5; Mic. 7:14), and for its spices (Gen. 37:35; Jer. 8:22, 46:11). Amos condemns **Damascus** (Am. 1:3f.) and **Ammon** (Am. 1:13) for their treatment of Gilead, and Obadiah promises Gilead to **Benjamin** (Ob. 19). Gilead is said to have refused to help Nebuchadnezzar (Jdt. 1:8, 15:5), but the Gentiles in Gilead attacked the Jews in the time of Judas (1 Mac. 5:9ff.).

2. A city mentioned in Hos. 6:8 (cf. 12:11); but elsewhere no city of this name is known, and the reference may be to the chief town of **Gilead** (1).

GILEAD, MOUNT: Mentioned in RSVm in Jg. 7:3, where it is out of place, as the context is concerned with W. of **Jordan**. RSV emends to read 'And Gideon tested them' (cf. JB).

GILGAL (*'circle'*): 1. A place on the E. border of **Jericho**, where the Israelites encamped and set up twelve stones (Jos. 4:19f.), and where they kept the Passover (Jos. 5:10). Here they received the Gibeonites (Jos. 9:6), and from here they went to their defence (Jos. 10:6ff.); here, too, Joshua received the Judahites (Jos. 14:6). Ehud turned back to **Eglon** from here (Jg. 3:19). Gilgal was one of the places where Samuel judged Israel (1 Sam. 7:16), and he arranged to sacrifice here (1 Sam. 10:8). Here the kingdom was confirmed for Saul (1 Sam. 11:14ff.). Saul's impatience to await Samuel here angered the prophet (1 Sam. 13:4ff.), and it was at Gilgal that Samuel met him after the Amalekite campaign and slew Agag (1 Sam. 15:12–13). Here the elders of **Judah** met David after the rebellion of Absalom (2 Sam. 19:15, 40). An important shrine was here, and its worship is condemned in Hos. 4:15, 9:15, 12:11; Am. 4:4, 5:5. It is mod. *Khirbet el-Mefjer*. See **Beth-gilgal**.

2. A place near **Dor**, whose king Joshua conquered (Jos. 12:23, RSVm). But LXX has **Galilee**, and so RSV and JB.

3. A place W. of **Bethel**, from which Elijah and Elisha left before Elijah was taken up (2 Kg. 2:1, 4:38); perhaps mod. *Jiljûlieh*.

4. A place near **Mount Ebal** and **Mount Gerizim** (Dt. 11:30); possibly *Juleijil*. S.E. of Shechem.

5. A place near the **Ascent of Adummim** (Jos. 15:7); called **Geliloth** in Jos. 18:17. See **Beth-gilgal**.

GILO: *See* **Giloh**.

GILOH: A place in the hill country of **Judah** (Jos. 15:51), from which Ahithophel came (2 Sam. 15:12); called **Gilo** in 2 Sam. 23:34. It is possibly mod. *Khirbet Jâlâ*.

GIMZO: A place in **Judah** raided by the Philistines (2 Chr. 28:18); mod. *Jimzû*.

GITTAIM (*'the two wine-presses'*): An unidentified place to which the Beerothites fled (2 Sam. 4:3); it was resettled after the exile (Neh. 11:33).

GOB (*'cistern'*): The scene of a battle with the Philistines (2 Sam. 21:18f.); replaced by **Gezer** in 1 Chr. 20:4. Its location is unknown.

GOIIM: 1. The country ruled over by Tidal (Gen. 14:1, 9), who is sometimes identified with the Hittite king, Tudhalia.

2. A place whose king was conquered by Joshua (Jos. 12:23).

GOLAN: A city in **Bashan** (Dt. 4:43), within the borders of **Manasseh** (Jos. 20:7), allocated as a Levitical city (Jos. 21:27; 1 Chr. 6:71) and a city of refuge (Dt. 4:43; Jos. 20:8). It was the chief town of a district which in Hellenistic times was known as *Gaulanitis*, mod. *Jolân*. But the location of the city is unknown.

GOLGOTHA (*'skull'*): The place where Jesus was crucified (Mt. 27:33; Mk 15:22; Jn 19:17). In Lk. 23:33 RSV has 'the skull' (Greek here has *kranion* and Vulg. *calvaria*, whence AV **Calvary**). It was outside the city (Jn 19:20; Heb. 13:12), though its most favoured site lies within the expanded area walled in by Herod Agrippa I. It was probably on an eminence (Mk 15:40; Lk. 23:49).

GOMORRAH: One of the **Cities of the Valley** (Gen. 19:29), always associated with **Sodom**. It fought with Sodom against Chedorlaomer and his allies (Gen. 14:2ff.), and it shared the sin of Sodom (Gen. 18:20; Dt. 32:32; Jer. 23:14), and was destroyed with Sodom (Gen. 19:24ff.). This destruction was always remembered with horror (Dt. 29:23; Isa. 1:9f., 13:19; Jer. 49:18, 50:40; Am. 4:11; Zeph. 2:9). It is referred to in Wis. 10:6, and NT references are in Rom. 9:29; 2 Pet. 2:6; Jude 7. Jesus declared that it would be more tolerable for Sodom and Gomorrah than for those who rejected His disciples (Mt. 10:15). Its site is unknown, but it may be submerged under the **Dead Sea**.

GORTYNA: A city in **Crete**, to which the Roman consul wrote announcing the friendship of the Romans for the Jews (1 Mac. 15:23); mod. *Gortyn*.

GOSHEN: 1. A place in the hill country of **Judah** (Jos. 15:51); possibly mod. *edh-Dhāhirîyeh*.

2. A district in S. **Palestine** conquered by Joshua (Jos. 10:41; 11:16); perhaps the region surrounding 1.

3. A region in **Egypt** where Jacob and his family settled (Gen. 45:10; 46:28ff., 47:1ff., 27, 50:8), which was spared the plagues (Exod. 8:22, 9:26). It was probably mod. *Wâdī Ṭumilât*. In Jdt. 1:9 it would appear erroneously to include **Memphis**.

GOZAN: A place to which northern Israelites were deported (2 Kg. 17:6, 18:11). It was conquered by the Assyrians (2 Kg. 19:12; Isa. 37:12). It is probably mod. *Tell Ḥalâf*, on the river *Khābûr*. In 1 Chr. 5:26 it is wrongly cited as the name of the river.

GREAT SEA: One of the names of the **Mediterranean** used in the Bible (Num. 34:6f.; Jos. 1:4, 9:1, 15:12, 23:4 +).

GREECE: A country famous for its culture, in SE. Europe. It directly affected the Jews when Alexander the Great, the son of Philip (1 Mac. 6:2), became king (1 Mac. 1:1) and then conquered the Persian empire (1 Mac. 1:1; Dan. 8:20f.). His conquests were divided (Dan. 11:4) and the Ptolemies (the 'kings of the south 'of Dan. 11) and the Seleucids (the 'kings of the north' of Dan. 11) successively controlled **Palestine**. These were Greek kingdoms fostering Greek culture, though neither controlled the country of Greece. There are, accordingly, many references to Greeks, especially in the N.T. where the country is not indicated. Jl refers to Jewish prisoners being sold to Greeks (Jl 3:6), and Zech. 9:13 promises Jewish triumph over Greece. Some Greeks sought to see Jesus (Jn 12:20ff.), but whether they were from Greece we do not know. Paul preached in **Athens** (Ac. 17:15ff.) and **Corinth** (Ac. 18:1ff.) and later returned to Greece (Ac. 20:2). His Letters to the Corinthians were written to Greece. *See* **Javan**.

GUARDS, GATE OF THE: The gate of **Jerusalem** where guards were posted at the time of the enthronement of Joash (2 Kg.11:19; cf. 11:6). The parallel 2 Chr. 23:5 mentions gatekeepers, without specifying which gate they kept. Apparently the same gate is referred to in Neh. 12:39.

GUDGODAH. A stopping-place in the Wilderness wanderings (Dt. 10:7); called **Hor-haggidgad** in Num. 33:32f. It was probably in mod. *Wâdī Khaḍâkhid*.

GUR: An unidentified ascent near **Ibleam** (2 Kg. 9:27).

GUR-BAAL (*'dwelling of Baal'*): An unidentified place inhabited by Arabs (2 Chr. 26:7).

78

H

HABOR: A tributary of the **Euphrates** in N. **Mesopotamia**, on whose banks **Gozan** stood (2 Kg. 17:6, 18:11); mod. *Khābûr*. In 1 Chr. 5:26 it wrongly appears to be a town.

HACHILAH: A hill where David hid (1 Sam. 23:19; 26:1) and where Saul encamped (1 Sam. 26:3). Here David spared Saul's life (1 Sam. 26:5ff.). Its location is unknown.

HADASHAH (*'new'*): An unidentified place in the lowland of **Judah** (Jos. 15:37).

HADID: A place from which some returning exiles traced their descent (Ezr. 2:33; Neh. 7:37), where the parallel 1 Esd.5:22 has 'the other Elam' (RSV). It was resettled after the exile (Neh. 11:34). It is probably the same as **Adida** (1 Mac. 12:38, 13:13), mod. *el-Ḥadîtheh*.

HADRACH: A city in **Syria**, prophesied against in Zech. 9:1. It is known from inscriptions, but its precise location is unknown.

HA-ELEPH: A place in **Benjamin** (Jos. 18:28). It should probably be joined to the preceding word (so LXX), giving **Zela-haeleph** (so JB); *see* **Zela**.

HAHIROTH: A stopping-place in the Wilderness wanderings (Num. 33:8); called **Pi-hahiroth** in Exod. 14:2, 9; Num. 33:7 (so JB in 33:8). Its location is unknown.

HALAH: An unidentified place to which Israelites were deported (2 Kg. 17:6, 18:11; 1 Chr. 5:26; Ob. 20).

HALAK, MOUNT (*'bald mountain'*): The S. limit of Joshua's conquests (Jos. 11:17, 12:7); probably mod. *Jebel Ḥalâq*.

HALHUL: A place in the hill country of **Judah** (Jos. 15:58); mod. *Ḥalḥûl*.

HALI: An unidentified place in **Asher** (1) (Jos. 19:25).

HALICARNASSUS: A town on the coast of **Caria**, to which the Roman consul wrote announcing the Roman friendship for the Jews (1 Mac. 15:23); mod. *Bodrum*.

HAM: 1. A region occupied by the Zuzim (Gen. 14:15); mod. *Ḥâm*.
2. A poetic name for **Egypt** (Ps. 105:23, 27; 106:22).

HAMATH: A city on the Orontes in **Syria**, which gave its name to the region of which it was the capital (2 Kg. 23:33, 25:21). The en-entrance of Hamath, probably in the *Beqa'*, was the ideal northern limit of Israel (Num. 13:21, 34:8; Jos. 13:5; Jg. 3:3; Ezek. 47:15ff., 48:1), which was attained when Toi, the king of Hamath, made peace with David (2 Sam. 8:9; 1 Chr. 18:9ff.; cf. 1 Chr. 13:5), and continued into the reign of Solomon (1 Kg. 8:65; 2 Chr. 7:8), who built store cities here (2 Chr. 8:4). Control was later lost, but Jeroboam II restored it (2 Kg. 14:25, 28). Hamath was conquered by **Assyria** (2 Kg. 18:34, 19:13; Isa. 36:19, 37:11; cf. Isa. 10:9) and people from Hamath were transferred to **Israel** (2 Kg. 17:24, 30). Some Israelites were apparently taken to Hamath (Isa. 11:11). Before the battle of **Carchemish** Pharaoh Neco occupied it and deposed Jehoahaz at **Riblah** in Hamath (2 Kg. 23:33). At the same place Nebuchadrezzar made his headquarters, and here he blinded Zedekiah (2 Kg. 25:6f.; Jer. 39:5, 52:9) and killed other captives from Jerusalem (2 Kg. 25:20f.; Jer. 52:27). Prophecies against Hamath stand in Jer. 49:23; Zech. 9:2. Jonathan marched against Demetrius to Hamath (1 Mac. 12:25). The city is mod. *Ḥamā*.

HAMATH-ZOBAH: A place conquered by Solomon (2 Chr. 8:3). Its location is unknown. **Hamath** and **Zobah** were two separate Syrian states, but in the Persian period Zobah was in the province of Hamath. In 1 Chr. 18:3 we find 'Zobah toward Hamath.'

HAMMATH (*'hot spring'*): A fortified city of **Naphtali** (Jos. 19:35); probably the same as **Hammoth-dor** (Jos. 21:32) and **Hammon** (1 Chr. 6:76). It is mod. *Ḥammâm Ṭabarîyeh*, S. of **Tiberias**.

HAMMON (*'hot spring'*): 1. A Levitical city in **Naphtali** (1 Chr. 6:76); called **Hammoth-dor** in Jos. 21:32. It is probably the same as **Hammath** (Jos. 19:35), mod. *Ḥammâm Ṭabarîyeh*.
2. A place in **Asher** (Jos. 19:28); perhaps mod. *Umm el-'Awāmid*.

HAMMOTH-DOR: A Levitical city in Naphtali (Jos. 21:32); called Hammon in 1 Chr.6:76. It is probably the same as Hammoth (Jos. 19:35), mod. *Ḥammâm Ṭabarîyeh*.

HAMONAH (*'multitude'*): A city in the valley of Hamon-gog (Ezek. 29:16).

HAMON-GOG (*'multitude of Gog'*): A valley E. of the Jordan, where Gog will be buried (Ezek. 39:11, 15).

HANANEL, TOWER OF: A tower on the wall of Jerusalem on the N. side (Neh. 3:1, 12:39; Jer. 31:38; Zech. 14:10).

HANES: A place in Egypt to which Israelite envoys would come (Isa. 30:4). It is possibly the same as *Heracleopolis*, mod. *Aḥnâs el-Medîneh*.

HANNATHON: A place in Zebulun (Jos. 19:14); perhaps mod. *Tell el-Bedeiwîyeh*.

HAPHARAIM: A place in Issachar (Jos. 19:19); possibly *eṭ-Ṭaiyibeh*. N.W. of Beth-shan.

HARA: An unknown place to which Israelites from E. of the Jordan were deported (1 Chr. 5:26). In the parallel 2 Kg. 17:6, 18:11 it is unmentioned, and replaced by 'the cities of Media'.

HARADAH: An unidentified stopping-place in the Wilderness wanderings (Num. 33:24f.).

HARAN: The city to which Terah and his family went from Ur (Gen. 11:31f.; cf. Ac. 7:2ff.), and from which Abraham departed with Lot (Gen. 12:4f.). Here Laban lived (Gen. 27:43), and Jacob came here (Gen. 28:10) and served Laban (Gen. 29:4ff.). It is called the city of Nahor' in Gen. 24:10. Its conquest by Assyria is alluded to in 2 Kg. 19:12; Isa. 37:12. It is mentioned as trading with Tyre (Ezek. 27:23). It is mod. *Harrân* on the *Balîkh*, which flows into the Euphrates.

HAR-HERES (*'mountain of the sun'*): A place in Dan (1), from which the Amorites could not be expelled (Jg. 4:9; 2 Chr. 28:18) and Ir-shemesh (Jos. 19:41).

HARMON: An unknown place mentioned in Am. 4:3 as a place of exile.

HAROD: 1. A spring where Gideon encamped (Jg. 7:1); perhaps where Saul also encamped (1 Sam. 29:1). It is probably mod. *'Ain Jālûd*.

2. The birthplace of two of David's heroes (2 Sam. 23:25; 1 Chr. 11:27). Its location is unknown.

HAROSHETH-HA-GOIIM: The city where Sisera lived (Jg. 4:2, 13, 16); possibly mod. *Tell 'Amr*, near *el-Ḥarithîyeh*.

HASHMONAH: A stopping-place in the Wilderness wanderings (Num. 33:29f.); possibly mod. *Wâdī el-Hahsim*, near **Kadesh-barnea.** It may be the same as **Heshmon** (Jos. 15:27).

HAURAN: A district SE. of **Hermon,** contiguous with Ezekiel's ideal boundary of **Israel** (Ezek. 47:16, 18); mod. *Jebel Ḥaurân*.

HAVILAH: 1. A land around which the river **Pishon,** one of the rivers of the **Garden of Eden,** flows (Gen. 2:11), from which gold, bdellium, and onyx were obtained.

2. A place marking the boundary of Ishmaelite territory (Gen. 25:18). Here Saul defeated the Amalekites (1 Sam. 15:7). Its location is unknown. The relation of this Havilah to that occupied by the descendants of Joktan in Gen. 10:29; 1 Chr. 1:23 is obscure, but for the latter some scholars think of the neighbourhood of the Persian Gulf or of a region N. of the *Yemen*.

HAVVOTH-JAIR (*'tent villages of Jair'*): A group of villages in **Gilead** (Num. 32:41) or **Bashan** (Dt. 3:14; Jos. 13:30, here called 'the towns of Jair'). They are said to be named after Jair, the son of Manasseh (Num. 32:41; Dt. 3:14; 1 Kg. 4:13, here called 'the villages of Jair'), or after the minor Judge (Jg. 10:4). They were annexed by **Geshur** and **Aram** (1 Chr. 2:23).

HAZAR-ADDAR: A place in S. **Palestine,** near **Kadesh-barnea** (Num. 34:4); perhaps mod. *Khirbet el-Qudeirât. See* **Addar, Hezron.**

HAZAR-ENAN: A place in the N. of **Palestine** (Num. 34:9f.); called **Hazar-enon** in Ezek. 47:17f., 48:1. Its location is uncertain. It may be the same as **Hazer-hatticon** (Ezek. 47:16).

HAZAR-ENON: A place of uncertain location N. of **Damascus**, on Ezekiel's ideal boundary of **Israel** (Ezek. 47:17f.; 48:1; called Hazar-enan in Num. 34:9f.).

HAZAR-GADDAH: A place in S. **Judah** (Jos. 15:27); of unknown location.

HAZARMAVETH: The name of a S. Arabian state, represented as a son of Joktan (Gen. 10:26; 1 Chr. 1:20); mod. *Ḥaḍramaut*.

HAZAR-SHUAL: A place in S. **Judah** (Jos. 15:28; 1 Chr. 4:28) or **Simeon** (Jos. 17:3), which was early absorbed in Judah. It was resettled after the exile (Neh. 11:27). It is perhaps *Khirbet Waṭan*, near **Beersheba**.

HAZAR-SUSAH: A place in **Simeon** (Jos. 19:5); called **Hazar-susim** in 1 Chr. 4:31. It is perhaps mod. **Sbalat** *Abū Sûsein*.

HAZAR-SUSIM: *See* **Hazar-susah**.

HAZAZON-TAMAR: An Amorite city conquered by **Chedor-laomer** and his allies (Gen. 14:7); identified with **En-gedi** in 2 Chr. 20:2, but this may be a gloss. It is probably the same as **Tamar** (1) (1 Kg. 9:18). It was perhaps near *'Ainfiel-'Arûs*.

HAZER-HATTICON: A place on the border of Ezekiel's ideal **Israel** (Ezek. 47:16). It may be the same as **Hazar-enan** (Ezek. 47:17f., 48:1).

HAZEROTH: A stopping-place in the Wilderness wanderings (Num. 11:35, 12:16, 33:17f.; Dt. 1:1); perhaps mod. *'Ain Khaḍrā*.

HAZO: The name of a region in N. **Arabia**, mentioned in an inscription of **Esarhaddon**, represented as a 'son' of Nahor (Gen. 22:22).

HAZOR: 1. A Canaanite city situated in **Naphtali** (Jos. 19:36), raided by Jabin (Jos. 11:1; Jg. 4:2), who was defeated and killed by Joshua (Jos. 11:6ff.) or by **Zebulun** and Naphtali under Deborah and Barak (Jg. 4:4ff.; cf. 1 Sam. 12:9ff.). Hazor stood near **Kedesh** (3) (1 Mac. 11:63, 67), and modern excavations have disclosed its importance and confirmed its destruction (in the period of the Israelite settlement. Solomon rebuilt it and fortified it (1 Kg. 9:15), and it was captured by Tiglath-pileser (2 Kg. 15:29). Jonathan repulsed his enemies near here (1 Mac. 11:63ff.). It is mod. *Tell el-Qebaḥ*.

2. An unidentified place in S. **Judah** (Jos. 15:23).

3. Another place in S. **Judah**, identified with **Kerioth-hezron** (Jos. 15:25).

4. A place in **Benjamin**, resettled after the exile (Neh. 11:33); perhaps mod. *Khirbet Ḥazzûr*.

5. An unidentified region of **Arabia**, invaded by Nebuchadrezzar (Jer. 49:28ff.).

HAZOR-HADATTAH: An unknown place in S. **Judah** (Jos. 15:25).

HEBRON: A Canaanite city peopled by Anakim (Num. 13:22; Jos. 14:15, 15:13ff.), formerly called **Kiriath-arba** (Gen. 23:2; Jos. 14:15, 15:54; Jg. 1:10), and built seven years before **Zoan** (Num. 13:22). It was visited by Abraham (Gen. 13:18), and Sarah died here (Gen. 23:2) and was buried in the **Cave of Machpelah** (Gen. 23:7ff.). Here too Isaac sojourned (Gen. 35:27), and from Hebron Joseph was sent by Jacob to visit his brothers (Gen. 37:14). It was conquered by Caleb (Jos. 15:14; Jg. 1:20) or by Judah (Jg. 1:9f.) and given to Caleb (Jos. 14:13f., 15:14; Jg. 1:20) and lay within **Judah** (Jos. 15:54), where it was a city of refuge (Jos. 20:7) and a Levitical city (Jos. 21:11; 1 Chr. 6:55). A different account of its capture is given in Jos. 10:3ff., 36ff., 12:10. David sent spoils to Hebron (1 Sam. 20:31); here he became king of Judah (2 Sam. 2:3f.) and reigned for seven years (2 Sam. 5:5; 1 Kg. 2:11). Here Abner was killed (2 Sam. 3:27). Absalom raised the standard of revolt here (2 Sam. 15:7ff.). The city was fortified by Rehoboam (2 Chr. 11:10), and after the exile it was resettled (Neh. 11:25). Later it was occupied by Edomites, and it was recaptured by Judas (1 Mac. 5:65). It is mod. *el-Khalîl*.

HELAM: A place E. of the **Jordan**, where David defeated Hadadezer (2 Sam. 10:16ff.); perhaps mod. *'Almâ*.

HELBAH: A place in **Asher** (1) which successfully resisted the Israelites (Jg. 1:31). It is possibly a doublet of **Ahlab**, and perhaps the same as **Mahalob** (Jos. 19:29).

HELBON: A locality which traded with **Tyre** (Ezek. 27:18); probably mod. *Halbûn.*

HELEPH: A place in **Naphtali** (Jos. 19:33); possibly mod. *Khirbet 'Arbâdeh.*

HELIOPOLIS: An important city of **Egypt**, famous for its worship of Rē, the sun god. Its only mention by this name in the Bible is in Jer. 43:13, which foretells the destruction of its obelisks. Elsewhere it is called **On**, which represents the ancient Egyptian name. Joseph was given the daughter of its priest as wife (Gen. 41:45, 50, 46:20), and a prophecy against it stands in Ezek. 30:17. It is mod *Tell Ḥuṣn.*

HELKATH: A place in **Asher** (1) (Jos. 19:25), assigned as a Levitical city (Jos. 21:31); called **Hukok** in 1 Chr. 6:75. It is perhaps *Khirbet el-Harbaj.*

HELKATH-HAZZURIM (*'field of flints'*): The place at **Gideon** where twelve champions of Joab and twelve of Abner fought (2 Sam. 2:16).

HENA: An unknown city conquered by **Assyria** (2 Kg. 18:34, 19:13; Isa. 37:13).

HEPHER: 1. A Canaanite city conquered by Joshua (Jos. 12:17); possibly *Tell Ibshāh.*
    2. A district in Solomon's third district (1 Kg. 4:10,) possibly connected with 1.

HERES, ASCENT OF: The place of unknown location where Gideon came after defeating the Midianites (Jg. 8:13).

HERETH, FOREST OF: A place where David found refuge (1 Sam. 22:5); possibly near **Kharās.**

HERMON: A mountain of the **Anti-Lebanon** and the highest in **Syria**, the N. limit of the kindgom of Og (Dt. 3:8, 4:48; Jos. 12:1, 5; 13:11f.), conquered by the Israelites and occupied by them (Jos. 11:3ff., 17; 1 Chr. 5:23). It is frequently referred to in poetry (Ps. 42:6, 89:12, 133:3; Ca. 4:8; Sir. 24:13). It is also called **Sirion**

(Dt. 3:9, 4:48) and **Senir** (Dt. 3:9). It may have been the mount of the Transfiguration (Mt. 17:1ff.; Mk 9:2ff.; Lk. 9:28ff.), which is traditionally identified with **Mount Tabor**. Hermon is mod. *Jebel esh-Sheikh*.

HESHBON: A city E. of the **Jordan,** formerly the capital of Sihon (Num. 21:26, 34; Dt. 1:4 +), which he had taken from **Moab** (Num. 21:27ff.). It was taken by the Israelites (Dt. 2:30ff., 3:16) and assigned to **Reuben** (Num. 32:37; Jos. 13:17), or **Gad** (Jos. 13:26), as a Levitical city (Jos. 21:39; 1 Chr. 6:81). In Jg. 11:26 it is said to have been in Israelite hands for three hundred years, but Moab later recovered it (Isa. 15:4, 16:8; Jer. 48:2, 34ff., 45). It is referred to as Ammonite in Jer. 49:3 (cf. Jg. 11:26). Its pools were famous (Ca. 7:4). It is mod. *Ḥesbân*.

HESHMON: An unidentified place in S. **Judah** (Jos. 15:27), possibly the same as **Hashmonah** (Num. 33:29f.).

HETHLON: A place on Ezekiel's ideal border of **Israel** (Ezek. 47:15); possibly mod. *Ḥeitelâ*, near **Tripolis.**

HEZRON: A place in S. **Judah,** mentioned with **Addar** (Jos. 15:3), where the two names should perhaps be combined to give **Hazar-addar,** as in Num. 34:4.

HIDDEKEL: This name stood in early editions of RSV in Gen. 2:14, but was later changed to **Tigris,** as in Dan. 10:4.

HIERAPOLIS: A city in the *Lycus* valley, where Epaphras ministered (Col. 4:13); mod. *Pambuk Kalesi.*

HILEN: A Levitical city of **Judah** (1 Chr. 6:58); called **Holon** (1) in Jos. 15:51, 21:15. It is possibly mod. *Khirbet ʿAîln.*

HINNOM, VALLEY (OF THE SON, or SONS) OF; A valley near **Jerusalem** where children were sacrificed (2 Kg. 23:10; 2 Chr. 28:3, 33:6), whose evil reputation was denounced by Jeremiah (Jer. 7:31ff., 19:2ff., 32:35). Its name *Gê Hinnôm* gave rise to the use of *Gehenna* for Hell. The boundary between **Judah** and **Benjamin** passed through it (Jos. 15:8, 18:16). It was probably mod. *Wadî er-Rabâbi.*

HOBAH: A place N. of **Damascus** to which Abraham pursued the defeated kings (Gen. 14:15). Its location is unknown. **Choba** (Jdt. 4:4, 15:4f.) may be the same place.

HOLON: 1. A place in the hill country of **Judah** (Jos. 15:51), assigned as a Levitical city (Jos. 21:15); called **Hilen** in 1 Chr. 6:58. It is possibly mod. *Khirbet 'Aîln.*
2. A place in **Moab** (Jer. 48:21), of unknown location.

HOR, MOUNT: 1. A mountain on the border of **Edom** (Num. 20:23, 33:37), and a stopping-place in the Wilderness wanderings (Num. 20:22, 33:41), where Aaron died (Num. 20:27f., 33:38f.; Dt. 32:50). Its location is uncertain.
2. A mountain on the N. border of the Promised Land (Num. 34:7f.). It stands for an unknown spur of the **Lebanon** range.

HOREM: An unlocated place in **Naphtali** (Jos. 19:38).

HOREB, MOUNT: The name of the sacred mountain to which the Israelites went found in a number of passages, instead of **Sinai** (cf. Sir. 48:7). It is called 'the mountain of God' (Exod. 3:1) and here Moses received his call (Exod. 32:ff.). Moses led the Israelites to it, and brought water from the rock (Exod. 17:6f.). Here the people made the Golden Calf (Dt. 9:8ff.; Ps. 106:19), and afterwards stripped off their ornaments in grief (Exod. 33:4ff.). Here the Covenant was made (Dt. 4:10ff., 5:2, 29:1; 1 Kg. 8:9; 2 Chr. 5:10) and the commands received (Mal. 4:4), and from here the Israelites went to **Kadesh-barnea** (Dt. 1:2, 19f.). When Elijah fled from Jezebel he came to Horeb (1 Kg. 19:8), where he heard the 'still small voice' (1 Kg. 19:12).

HORESH (*'forest'*): A place in the wilderness where David took refuge (1 Sam. 23:15), and where Jonathan came to him and made a covenant with him (1 Sam. 23:16ff.). It is possibly mod. *Khirbet Khureisā.*

HOR-HAGGIDGAD: A stopping-place in the Wilderness wanderings (Num. 33:32f.); probably the same as **Gudgodah** (Dt. 10:7). It was probably in mod. *Wâdi Khaḍâkhid.*

HORMAH (*'destruction'*): A Canaanite city, formerly called **Zephath** (Jg. 1:17), where the Israelites were repulsed by the

Amalekites and the Canaanites (Num. 14:45), or by the Amorites
(Dt. 1:49). It was later taken and destroyed by the Israelites (Num.
21:3), or by Judahites and Simeonites (Jg. 1:17), a victory later
transferred to Joshua (Jos. 12:14). It was assigned to Judah (Jos.
15:30), or to Simeon (Jos. 19:4; 1 Chr. 4:30), which was early absorbed by Judah. David sent spoils here (1 Sam. 20:30). It is
probably mod. *Tell el-Mishâsh*.

HORONAIM: 1. A city in Moab (Isa. 15:5; Jer. 48:3, 5, 34), of
unknown location.

2. In 2 Sam. 13:34, the conjectural RSV 'the Horoniam road'
must be W. of the Jordan and therefore different from 1. It perhaps means 'the two Horons,' i.e. Upper and Lower Beth-Horon.
JB conjectures differently 'the Bahurim road.'

HORSE GATE: A gate of the royal palace in Jerusalem, where
Athaliah was slain (2 Chr. 23:15). It was on the E. side leading to the
Kidron valley (Jer. 31:40). It was repaired by the priests in
Nehemiah's time (Neh. 3:28).

HOSAH (*'refuge'*): An unlocated place in Asher (1) (Jos. 19:29).

HUKKOK: A place in Naphtali (Jos. 19:34); perhaps. mod
Yāqûq.

HUKOK: A Levitical city in Asher (1) (1 Chr. 6:75); called
Helkath in Jos. 19:25, 21:31. It is perhaps mod. *Khirbet el-Harbaj*.

HUMTAH: An unlocated place in Judah (Jos. 15:54).

HUNDRED, TOWER OF THE: A tower on the wall of Jerusalem on
the N. side (Neh. 3:1, 12:39).

HUSHAH: A village in Judah, founded by Ezer, who is called its
father (1 Chr. 4:4); two of David's heroes came from there (2 Sam.
21:18, 23:27; 1 Chr. 11:29); perhaps mod. *Ḥūsân*.

I

IBLEAM: A town in **Asher** (1) allotted to W. **Manasseh** (Jos. 17:11), where the Canaanites resisted successfully (Jos. 17:12; Jg. 1:27); called **Bileam** in 1 Chr. 6:7. In Jos 21:25 we should probably read 'Ibleam' for 'Gath-rimmon' (cf. JB). Near here Jehu killed Ahaziah (2 Kg. 9:27) and Shallum killed Zechariah (2 Kg. 15:10). It is probably mod. *Tell Bel'ameh. See* **Belmain.**

ICONIUM: A town in Asia Minor, ethnically in **Phrygia**, but administratively for a time the chief town of **Lycaonia**, and from 25 B.C. incorporated in the Roman province of **Galatia**. Paul preached here on his first missionary journey (Ac. 13:51, 14:1ff., 21ff.) and perhaps subsequently (*see* **Galatia**). In 2 Tim. 3:11 Paul refers to his sufferings there. It is mod. *Konya.*

IDALAH: A place in **Zebulun** (Jos. 19:15); perhaps mod. *Khirbet el-Ḥawârah.*

IDUMEA: The Greek equivalent of **Edom**, which after the exile included part of S. **Judah**, including **Hebron** (1 Mac. 5:65) and **Beth-zur** (1 Mac. 4:29, 61, 6:31). In the Maccabean period Gorgias was its governor (2 Mac. 12:32), and it was hostile to the Jews (2 Mac. 10:15ff.). Judas won victories here (1 Mac. 4:15, 6:31). Some people from Idumea came to hear Jesus (Mk 3:8).

IIM: An unidentified place in S. **Judah** (Jos. 15:59).

IJON: A town in **Naphtali** annexed by Benhadad (1 Kg. 15:20; 2 Chr. 16:4). It was later taken by Tiglath-pileser and its people deported (2 Kg. 15:29). It is perhaps mod. *Tell Dibbîn.*

ILLYRICUM: A Roman province on the E. side of the Adriatic Sea, which Paul visited on some unknown occasion (Rom. 15:29).

IMMER: An unknown place in **Babylonia** from which some who could not prove their descent came (Ezr. 2:59; Neh. 7:61; 1 Esd. 5:36).

INDIA: The E. boundary of the kingdom of Ahasuerus (Est. 1:1, 8:9) and of Artaxerxes (Ad. Est. 13:1, 16:1) and Darius (1 Esd. 3:2). The name is derived from the name of the *Indus*, and the reference is to that part of the country watered by the **Indus**. This region was conquered by Alexander the Great and was claimed as part of the kingdom of the Seleucids, though it was not continuously controlled by them. Antiochus the Great is incorrectly said to have been compelled by the Romans to surrender it (1 Mac. 8:6ff.).

IPHTAH: A place in the lowland of **Judah** (Jos. 15:43); perhaps mod. *Tarqûmiya*.

IPHTAH-EL, VALLEY OF: Part of the border of **Zebulun** (Jos. 19:14) and **Asher** (1) (Jos. 19:27); perhaps mod. *Sahl el-Battôf*.

IRNAHASH (? *'city of a serpent'*): A town in **Judah** (1 Chr. 4:12); possibly mod. *Deir Nakhkhâs*.

IRPEEL: A town in **Benjamin** (Jos. 18:27); possibly mod. *Rafât*.

IR-SHEMESH (*'city of the sun'*): A town in **Dan** (1) (Jos. 19:41), perhaps the same as **Har-Heres** (Jg. 1:34f.); later in **Judah**, and called **Bethshemesh** (Jos. 15:10). It is mod. *Tell er-Rumeileh*.

ISRAEL: The territory occupied by the twelve tribes of Israel (Jg. 19:29; 1 Sam. 13:19, 27:1; 2 Sam. 21:5; 1 Kg. 1:3), and, after the disruption of the kingdom (1 Kg. 12:16ff.), used for the northern kingdom (1 Kg. 15:33; 2 Kg. 5:2, 6:23) until its extinction. The term is sometimes used for the southern kingdom (Isa. 5:7; Mic. 3:1, 9f.), or it may stand for the restored land to which Ezekiel looked (Ezek. 11:17, 47:13ff.). Only the context can determine which of its uses is relevant.

ISSACHAR: The territory occupied by the tribe of Issachar. Its ideal limits are stated in Jos. 19:17ff.

ITALY: This country is mentioned in the Bible only four times. Aquila and Priscilla came to **Corinth** when they were expelled from **Rome** as Jews (Ac. 18:2), and Paul sailed as a prisoner for Italy for his trial (Ac. 27:1, 6). The greeting of Christians from Italy was sent in Heb. 13:24. One of Paul's letters was sent to Rome (Rom. 1:7). In addition to Rome, places in Italy mentioned in the NT are **Forum of Appius**, **Puteoli**, **Rhegium**, and **Three Taverns**.

ITHLAH: An unidentified place in Dan (1) (Jos. 19:42).

ITHNAN: A place in S. Judah (Jos. 15:23), of unknown location.

ITURAEA: A region NE. of the Sea of Galilee ruled over by Herod Philip (Lk. 3:1).

IVVAH: A city conquered by Assyria (1 Kg. 18:34, 19:13; Isa. 37:13); probably the same as Avva (2 Kg. 17:24, 31). It is possibly mod. *Tell Kefr 'Ayā*.

IYE-ABARIM: A stopping-place in the Wilderness wanderings (Num. 21:11), in Moab (Num. 33:44); also called Iyim (Num. 33:45). It is possibly mod. *Maḥaiy. See* Abarim.

IYIM: *See* Iye-abarim.

J

JAAR: A shortened form of Kiriath-jearim (Ps. 132:6). It is here parallel to Ephrathah (2); cf. 1 Chr. 2:50, where Kiriath-jearim and Ephrathah are associated.

JABBOK, RIVER: A river flowing into the Jordan from the E., beside which Jacob wrestled with the angel (Gen. 32:22ff.). It is elsewhere mentioned as a boundary (Num. 21:24; Dt. 2:37, 3:16; Jg. 11:13, 22). It is mod. *Nahr ez-Zerqâ*.

JABESH: *See* Jabesh-gilead.

JABESH-GILEAD: A town E. of the Jordan which did not join in the war against Benjamin, and which supplied brides to the Benjaminites (Jg. 21:8ff.). When later it was besieged by the Ammonites (1 Sam. 11:1ff.), it appealed for help, which it received under the leadership of Saul of Gibeah (1 Sam. 11:4ff.). When Saul's body was fastened to the wall of Beth-shan, the men of Jabesh-gilead removed it and buried it (1 Sam. 31:10ff.; 2 Sam. 2:4; 1 Chr.10:11f.)

for which act David blessed them (2 Sam. 2:5ff.). David subsequently transferred the body and those of others of Saul's family to the family tomb (2 Sam. 21:12ff.). Jabesh-gilead is called simply Jabesh in 1 Sam. 11:1, 3, 5, 9f., 31:12f.; 1 Chr. 10:12). It is mod. *Tell Abū Kharâz*, in the *Wâdi Yâbis*.

JABEZ: A town in Judah inhabited by scribes (1 Chr. 2:55), of unknown location.

JABNEEL: 1. A town on the border of Judah, near the sea (Jos. 15:11); called Jabneh in 2 Chr. 26:6, where it is in Philistine hands and attacked by Uzziah. In the Apocrypha it is called Jamnia (1 Mac. 4:15, 5:58), and after the destruction of Jerusalem in A.D. 70, the rabbis gathered here. It is mod. *Yebnâ*.
  2. A place in Naphtali (Jos. 19:33); perhaps mod. *Khirbet Yemmâ*.

JABNEH: A Philistine town attacked by Uzziah (2 Chr. 26:6); called Jabneel (1) in Jos. 15:11, where it is said to be in Judah. *See* Jamnia.

JACOB'S WELL: The well at Sychar beside which Jesus met the Samaritan woman (Jn 4:6ff.). It is unmentioned in the OT.

JAGUR: A place in S. Judah (Jos. 15:21); possibly mod. *Tell Ghurr*.

JAHAZ: The scene of Sihon's defeat (Num. 21:23f.; Dt. 2:32ff.; Jg. 11:20ff.). It was assigned to Reuben (Jos. 13:18), and became a Levitical city (Jos. 21:36f.). It later became Moabite (Isa. 15:4; Jer. 48:34). It is called Jahzah in 1 Chr. 6:78 and Jer. 48:21. It is mentioned on the Moabite Stone, but is site is unidentified.

JAHZAH: A city in Reuben which became a Levitical city (1 Chr. 6:78), but was which subsequently Moabite (Jer. 48:21). It is elsewhere called Jahaz.

JAIR, TOWNS OF: *See* Havvoth-jair.

JAIR, VILLAGES OF: *See* Havvoth-jair.

JAMNIA: The name of Jabneel (1) in the Apocrypha. Judas pursued his foes to this city (1 Mac. 4:15), and it was unsuccessfully attacked by Jews under Joseph and Azariadash (1 Mac. 5:58ff.). Judas attacked it and burned its harbour and fleet (2 Mac. 12:8ff.), but a subsequent defeat was attributed to the fact that his soldiers took from here idolatrous tokens (2 Mac. 12:40). Appollonius encamped against it (1 Mac. 10:69), and Cendebaeus roused its people against the Jews (1 Mac. 15:40). In Jdt. 2:28 the fear of Holofernes is said to have fallen on it. After the destruction of Jerusalem by Titus, the Jewish rabbis gathered here. It is mod. *Yebnâ*.

JANIM: A place in the hill country of Judah (Jos. 15:53); perhaps mod. *Benî Na'îm*.

JANOAH: 1. A place in Naphtali, captured by Tiglath-pileser (2 Kg. 15:29); perhaps mod. *Yānûḥ*.

2. A place in Ephraim (1) (Jos. 16:6f.); perhaps mod. *Khirbet Yānûn*.

JAPHIA: A place in Zebulun (Jos. 19:12); perhaps mod. *Yâfā*.

JARMUTH: 1. A Canaanite city whose king joined the alliance against Joshua (Jos. 10:3ff.) and was defeated and slain (Jos. 10:23ff., 12:11). It was assigned to Judah (Jos. 16:35). After the exile it was resettled (Neh. 11:29). It is perhaps mod. *Khirbet Yarmûk*.

2. A place in Issachar assigned as a Levitical city (Jos. 21:29); called Ramoth in 1 Chr. 6:73), and probably the same as Remeth in Jos. 19:21. It is possibly mod. *Kôkab el-Hawâ*.

JATTIR: A town in the hill country of Judah (Jos. 15:48), assigned as a Levitical city (Jos. 21:14; 1 Chr. 6:57). David sent spoils to it (1 Sam. 30:27). It is mod. *Khirbet 'Attîr*.

JAVAN: This term is used in the OT for the Greeks. Etymologically it is connected with 'Ionians', and it nowhere stands for the mainland of Greece. Javan is the 'father' of certain peoples, where the reference is to Cyprus and other islands of the Mediterranean (Gen. 10:2, 4; 1 Chr. 1:5, 7). The coasts of Asia Minor are referred to as Javan in Isa. 66:19; Ezek. 27:13, and in Jl 3:6, where RSV renders the gentilic by 'Greeks'. (In Ezek. 27:19 RSV has 'wine', *yayin*, for MT Javan, *yāwān*.) Javan stands for the kingdoms of Alexander and his successors in Dan. 8:21, 10:20, 11:12, where RSV renders by Greece.

JAZER: An Amorite town on the boundary of **Ammon** (Num. 21:24), E. of the **Jordan,** taken by the Israelites (Num. 21:32). It was assigned to **Gad** (Jos. 13:25; cf. 32:1ff.). It was fortified (Num. 32:35) and became a Levitical city (Jos. 21:39; 1 Chr. 6:81). In David's time able men from **Hebron** were found here (1 Chr. 26:31), and it was Israelite at the time of the census (2 Sam. 24:5), but was in Moabite hands later (Isa. 16:8f.; Jer. 48:32). It was aparently famous for its vines (Isa. 16:9; Jer. 48:32). In the Maccabean age it was held by the Ammonites, and was captured by Judas (1 Mac. 5:8). *See* **Gazara.** It is probably mod. *Khirbet Jazzir.*

JEARIM, mount: A mountain in **Judah,** identified with **Chesalon** (Jos. 15:10).

JEBUS: A name for **Jerusalem** (Jos. 18:28, 19:10f., 1 Chr. 11:4f.), whose people are called Jebusites (Jos. 15:63; Jg. 1:21, 19:11; 2 Sam. 5:6, 8).

JEGAR-SAHADUTHA (*'cairn of witness'*): Laban's name (aramaic) for the heap of stones made by Jacob and himself (Gen. 31:47), of the same meaning as **Galeed.**

JEHOSHAPHAT, valley of: The scene of the coming judgment of the nations (Jl 3:2, 12). Tradition has located it near **Jerusalem,** but it is probable that the name is symbolical rather than geographical; it means *'the valley where Yahweh will judge'.*

JEHUD: A place in **Dan** (1) (Jos. 19:45); perhaps mod. *el-Yehûdîyeh.*

JEKABZEEL: A place in **Judah** (Neh. 11:25); called **Kabzeel** in Jos. 15:21. It is perhaps mod. *Khirbet Ḥôrah.*

JERAH: A 'son' of **Jokton** (Gen. 10:26; 1 Chr. 1:20), possibly a locality in S. **Arabia.**

JERICHO: A city W. of the Jordan, about 5 miles from the **Dead Sea.** Moses led the Israelites to a position opposite Jericho on the E. of the Jordan (Num. 22:1; Dt. 32:49), and after his death Joshua sent spies into the city (Jos. 2:1ff.), and subsequently captured and destroyed it (Jos. 4:13–6:21) and cursed anyone who should rebuild it (Jos. 6:26f.). The curse was fulfilled on Hiel (1 Kg. 16:34f.). The city was reckoned to **Benjamin** (Jos. 18:21), and some small settlement in or near Jericho probably existed before the time of Hiel. Eglon of **Moab** took possession of the **City of Palms** (Jg. 3:13), where he was killed (Jg. 3:15 ff.). This must have been in the neighbourhood of Jericho, and the City of Palms is equated with Jericho in Dt. 34:3; 2 Chr. 28:15. David's abused messengers to **Ammon** stayed at Jericho (2 Sam. 10:3; 1 Chr. 19:5), and in Elijah's time there was a company of prophets here (2 Kg. 2:4ff.). Zedekiah was captured near Jericho (2 Kg. 25:5f.; Jer. 39:5, 52:8f.). Some of the returning exiles traced their descent from here (Ezr. 2:34; Neh. 7:36; 1 Esd. 5:22), and men of Jericho shared in the rebuilding of the walls of **Jerusalem** (Neh. 3:2). Jericho is said to have been appealed to for help against Holofernes (Jdt. 4:4). In the Maccabean period Bacchides fortified it (1 Mac. 9:50), and Judas captured it (2 Mac. 12:15f.). Some years later Ptolemy was its governor and there treacherously killed Simon, his father-in-law (1 Mac. 16:11, 14). In the Gospels Jericho is the place where Bartimaeus was healed (Mt. 20:29ff.; Mk 10:46ff.; Lk. 18:35ff.) and where Zacchaeus was converted (Lk. 19:1ff.). In the Parable of the Good Samaritan the attacked Jew was journeying from Jerusalem to Jericho (Lk. 10:30). The site of OT Jericho is mod. *Tell es-Sulṭân*, and that of NT Jericho mod. *Tulûl Abû el-'Alayiq.*

JERUEL: A wilderness region where Jehoshaphat defeated his foes (2 Chr. 20:16ff.).

JERUSALEM: The chief city of **Palestine**. It is probably to be identified with Melchizedek's city, **Salem** (Gen. 14:18ff.), and the place where Abraham almost sacrificed Isaac in the land of **Moriah** (Gen. 22:2) is traditionally identified with the site of the Temple (cf. 2 Chr. 3:1). Joshua is said to have conquered Adonizedek, the king of Jerusalem (Jos. 10:1ff.) and to have killed him (Jos. 10:23ff.), but elsewhere the king is called Adonibezek and the victory ascribed to **Judah** and **Simeon** after the death of Joshua (Jg. 1:1ff.). Judah is said to have conquered and burned Jerusalem (Jg. 1:8), but we are also told that Judah could not drive out the Jebusites (Jos. 15:63) and neither could **Benjamin** (Jg. 1:21), to which tribe Jerusalem was allotted (Jos. 18:28). It was in Jebusite hands (Jg. 19:10) when the Bethlehem Levite was returning to **Ephraim** (1) with his concubine (Jg. 19:1ff.), but it was captured by David (2 Sam. 5:6ff.; 1 Chr. 11:4ff.) and made his capital (2 Sam. 5:5). It continued to be

JES

the capital of the kingdom during the rest of the united monarchy, and of Judah after the disruption to its destruction. Solomon built the Temple (1 Kg. 6), which inspired Psalmists (Pss. 48, 122, 125), and especially under the name **Zion**, which was used as a synonym for it. During the monarchy the city was frequently despoiled (1 Kg. 14:25ff.; 2 Kg. 12:18, 14:13f., 18:13ff.), but it was never captured by a foreign foe until the time of Nebuchadrezzar. Hezekiah improved its water supply by cutting the **Siloam** tunnel (2 Kg. 20:20; 2 Chr. 32:30; Sir. 48:17), and in his reign Jerusalem was miraculously delivered (2 Kg. 19:35; 2 Chr. 32:21; Isa. 37:36). Nebuchadrezzar beseiged the city, but Jehoiachin surrendered it and it was despoiled and many of its people deported (2 Kg. 24:10ff.); when Zedekiah rebelled the Babylonian army again besieged it, and captured and destroyed both it and the Temple (2 Kg. 25:1ff.; 2 Chr. 36:17ff.). After the exile the Temple was rebuilt by Zerubbabel (Ezr. 5f.; Hag. 1:1ff.), and the walls of the city were rebuilt by Nehemiah (Neh. 2:11ff., 3:1ff., 6:15). In the time of Antiochus Epiphanes a Greek gymnasium was built in the city (1 Mac. 1:14), and the Temple was despoiled (1 Mac. 1:21ff.) and desecrated (1 Mac. 1:54ff.; 2 Mac. 6:2). It was cleansed by Judas (1 Mac. 4:36ff.), but the citadel remained in enemy hands (1 Mac. 19:6ff.). Jerusalem was Herod's capital, to which the Wise Men came (Mt. 2:1), and Jesus was presented as a babe in the Temple (Lk. 2:22), and taken for the Passover when He was twelve (Lk. 2:4ff.). John records visits of Jesus during His ministry (Jn 2:13ff., 5:1ff., 7:10ff., 10:22ff.); but these are not recorded in the other Gospels, which record only the visit which ended in His Crucifixion and Resurrection (Mt. 20:17ff.; Mk 10:32ff.; Lk. 13:22). In Mt. 23:37 and Lk. 13:34, however, there is an implied reference to other visits. After the Ascension the disciples returned to Jerusalem (Ac. 1:12), and the Church was largely concentrated there until after the martyrdom of Stephen (Ac. 7:58), when the disciples were scattered abroad (Ac. 8:1). Saul and Barnabas came to Jerusalem bringing relief funds (Ac. 11:29f.), and after their first missionary journey the Council of Jerusalem was held here (Ac. 15:4ff.). After his third missionary journey Paul was arrested in Jerusalem (Ac. 21:30), but later sent to **Caesarea** (Ac. 24:23ff.). *See* **Jebus**.

JESHANAH: A place near **Mizpah** (3) (1 Sam. 7:12); lost by Abijah to Jeroboam I (2 Chr. 13:19). It may be mod. *Burj el-Isâneh*, N. of **Jerusalem**.

JESHIMON: A wilderness region near Ziph where David took refuge (1 Sam. 23:19, 24, 26:1, 3).

JEZREEL ('*God sows*'): 1. A town in Issachar (Jos. 19:18). Here Saul encamped before the battle of Gilboa (1 Sam. 29:1, 11), and it was included in the kingdom of Ishbosheth (2 Sam 2:9). It was here that Mephibosheth was dropped by his nurse and became lame (2 Sam. 4:4). It was in Solomon's fifth district (1 Kg. 4:12), and here Ahab had a residence (1 Kg. 18:45f.), beside which was Naboth's vineyard (1 Kg. 21:1ff.). To it Joram was brought when wounded (2 Kg. 8:29, 9:15; 2 Chr. 22:6), and was shot near here (2 Kg. 9:21ff.), while Jezebel was killed in the city (2 Kg. 9:30ff.). The heads of seventy princes were sent to Jehu here (2 Kg. 10:7). All this bloodshed was condemned by Hosea (Hos. 1:4). Jezreel is mod. *Zer'în*.
   2. A place in Judah (Jos. 15:56), from which one of David's wives came (1 Sam. 25:43, 27:3, 30:5; 2 Sam. 2:2, 3:2); its location is unknown.

JEZREEL, VALLEY OF: The valley lying between the central highlands of Palestine and Galilee. It derived its name from Jezreel (1) (Jos. 17:16; Jg. 6:33). Hosea predicted that the house of Jehu would fall here (Hos. 1:5). The Greek name Esdraelon is derived from Jezreel, but is usually reserved for the western part of the valley.

JOGBEHAH: A town in Gad (Num. 32:35), to which Gideon pursued his foes (Jg. 8:11); mod. *Khirbet Jubeihât*.

JOKDEAM: A place in Judah (Jos. 15:56); called Jorkeam in 1 Chr 2:44. It is perhaps mod. *Khirbet Raqa'*.

JOKMEAM: 1. A Levitical city in Ephraim (1) (1 Chr. 6:68); corresponding to Kibzaim in Jos. 21:22. Its site is unknown.
   2. A place in Solomon's fifth district (1 Kg. 4:12); called Jokneam in Jos. 12:22, 19:11.

JOKNEAM: A Canaanite city defeated by Joshua (Jos. 12:22); allocated to Zebulin (Jos. 19:11) and a Levitical city (Jos. 21:34). It is called Jokmean in 1 Kg. 4:12, and is perhaps mod. *Tell Qeimûn*. It is probably the same as Cyamon (Jdt. 7:3).

JOKTHEEL: 1. An unidentified place in the lowland of Judah (Jos. 15:38).

2. The name given by Amaziah to the captured Edomite city of Sela (2 Kg. 14:7).

JOPPA: A seaport of **Palestine** (2 Chr. 2:16; Ezr. 3:7), allotted to **Dan** (1) (Jos. 19:46), but in the territory which Dan was forced to vacate (cf. Jg. 1:34, 18:1), and it was never effectively occupied by this tribe. Jonah embarked for **Tarshish** from here (Jon. 1:3). It was attacked by Jonathan (1 Mac. 10:74ff.) and Jonathan met Ptolemy VI here (1 Mac. 11:6). Simon captured it (1 Mac. 12:33, 14:5, 34, 15:28, 35) and Jonathan, son of Absalom, was sent with an army to it (1 Mac. 13:11). Here Peter raised Tabitha (Ac. 9:36ff.), and he was staying here when Cornelius sent for him from **Caesarea** (Ac. 10:5ff., 23f., 11:5, 13). It is mod. *Jaffa*.

JORDAN, RIVER: The longest river of **Palestine**, rising at the foot of Mount **Hermon** and flowing through the **Sea of Galilee** to the **Dead Sea**, much of its course being below sea level. It was crossed by the Israelites under Joshua (Jos. 3:14ff.). and the tribes E. of Jordan built an altar beside it (Jos. 22:10), which created strife (Jos. 22:12ff.). The fords of the Jordan were held against the Moabites (Jg. 3:28) and later against the Ephraimites (Jg. 12:5ff.). David found refuge from Absalom by crossing to the E. of the river (2 Sam. 17:22), and it was after crossing the Jordan that Elijah was taken up (2 Kg. 2:6ff.). Naaman washed in the river and was healed (2 Kg. 5:14). Part of the course of the river is very winding and through wooded country, in which wild beasts were found (Jer. 12:5, 49:19, 50:44; Zech. 11:3). In the marshes of the Jordan the Jewish patriots found refuge (1 Mac. 9:42). John the Baptist baptized in the river (Mk 3:5f.; Mk 1:5, Lk. 3:3; Jn 1:28) and Jesus was baptized in its waters (Mt. 3:13; Mk 1:9; Lk. 3:31 Jn 1:29ff.). Its mod. name is *esh-Sherî'ah el-Kabîreh*.

JORKEAM: The 'son' of Raham, probably indicating a village founded by him (1 Chr. 2:44); called **Jokdeam** in Jos. 15:56, where LXX[B] reads Jorkeam.

JOTBAH: The birthplace of king Amon's mother (2 Kg. 21:19); perhaps mod. *Khirbet Jefât*.

JOTBATHAH: A stopping-place in the Wilderness wanderings (Num. 33:33f.; Dt. 10:7); perhaps mod. *'Ain Ṭâbah*.

JUDAH: The territory occupied by the tribe of Judah, whose ideal limits are stated in Jos. 15. After the disruption of the kingdom it is used for the southern kingdom (1 Kg. 12:21, 15:1), which included the tribes of Judah and **Benjamin** (1 Kg. 12:21). It also included what survived of the tribe of **Simeon**, which was early absorbed by Judah, so that many places listed as belonging to Simeon (Jos. 19:1ff.) are elsewhere given as in Judah. *See also* **Judea**. (In Jos. 19:34 Judah is mentioned as contiguous to **Naphtali**. This is doubtless an error, and LXX omits; so also JB. Apparently the reference is to a tribal territory and not a town, and in any case no town of this name is known.)

JUDAH, HILL COUNTRY OF: The name for the southern highlands (Jos. 11:21, 15:48, 20:7, 21:11; 2 Chr. 21:11, 27:4; cf. Jer. 32:44, 33:13). Its area is indicated in Jos. 15:48ff.

JUDAH, WILDERNESS OF: A region along the W. side of the **Dead Sea** (Jg. 1:16; Ps. 63 heading), in which David found refuge (1 Sam. 24:1). It was the scene of the preaching of John the Baptist (Mt. 3:1), where it is called the **Wilderness of Judea**.

JUDEA: The Graeco-Latin form of **Judah**, used for the southern part of western Palestine, of which **Jerusalem** was the capital, in Ezr. 9:9 and in the Apocrypha (Jdt. 4:7, 8:21, 11:19; 1 Mac. 14:33, 15:40; 2 Mac. 5:11, 11:5, 13:1) and the NT (Mt. 2:1, 5, 3:1; Lk. 1:65, 2:4, 3:1; Jn 4:3; Ac. 8:1). It is sometimes used to include **Galilee** (Lk. 4:44, 7:17, 23:5; Ac. 10:37), but sometimes clearly distinguished from Galilee (Mk 3:7; Lk. 3:1, 5:17; Jn 4:47, 54; Ac. 9:31). It is even used for the country E. of the **Jordan** (Mt. 19:1; Mk 10:1). In 1 Mac. the form Judah is sometimes found (1 Mac. 6:5, 9:1, 10:30, 13:1).

JUDEA, WILDERNESS OF: *See* **Judah, Wilderness of**.

JUTTAH: A town in **Judah** (Jos. 15:55), which became a Levitical city (Jos. 21:16; omitted from 1 Chr. 6:59); perhaps mod. *Yaṭṭâ*.

K

KABZEEL: A place in S. Judah (Jos. 15:21), the birthplace of Benaiah (2 Sam. 23:20; 1 Chr. 11:22); called Jekabzeel in Neh. 11:25, where its resettlement after the exile is recorded. It is perhaps mod. *Khirbet Ḥôrah*.

KADESH: 1. *See* Kadesh-barnea.

2. A city in Syria on the *Orontes* (2 Sam. 24:6). A famous battle between Rameses II and the Hittites took place here in the thirteenth century B.C.

3. *See* Kedesh (3).

KADESH-BARNEA: A place referred to by this name in Num. 32:8, 34:4; Dt. 1:2, 19, 2:14, 9:23; Jos. 10:41; 14:6f., 15:3, and elsewhere simply as Kadesh (1). It was an oasis in the **Wilderness of Zin** (Num. 20:1, 33:36), on the edge of **Edom** (Num. 20:16). It was conquered by Chedorlaomer and his allies (Gen. 14:7), and near here Hagar saw an angel (Gen. 16:14). The Israelites came here after the Exodus (Dt. 1:19) and spent much time here (Dt. 1:46). Here Mirian died (Num. 20:1) and here Moses brought water from the rock (Num. 20:2ff., 27:14). The spies were sent into **Canaan** (Num. 13:26, 32:8; Dt. 1:22ff.; Jos. 14:7) and messengers to Edom (Num. 20:14ff.; Jg. 11:16ff.) from Kadesh. Joshua's conquests are represented as reaching this place (Jos. 10:41). It is called Kedesh (1) in Jos. 15:23, En-mishpat in Gen. 14:7, and Meribath-kadesh in Dt. 32:51; Ezek. 47:19, 48:28. It is mod. *'Ain Qedeirât*.

KAIN: A city in the hill country of **Judah** (Jos. 15:57); probably mod. *Khirbet Yâqîn*.

KAMON: An unlocated place in **Gilead** (1), where Jair was buried (Jg. 10:5).

KANAH: A place in **Asher** (1) (Jos. 19:28); probably mod. *Qânah*, near Tyre.

KANAH, BROOK: A wady in Ephraim (1) (Jos. 16:8, 17:9); probably mod. *Wâdī Qânah*, near Shechem.

KAREM: A place in the hill country of Judah (Jos. 15:59, in an addition in LXX and JB Carem, not in MT and RSV).

KARKA: An unidentified place in S. Judah (Jos. 15:3).

KARKOR: An unknown place in Gilead (1) (Jg. 8:10).

KARNAIM: A place mentioned in Am. 6:13; possibly the same as Ashteroth-karnaim (Gen. 14:5) and Carnaim (1 Mac. 5:26, 43f., 2 Mac. 12:21, 26); mod. *Sheikh Saʿad*.

KARTAH: An unidentified Levitical city in Zebulun (Jos. 21:34), unmentioned in 1 Chr. 6:77.

KARTAN: A Levitical city in Naphtali (Jos. 21:32); called Kiriathaim in 1 Chr. 6:76. It is perhaps *Khirbet el-Qureiyah*.

KATTATH: A place in Zebulun (Jos. 19:15); possibly the same as Kitron (Jg. 1:30). It is perhaps mod. *Khirbet Quṭeineh*.

KEDEMOTH: A town in Reuben (Jos. 13:18), which became a Levitical city (Jos. 21:37; 1 Chr. 6:79). Messengers were sent from near here to Sihon (Dt. 2:26). It is perhaps *Qaṣr ez-Zaʿferân*.

KEDESH: 1. A city in S. Judah (Jos. 15:23); the same as Kadesh (1).

2. A Levitical city in Issachar (1 Chr. 6:72); called Kishion in Jos. 21:28. It is possibly mod. *Tell Abū Qedeis*.

3. A Canaanite city, conquered by Joshua (Jos. 12:22) and assigned to Naphtali (Jos. 19:37). It was the home of Barak (Jg. 4:6) and here Deborah and Barak gathered the men of Naphtali and Zebulun to fight Jabin (Jg. 4:9f.), and the tent of Heber the Kenite was near by (Jg. 4:11). It became a city of refuge (Jos. 20:7) and a Levitical city (Jos. 21:32; 1 Chr. 6:76). It was captured by Tiglath-pileser (2 Kg. 15:29), and in the Maccabean age Jonathan won a victory here (1 Mac. 11:63ff., called Kadesh (3) in Galilee). It is called 'Kedesh in Galilee' in Jos. 20:7, 21:32; 1 Chr. 6:76, and 'Kedesh in Naphtali' in Jg. 4:6. It is mod. *Tell Qades*.

KEDRON: A place fortified by Cendebaeus (1 Mac. 15:39, 41), to which he fled before Simon (1 Mac. 16:9). It is probably mod. *Qaṭra*. It is sometimes identified with **Gedoreth**, but this is doubtful.

KEHELATHAH: An unidentified stopping-place in the Wilderness wanderings (Num. 33:22f.).

KEILAH: A town in the lowland of **Judah** (Jos. 15:44). David saved it from a Philistine attack (1 Sam. 23:1ff.) and dwelt there (2 Sam. 23:6ff.) until he had reason to fear betrayal by its people (1 Sam. 23:10ff.). It helped to rebuild the walls of **Jerusalem** (Neh. 3:17f.). It is perhaps mod. *Khirbet Qîlā*.

KENATH: A place E. of the **Jordan**, taken by Nobah and called **Nobah** (1) after him (Num. 32:42). **Geshur** and **Aram** annexed it. It was later called *Kanatha* and was one of the cities of the **Decapolis**. It is probably mod. *Qanawât*.

KERIOTH: A city in **Moab** (Jer. 48:24, 41; Am. 2:2), mentioned on the Moabite Stone. Its site is unknown.

KERIOTH-HEZRON: A place in S. **Judah** (Jos. 15:25), identified with **Hazor** (3).

KIBROTH-HATTAAVAH (*'graves of lust'*): A stopping-place in the Wilderness wanderings where the people were punished by disease (Num. 11:34f., 33:16f.; Dt. 9:22). It is perhaps mod. *Erweis el-Eberij*.

KIBZAIM: An unidentified Levitical city in **Ephraim** (1) (Jos. 21:22); called **Jokmean** (1) in 1 Chr. 6:68.

KIDRON, BROOK: A torrent valley E. of **Jerusalem**, crossed by David when he fled before Absalom (2 Sam. 15:23). Shimei was forbidden to cross it (2 Kg. 2:37). Here Asa burned his mother's idol (1 Kg. 15:13; 2 Chr. 15:16) and here Josiah destroyed the idolatrous symbols from the Temple (2 Kg. 23:4, 6, 12). The Chronicler records a similar action by Hezekiah (2 Chr. 29:16; 30:14). Its future sacredness is predicted in Jer. 31:40. Jesus crossed it with His disciples to go to **Gethsemane** (Jn 18:1). It is known in its different sections as mod. *Wâdî el-Jawz*, *Wâdî Sittî Maryam*, and the *Wâdî en-Nâr*.

KINAH: An unidentified place in S. Judah (Jos. 15:22). Its name is perhaps preserved in *Wâdî el-Qeini*.

KING'S GARDEN: A royal estate close to **Jerusalem**, by way of which Zedekiah left Jerusalem (2 Kg. 25:4; Jer. 39:4, 52:7). It was near the **Pool of Shelah** (Neh. 3:15).

KING'S HIGHWAY: The road by which Moses promises to pass peacefully through **Edom** (Num. 20:17) and through Sihon's territory (Num. 21:22; cf. Dt. 2:27). It was probably the road from **Damascus** to the Gulf of *'Aqaba*.

KING'S POOL: A pool mentioned only in Neh. 2:14; probably the same as the **Pool of Shelah** (Neh. 3:15).

KING'S VALLEY: Another name for the **Valley of Shaveh** (Gen. 14:17). Absalom set up a pillar for himself here (2 Sam. 18:18).

KIR: 1. The place from which Amos said the Syrians had come (Am. 9:7) and to which they would go into exile (Am. 1:5), a prophecy which was fulfilled (2 Kg. 16:9). Kir is mentioned with **Elam** as supplying Assyria with soldiers (Isa. 22:6). Its location is unknown.
  2. A place in **Moab** (Isa. 15:1); probably the same as **Kir-hareseth** (Isa. 16:7), mod. *el'Kerak*.

KIR-HARESETH: An important city in **Moab** (2 Kg. 3:25), famous for its raisin-cakes (Isa. 16:7); called **Kir-heres** in Isa. 16:11; Jer. 48:31, 36, and **Kir** (2) in Isa. 15:1. It is mod. *el-Kerak*.

KIR-HERES: *See* **Kir-hareseth**.

KIRIATHAIM (*'two cities'*): 1. A place E. of the **Jordan** in **Reuben** (Num. 32:37; Jos. 13:19), which was later in Moabite hands (Jer. 48:1, 23; Ezek. 25:9); mentioned on the Moabite Stone. It is possibly mod. *Khirbet el-Qureiyât*.
  2. A Levitical city in **Naphtali** (1 Chr. 6:76); called **Kartan** in Jos. 21:32. It is perhaps mod. *Khirbet el-Qureiyah*.

KIRIATH-ARBA (*'city of four'*): The earlier name of **Hebron** (Gen. 23:2, 35:27; Jos. 14:15, 15:13, 54, 20:7, 21:11; Jg. 1:10). It is curious that it should appear under its ancient name in the post-exilic period (Neh. 11:25).

KIRIATH-ARIM: The form of the name of **Kiriath-jearim** found in Ezr. 2:25; 1 Esd. 5:19 (cf. the parallel Neh. 7:29, Kiriath-jearim).

KIRIATH-BAAL (*'city of Baal'*): Alternative name of **Kiriath-jearim** found in Jos. 15:60, 18:14.

KIRIATH-HUZOTH (*'city of streets'*): An unidentified place to which Balaam took Balak (Num. 22:39).

KIRIATH-JEARIM (*'city of woods'*): One of the four Gibeonite towns that made peace with Joshua (Jos. 9:17). It was on the border of **Benjamin** and **Judah** (Jos. 15:9, 18:14), and alternatively assigned to Benjamin (Jos. 18:28) and to Judah (Jos. 15:60; 18:14; 1 Chr. 13:6). The migrating Danites encamped near here at **Mahaneh-dan** (Jg. 18:12). The Ark was brought here when it came back from the Philistines (1 Sam. 6:21, 7:1f.), and from here it was brought to **Jerusalem** (2 Sam. 6:2ff.; 1 Chr. 13:5f.; 2 Chr. 1:4). Uriah the prophet came from this town (Jer. 26:20), which is said to have been founded by Shobal (1 Chr. 2:50). Some who traced their descent from here returned from the exile (Neh. 7:29). It is called Baalah in Jos. 15:9; 1 Chr. 13:6, Baale-judah in 2 Sam. 6:2, Kiriath-arim in Ezr. 2:25; 1 Esd. 5:19, Kiriath-baal in Jos. 15:60, 18:4, and Jaar in Ps. 132:6. It is probably mod. *Tell el-Azhar*. *See* **Ephrathah** (2).

KIRIATH-SANNAH: An alternative name for **Debir** (1) or **Kiriath-sepher**, found in Jos. 15:49.

KIRIATH-SEPHER (*'city of writing'*): An older name for **Debir** (1) (Jos. 15:15f.; Jg. 1:11f.).

KISHION: A place in **Issachar** (Jos. 19:20), which became a Levitical city (Jos. 21:21); called **Kedesh** (2) in 1 Chr. 6:72. It is probably mod. *Tell Abū Qedeis*.

KISHON, RIVER: A stream which becomes a torrent after rains (Jg. 5:21), and which flows through the **Plain of Esdraelon** to the

Mediterranean. It figures especially in the story of the fight against Sisera (Jg. 4:7, 13, 5:21; Ps. 83:9), when it swept away the fleeing Canaanites. It was here that Elijah killed the prophets of Baal (1 Kg. 18:40). It is mod. *Nahr el-Mukaṭṭaʿ*.

KITRON: A place in **Zebulun**, whose Canaanite inhabitants could not be ejected (Jg. 1:30). Possibly the same as **Kattath** (Jos. 19:15); perhaps mod. *Khirbet Quṭeineh*.

KITTIM: The Hebrew name for **Cyprus** (so rendered in Isa. 23:1, 12; Jer. 2:10; Ezek. 27:6). It stands for Cyprus in Gen. 10:4; 1 Chr. 1:7; the name was derived from the Phoenician settlement at *Kition* (mod. *Larnaka*) on the island. In Num. 24:24 it stands for Cyprus, but in Dan. 11:30 it stands for **Rome**, and it is here probably an interpretation of the Numbers passage. In 1 Mac. 1:1 it stands for **Greece** or **Macedonia**, and in 1 Mac. 8:5 RSV renders by 'Macedonians'.

KOA: A district or people mentioned in Ezek. 23:23; sometimes identified with the *Kutū* mentioned in Assyrian texts. The location cannot be certainly determined.

KOLA: An unidentified place mentioned in Jdt. 15:4.

KONA: An unidentified locality in **Palestine**, mentioned in Jdt. 4:4.

KOULON: A place in the hill country of **Judah** (Jos. 15:59, in an addition in LXX, JB **Kulon**, not in MT and RSV).

KUE: A place from which horses were imported by Solomon (1 Kg. 10:28; 2 Chr. 1:16). It was a region in the E. part of **Cilicia**.

KULON: *See* **Koulon**.

L

LABAN: An unidentified stopping-place in the Wilderness wanderings (Dt. 1:1).

LACHISH: A Canaanite city which joined the coalition against Joshua (Jos. 10:3ff.), whose king was defeated and slain (Jos. 10:23f., 12:11), and which was captured and its people massacred (Jos. 10:31f.). It was allotted to **Judah** (Jos. 15:39), and fortified by Rehoboam (2 Chr. 11:9). Amaziah fled to Lachish, and was assassinated there (2 Kg. 14:19; 2 Chr. 25:27). Sennacherib besieged it, and sent envoys to Hezekiah from there (2 Kg. 18:14, 17, 19:18; 2 Chr. 32:9; Isa. 36:2, 37:8), and in the resistance to Nebuchadrezzar Lachish, **Azekah**, and **Jerusalem** were the last places to hold out (Jer. 34:7). The Lachish letters come from this period. Lachish was resettled after the exile (Neh. 11:30). The reference in Micah's denunciation (Mic. 1:13) is unknown. Lachish is mod. *Tell ed-Duweir*.

LAHMAM: A place in **Judah** (Jos. 15:40); perhaps mod. *Khirbet el-Laḥm*.

LAISH: The original name of **Dan** (2) (Jg. 18:7, 14, 27, 29); called **Leshem** in Jos. 19:47.

LAISHAH: A place in **Benjamin** on the expected route of the Assyrian advance (Isa. 10:30); possibly mod. *el-Isāwîyeh*.

LAKKUM: A place in **Naphtali** (Jos. 19:33); possibly mod. *Khirbet el-Manṣûrah*.

LAODICEA: A city in the *Lycus* valley in Asia Minor. It was not visited by Paul (Col. 2:1), but his letter to the Colossians was addressed also to the church there (Col. 4:16) and included greetings to it (Col. 4:15). Epaphras had ministered there (Col. 4:13). The church there was one of the seven churches addressed by John (Rev. 1:11, 3:14ff.) and rebuked for its lukewarmness. It is mod. *Eski Hisar*.

LASEA: A town in **Crete**, near **Fair Havens** (Ac. 27:8).

LASHA: An unidentified Canaanite border town (Gen. 10:19).

LASHARON: A Canaanite city whose king was conquered by Joshua (Jos. 12:18). Its site is unknown. Many scholars think it denotes the location of **Aphek** (1) as 'in **Sharon**' (JB renders 'the king of Sharon').

LEBANON (*'white'*): The western mountain range, roughly parallel to the Anti-Lebanon, in N. Syria, separated from it by the valley now called *el-Beqa'*. Lebanon is mod. *Jebel Libnân*. Its name is due to the snow on its summit (Jer. 18:14). It was famous for its fragrance and beauty (Ca. 4:11, 15; Hos. 14:6f.; Nah. 1:4; Isa. 35:2, 60:13), and especially for its cedars (Jg. 9:15; 1 Kg. 5:6; 2 Kg. 14:9; Ps. 29:5, 37:35, 92:12, 104:16; Isa. 2:13, 14:8; Ezek. 27:5, 31:3; 1 Esd. 4:48, 5:55; Sir. 24:13, 50:12), from which timber for the Temple was supplied (1 Kg. 5:6, 9; 2 Chr. 2:8, 16) and for Solomon's palace (1 Kg. 7:2f.), and also for the Second Temple (Ezr. 3:7). It is mentioned as a boundary (Dt. 3:25, 11:24; Jos. 9:1; 2 Esd. 15:20).

LEBANON, VALLEY OF: The valley between the Lebanon and the Anti-Lebanon (Jos. 11:17); mod. *el-Beqa'*.

LEBAOTH (*'lions'*): A place in S. Judah (Jos. 15:32); called Beth-lebaoth in Jos. 19:6, and assigned to Simeon, which was early absorbed in Judah. Its location is unknown.

LEBONAH (*'frankincense'*): A place near Shiloh (Jg. 21:19); probably mod. *Lubbân*.

LEHABIM: *See* Libya.

LEHEM: An unknown place mentioned in RSV in 1 Chr. 4:22, where the reading is conjectural. JB reads Bethlehem.

LEHI (*'jawbone'*): The unknown scene of an exploit of Samson's (Jg. 15:9, 14, 19; cf. 2 Sam. 23:11); called Ramath-lehi in Jg. 15:17.

LESHEM: An alternative form (Jos. 19:47) of Laish (Jg. 18:7), the original name of Dan (2).

LIBNAH (*'white'*): 1. An unknown stopping-place in the Wilderness wanderings (Num. 23:20f.).

2. A Canaanite city which Joshua conquered and whose people he massacred (Jos. 10:29f., 12:15). It was situated in the lowland of Judah (Jos. 15:42), and became a Levitical city (Jos. 21:13; 1 Chr. 6:57). It revolted with Edom against Joram (2 Kg. 8:22; 2 Chr. 21:10). It was attacked by Sennacherib (2 Kg. 19:8; Isa. 37:8). It was

the birthplace of the mother of Jehoahaz and Zedekiah (2 Kg. 23:31, 24:18; Jer. 52:1). It is perhaps mod. *Tell eṣ-Ṣâfī*.

LIBYA: A region of N. Africa, mentioned in Ezek. 30:5 (RSV, but not MT). Some Jews or proselytes from Libya were in **Jerusalem** at Pentecost (Ac. 2:10). Some of its people were in Shishak's army (2 Chr. 12:3), and Asa is said to have destroyed a large army of them (2 Chr. 16:8). Their support of Egypt is referred to in Nah. 3:9, and in Dan. 11:43 their conquest by the 'king of the north' is predicted. It is possible that the Libyans are meant by the **Lehabim** in Gen. 10:13; 1 Chr. 1:11.

LIDEBIR: *See* **Lo-debar.**

LOD: A town in **Benjamin** built by Shemed (1 Chr. 8:12). Some who traced their descent from here returned after the exile (Ezr. 2:23; Neh. 7:37), where the parallel 1 Esd. 5:22 has 'the other Elam' (RSV). It is called **Lydda** in 1 Mac. 11:34; Ac. 9:32, 35, 38. It is mod. *Ludd.*

LO-DEBAR: A place in **Gilead** where Mephibosheth was until David provided for him (2 Sam. 9:4f.). Machir from Lo-debar supported David when he fled before Absalom (2 Sam. 17:27). It is mentioned in Am. 6:13. We should perhaps read Lo-debar in Jos. 13:26 (so JB), where MT has **Lidebir** (RSVm), and where RSV has **Debir** (3). Lo-debar is perhaps mod. *Ummed-Dabar.*

LUD: 1. In the table of nations in Gen. 10:22; 1 Chr. 1:17 Lud, the 'son' of Shem, is apparently a geographical term, and it is probable that it refers to **Lydia**, in Asia Minor.
 2. In Isa. 66:19; Jer. 46:9; Ezek. 27:10, 30:5, Lud is apparently associated with Africa, and the **Ludim** of Gen. 10:13; 1 Chr. 1:11 are connected with Egypt. The reference may be to an unknown region in Africa, or possibly to 1, which supplied mercenaries to the Egyptian armies. The double affiliation in the table of nations favours the former view.

LUDIM: *See* **Lud** (2).

LUHITH, ASCENT OF: A location in Moab, near Horonaim (1) (Isa. 15:5; Jer. 48:5).

LUZ: 1. The former name of **Bethel** (1) (Gen. 28:19, 35:6; Jos. 18:13; Jg. 1:23), or a nearby site (Jos. 16:2).

2. An unknown place in Hittite territory (Jg. 1:26).

LYCAONIA: A region of Asia Minor, part of which in NT times was incorporated administratively in **Galatia**. This part included Lystra and **Derbe**, which Paul evangelized (Ac. 14:6, 11).

LYCIA: A region in SW Asia Minor, a port of which was **Myra**, where Paul transhipped on his journey to **Rome** (Ac. 27:5). **Patara**, where he embarked on an earlier occasion (Ac. 21:1), was also in Lycia.

LYDDA: The Greek name for **Lod**. It was one of the cities (1 Mac. 11:34) ceded to Jonathan by Demetrius (1 Mac. 10:30, 38, 11:28). It was here that Peter healed Aeneas (Ac. 9:32ff.), and from here he went to **Joppa** (Ac. 9:38). It is mod. *Ludd*.

LYDIA: A region of Asia Minor once ruled by Croesus, with its capital at **Sardis**. It was conquered by Cyrus before he conquered Babylon. It is mentioned in 1 Mac. 8:8 as surrendered by Antiochus III when he was defeated by **Rome**. Lydia (Ac. 16:14, 40), whom Paul converted at Philippi, was from **Thyatira**, a city of Lydia, and it is possible that Lydia was not her name but the term by which she was known: 'the Lydian woman'. Lydia is probably referred to in the OT as **Lud** (1).

LYSTRA: A city in the Roman province of **Galatia**, but in the ethnic area of **Lycaonia** (Ac. 14:6, 11). Paul came here from **Iconium** on his first missionary journey (Ac. 14:6ff.). Here he healed a cripple and was hailed as a god (Ac. 14:8ff.), but was afterwards stoned at the instigation of Jews from Iconium (Ac. 14:19; cf. 2 Tim. 3:11). After going to **Derbe** (Ac. 14:20), he returned to Lystra (Ac. 14:2). On his second missionary journey he visited it again (Ac. 16:1). Timothy was a native of Lystra (Ac. 16:1ff.). It is mod. *Zoldera*.

M

MAACAH: A region E. of the **Jordan**, associated with **Geshur** as conquered but not dispossessed by the Israelites (Dt. 3:14; Jos. 12:5, 13:11ff.), which later was independent and assisted **Ammon** against David (2 Sam. 10:6ff.; 1 Chr. 19:6ff.); called **Aram-maacah** in 1 Chr. 9:6, and **Maacath** in Jos. 13:13. One of David's heroes came from here (2 Sam. 23:34).

MAACATH: *See* **Maacah.**

MAARATH: A place in **Judah** (Jos. 15:59); perhaps mod. *Beit Ummâr*. It is possibly the same as **Maroth.**

MACEDONIA: A region in the Balkan peninsula from which Alexander the Great, the son of Philip, came (1 Mac. 1:1, 6:2, 8:5). In response to a vision of a man of **Macedonia** (Ac. 16:9), Paul entered Europe here and preached in **Philippi,** the chief city of one of its districts (Ac. 16:12ff.), and in **Thessalonica** (Ac. 17:1ff.) and **Beroea** (Ac. 17:10ff.), where he left Silas and Timothy (Ac. 17:14), who later joined him in **Corinth** (Ac. 18:5). Paul visited Macedonia again later (Ac. 21:1ff.), and makes many references to Macedonia and its several churches in his letters, three of which (Phil. and 1 & 2 Th.) are addressed to Macedonian churches.

MACHBENAH: The 'son' of Sheva, or a place in **Judah** founded by him (1 Chr. 2:49). It is possibly the same as **Meconah** (Neh. 11:28). Its location is unknown.

MACHPELAH: A locality near **Hebron** (Gen. 23:2, 19), in which was the cave which Abraham bought to bury Sarah in (Gen. 23:9ff.). Here too Abraham (Gen. 25:9), Isaac and Rebekah and Leah (Gen. 49:31), and Jacob (Gen. 50:13) were buried.

MADMANNAH: A place in S. **Judah** (Jos. 15:31), called the 'son' of (i.e. a place founded by' Shaaph (1 Chr. 2:49); probably the same as **Beth-marcaboth** (Jos. 19:5; 1 Chr. 4:31) in **Simeon**, which was early absorbed in Judah. It is perhaps mod. *Umm Deimneh*.

MADMEN: A place in **Moab**, mentioned only in Jer. 48:2; perhaps the same as **Dimon** (Isa. 15:9, MT), and possibly mod. *Khirbet Dimneh*.

MADMENAH: An unidentified place on the expected route of the Assyrian approach to **Jerusalem** (Isa. 10:31).

MADON: A Canaanite city allied with Jabin against Joshua (Jos. 11:1) and defeated by the Israelites (Jos. 12:19); probably mod. *Qarn Ḥaṭṭîn*.

MAGADAN: A place not certainly known on the W. shore of the Sea of Galilee (Mt. 15:39), corresponding to **Dalmanutha** in Mk 8:10.

MAGDALA: A place from which Mary Magdalene (Mt. 27:56; Mk 15:40; Lk. 8:2, 24:10; Jn 19:25) came. It was on the W. shore of the Sea of Galilee, and is probably mod. *Mejdel*.

MAGOG: The land ruled over by Gog (Ezek. 38:2, 39:6), in the far north (Ezek. 39:2), represented as a 'son' of Japheth in Gen. 10:2; 1 Chr. 1:5. In Rev. 20:8 Magog is a symbol of the hosts of Satan.

MAHALAB: A place in **Asher** (Jos. 19:29), perhaps the same as **Ahlab** (Jg. 1:31) and **Helbah** (Jg. 1:31). It is probably mod. *Khirbet el-Maḥālib*, NE. of Tyre.

MAHANAIM ('*two camps*'): A city E. of the **Jordan**, on the border between **Gad** (Jos. 13:26) and **Manasseh** (Jos. 13:30), which became a Levitical city (Jos. 21:38; 1 Chr. 6:80). Jacob came to it before crossing the **Jabbok** when he returned from his sojourn with Laban (Gen. 32:2, 22). It was the capital of Ishbosheth (2 Sam. 2:8, 12, 29), and David made it his headquarters when he fled before Absalom (2 Sam. 17:24, 27, 19:32; 1 Kg. 2:8). It was in Solomon's seventh district (1 Kg. 4:14). Of the proposed identifications, mod. *Khirbet Maḥneh* is the most favoured.

MAHANEH-DAN ('*camp of Dan*'): A place near **Kiriath-jearim**, where the migrating Danites encamped (Jg. 18:12). The site is unidentified.

MAKAZ: A place in Solomon's second district (1 Kg. 4:9); possibly mod. *Khirbet el-Mukheizin*, S. of Ekron.

MAKED: A fortified town in **Gilead** (1) (1 Mac. 5:26, 36); possibly mod. *Tell Miqdâd*.

MAKHELOTH: An unidentified stopping-place in the Wilderness wanderings (Num. 33:25f.).

MAKKEDAH: A Canaanite city taken by Joshua and its people massacred (Jos. 10:28). In a cave near here he captured the five kings who headed the alliance against him, and killed them (Jos. 10:16ff.; cf. 12:16). The city was allotted to **Judah**, and was in the lowland (Jos. 15:41). It is perhaps mod. *Khirbet el-Kheishûm*, N. of Azekah.

MALLUS: A city in **Cilicia**, which revolted with **Tarsus** against Antiochus Epiphanes (2 Mac. 4:30). It is mod. *Kara Tash*.

MALTA: An island in the **Mediterranean** on which Paul was shipwrecked (Ac. 27:39ff., 28:1). Here a viper fastened on Paul's hand without harming him (Ac. 28:3ff.). Paul also healed the father of Publius (Ac. 28:8). After a stay of three months, he proceeded to **Rome** (Ac. 28:11).

MAMRE: An ancient name either for **Hebron** or for an adjoining site (Gen. 23:19, 35:27), where were some oaks near which Abraham stayed (Gen. 13:18, 14:13). Here three angels came to him (Gen. 18:1ff.), and here he bought the cave of **Machpelah** (Gen. 23:17f., 25:9, 49:30, 50:13). The name appears to come from the Mamre who was a local chief in Abraham's time (Gen. 14:24). It is probably mod. *Râmet el-Khalîl*, near **Hebron**.

MANACH: *See* **Manahath**.

MANAHATH: A place, probably in **Judah** (cf. 1 Chr. 2:54, where the Manahathites belong to Judah), to which Benjaminites were forcibly removed (1 Chr. 8:6). It is perhaps mentioned in Jos. 15:59, where LXX adds several names omitted from MT and RSV, among which is **Manocho** (JB **Manach**). Manahath is perhaps mod. *Mâlhâ*, SW. of **Jerusalem**.

MANASSEH: The territory occupied by the tribe of Manasseh, part of which was E. of the Jordan and part W. The ideal limits of the former are stated in Jos. 13.29ff., and of the latter in Jos. 17:7ff.

MANOCHO: *See* **Manahath.**

MAON: 1. A place in the hill country of Judah (Jos. 15:55). Nabal dwelt here (1 Sam. 25:2), and David twice spent periods here when he was an outlaw (1 Sam. 23:24ff., 25:2ff.). It is mod. *Tell Ma'in.*

2. In Jg. 10:12 reference is made to the deliverance of the Israelites from Maonite foes. The Maon where they dwelt is probably the place from which came the Meumin (1 Chr. 4:41), who were driven out by Simeonites, in which case it was in the region of Mount Seir, S. of the Dead Sea. These are the Meunites who were fought by Jehoshaphat (2 Chr. 20:1) and Uzziah (2 Chr. 26:7).

MARAH (*'bitter'*): The first stopping place in the Wilderness wanderings after crossing the sea (Exod. 15:23; Num. 33:8f.). It is perhaps mod. *'Ain Harâwah.*

MAREAL: A place in Zebulun (Jos. 19:11); possibly mod. *Tell Ghaltah.*

MARESHAH: A town in the lowland of Judah (Jos. 15:44). It was fortified by Rehoboam (2 Chr. 11:8), and here Asa is said to have conquered a million Ethiopians (2 Chr. 14:9ff.). Micah prophesied disaster for Mareshah (Mic. 1:15), and a prophet from here condemned Jehoshaphat (2 Chr. 20:37). In the Hellenistic period it was called Marisa. It is mod. *Tell Sandahannah.*

MARISA: The Greek name for **Mareshah.** Gorgias escaped here (2 Mac. 12:35) and Judas marched through it and plundered it (1 Mac. 5:66ff.).

MAROTH (*'bitterness'*): A place mentioned only in Mic. 1:2. It may be the same as **Maarath** (Jos. 15:59), possibly mod. *Beit Ummâr.*

MASH: One of the 'sons' of **Aram** (Gen. 10:23). It is possible that a geographical reference is intended, and this may be either *Mons Masius,* S. of **Armenia,** or a region in the Syro-Arabian desert. *See* **Meshech** (2).

MASHAL: A Levitical city in **Asher** (1) (1 Chr. 6:74); called Mishal in Jos. 19:26, 21:30. Its site is unknown.

MASREKAH: An unidentified place in **Edom** (Gen. 36:36; 1 Chr. 1:47).

MASSA: The country of Lemuel (Prov. 31:1) and of Agur (Prov. 30:1). This is probably the territory of an Arabian tribe descended from Ishmael (Gen. 25:14; 1 Chr. 1:30). Its location is not certainly known. *See* **Mesha.**

MASSAH (*'testing'*) A place where Moses brought water from the rock (Exod. 17:7). This was near **Horeb,** and within three months of leaving **Egypt** (Exod. 19:1). From Exod. 17:7 **Meribah** would seem to be the same place as Massah, and Massah and Meribah are associated also in Dt. 33:8 (which would seem to be a different incident, which concerned the tribe of Levi only) and Ps. 95:8. In Num. 20:2ff. the bringing of water from the rock at Meribah is placed at **Kadesh** (1) (and so Num. 27:14). Here Moses and Aaron are condemned to die before reaching the Land of Promise (Num. 20:12), and this story appears to be referred to in Ps. 106:32. Massah alone is referred to in Dt. 6:16, 9:22, and the Massah and Meribah traditions may once have been quite separate.

MATTANAH: A stopping-place in the Wilderness wanderings (Num. 21:18f.); possibly mod. *Khirbet el-Medeiyineh.*

MEARAH (*'cave'*): A district yet to be possessed after Joshua's conquests (Jos. 13:4). We should perhaps read *mē-'ārāh,* 'from **Arah'** (so JB). Arah is perhaps *Tell 'Arah.*

MECONAH: An unknown place which was resettled after the exile (Neh. 11:28). It is possibly the same as **Machbenah.**

MEDAN: An unknown region or tribe (Gen. 25:2; 1 Chr. 1:32).

MEDEBA: A Moabite city captured by Sihon (Num. 21:26), which became Israelite when Sihon was conquered and was allotted to **Reuben** (Jos. 13:9, 16). In the time of David it appears to have been in Ammonite hands (1 Chr. 19:7, 9), and then fell to David. (It is unmentioned in the account of this war in 2 Sam. 10:6ff.). When

Moab recovered her independence, Medeba was Moabite, but the Moabite Stone says it was in Israelite hands for forty years until Mesha recovered it. It is mentioned in Isa. 15:2 in a prophecy against Moab. John, the brother of Judas Maccabeus, was seized here (1 Mac. 9:36), a deed which was avenged (1 Mac. 9:37ff.). Medeba is mod. *Mâdebâ*.

MEDIA: A country to the E. of **Assyria**, whose capital was **Ecbatana** (Ezr. 6:2). It came under Assyrian control, and some northern Israelites were deported to Media (2 Kg. 17:6, 18:11). Later it became independent, and it was the ally of **Babylonia** in the overthrow of Assyria, The prophets believed that it would overthrow **Babylon** (Isa. 13:17, 21:2; Jer. 51:11, 28), and Dan. 5:31 represents Babylon as ruled by a Mede after its fall (cf. Dan. 9:1, 11:1). But before Babylon fell Cyrus had brought Media under his control, and the Persian empire succeeded the Babylonian. **Persia** and Media are named together in Est. 1:3, 14, 18, 10:2), Tobit had deposited his silver in Media (Tob. 1:14), and the angel Raphael went there to recover it (Tob. 9:2ff.). Some Jews or proselytes from Media were in Jerusalem at Pentecost (Ac. 2:9).

MEDITERRANEAN SEA: This name is not found in the Bible, where this sea is called the **Great Sea** (Num. 34:6f.; Jos. 1:4, 9:1, 15:12, 23:4 +), or the **Sea** (Jos. 16:8; 1 Kg. 5:9; Ac. 10:6), or the **Sea of the Philistines** (Exod. 23:31), or the **Western Sea** (Dt. 11:24; Jl 2:20; Zech. 14:8).

MEGIDDO: A Canaanite city, whose king was defeated by Joshua (Jos. 12:21), but which was not occupied by the Israelites (Jg. 1:27), though it was allotted to **Manasseh** (Jos. 17:11; 1 Chr. 7:29). Near Megiddo Sisera was defeated (Jg. 5:19). It was in Solomon's fifth district (1 Kg. 4:12), and fortified by him (1 Kg. 9:15). Ahaziah died in Megiddo (2 Kg. 9:27), and Josiah was killed here by Pharaoh Neco (2 Kg. 23:29f.; 2 Chr. 35:20f.). It is possible that there is an allusion to this in Zech. 12:11, but this is far from certain. Megiddo is mod. *Tell el-Mutesellim. See* **Armageddon.**

MEGIDDO. PLAIN OF: This plain (2 Chr. 35:22; Zech. 12:11) is the same as the **Plain of Esdraelon.**

MEGIDDO, WATERS OF: The scene of Sisera's defeat (Jg. 5—19); probably mod. *Wâdî el-Lejjûn.*

ME-JARKON: A watercourse in **Dan** (1) (Jos. 19:46); perhaps mod. *Nahr el-'Aujâ*.

MEMPHIS: The ancient capital of **Egypt**, S. of *Cairo*. Jeremiah condemned the trust of Judah in Memphis as fraught with harm for her (Jer. 2:16; cf. Hos. 9:6), and prophecies against Memphis stand in Isa. 19:13; Jer. 46:14, 19; Ezek. 30:13. Jeremiah addressed a message to the Jews here (Jer. 44:1ff.). It is mod. *Mît Rahîneh*.

MEPHAATH: A city in **Reuben** (Jos. 13:15), which became a Levitical city (Jos. 21:37; 1 Chr. 6:79).. It was later retaken by Moab (Jer. 48:21). It is perhaps mod. *Tell el-Jâwah*, near *Khirbet Nefa'ah*, which reflects the ancient name.

MERATHAIM (*'double rebellion'*): The region where the **Tigris** and the **Euphrates** reached the ocean, used as a symbolic name for **Babylon** (Jer. 50:21).

MERIBAH: *See* Massah.

MERIBATH-KADESH, WATERS OF: These are referred to in Dt. 32:51; Ezek. 47:19, 48:28, and they support the tradition which links the incident at **Meribah** (*see* **Massah**) with **Kadesh** (1).

MEROM, WATERS OF: The scene of Joshua's victory over Jabin and his allies (Jos. 11:5, 7). It was probably a wady near mod. *Meirûn*.

MERRAN: A place from which merchants came (Bar. 3:23). But Midian (so JB) should probably be read (cf. Gen. 37:28; Hab. 3:7).

MESALOTH: A place where Bacchides encamped (1 Mac. 9:2). It was situated in **Arbela**, but its location is unknown.

MESHA: A region mentioned in Gen. 10:30 as one limit of the peoples descended from Joktan. It is possibly to be identified with **Massa**.

MESHECH: 1. A region and people of Asia Minor (Gen. 10:2; 1 Chr. 1:5), perhaps referred to in Isa. 66:19, where Meshech should possibly be read instead of 'who draw the bow' (JB **Moshech**). Meshech traded with **Tyre** (Ezek. 27:13), and was a land of warlike people (Ezek. 32:26; 38;2; cf. Ps. 120:5), whose chief prince is Gog (Ezek. 38:3, 39:1). They figure in Assyrian inscriptions as *Mushki*, and in classical texts as *Moschi*.

2. One of the 'sons' of Aram (1 Chr. 1:17). The name corresponds to Mash in Gen. 10:23, and this should perhaps be read here (so JB).

MESOPOTAMIA: A term properly used for the land between the Tigris and the Euphrates, but frequently used more widely to include Babylonia. In RSV of the OT it always translates Aram-naharaim (save in the heading of Ps. 60), a state in the Upper basin of the Euphrates. The city of Haran was here (Gen. 24:10), and so was the home of Balaam (Dt. 23:4), while the Ammonites sought help from here against David (1 Chr. 19:6). Cushan-rishathaim is said to have come from here (Jg. 3:8, 10), though it is probable that we should read Edom (so JB) instead of Aram-naharaim (Mesopotamia), since the deliverer was from the S., which was neighbour to Edom, and Edom and Aram are frequently confused in Hebrew (the word *naharaim* may have been added after the confusion arose). Mesopotamia occurs several times in Judith (Jdt. 2:24, 5:7f., 8:26), where we find Jacob's residence with Laban described as 'in Meso-potamia in Syria' (Jdt. 8:26). Jews or proselytes from Mesopotamia were in Jerusalem at Pentecost (Ac. 2:9), while Stephen in his speech used Mesopotamia where his reference is to Abraham's resi-dence in Ur, in Babylonia (Ac. 7:2).

ME-ZAHAB ('*waters of gold*'): Apparently the father of Matred (Gen. 36:39; 1 Chr. 1:50). But it looks more like a place name than a personal name, and for 'daughter of Me-zahab' we should probably read 'from Me-zahab' (so JB), or 'from Dizahab' (Dt. 1:1). In either case the location is unknown.

MICHMAS: The spelling of Michmash in Ezr. 2:27; Neh. 7:31; 1 Esd. 5:21.

MICHMASH: A location in Benjamin, where Saul gathered part of his army (1 Sam. 13:2), and where the Philistines encamped against him (1 Sam. 13:5, 11, 16), before moving out to the pass (1 Sam. 13:23). Here Jonathan and his armour-bearer surprised the Philistine outpost by climbing a crag at the entrance to the pass (1 Sam. 14:5ff.), and this led to the defeat of the Philistines (1 Sam. 14:16ff.) and their pursuit from Michmash to Aijalon (1 Sam. 14:31).

Some who traced their descent from here (**Michmas**) returned after the exile (Ezr. 2:27; Neh. 7:31; 1 Esd. 5:21), and it was resettled (Neh. 11:31). It lay on the expected line of the Assyrian approach to Jerusalem (Isa. 10:28). It is mod. *Mukhmâs*.

MICHMETHATH: A place on the border of **Ephraim** (1) (Jos. 16:6) and **Manasseh** (Jos. 17:7); perhaps mod. *Khirbet Juleijil*.

MIDDIN: A place in the **Wilderness of Judah** (Jos. 15:61); possibly mod. *Khirbet Abū Ṭabaq*.

MIDIAN: The territory in NW. **Arabia** occupied by the Midianites (Exod. 2:15; Hab. 3:7). Here Moses stayed with Jethro (Exod. 2:15ff., 4:19), and here he received his call (Exod. 3:1ff.). The elders of Midian were associated with Balak in the appeal to Balaam (Num. 22:4, 7), and Midian was attacked by the Israelites (Num. 25:16ff., 31:2ff.; Jos. 13:21). Midian established some control in central **Palestine** until ejected by Gideon (Jg. 6ff.), whose victory was long remembered (Ps. 83:9; Isa. 9:4, 10:26).

MIGDAL-EL (*'tower of El'*); An unidentified place in **Naphtali** (Jos. 19:38).

MIGDAL-GAD (*'tower of Gad'*): A place in the lowland of **Judah** (Jos. 15:37); perhaps mod. *Khirbet el-Mejdeleh*.

MIGDOL (*'tower'*): 1. A place on the border of **Egypt**, near which the Israelites crossed the sea (Exod. 14:2; Num. 33:7), probably a military post.

2. A place marking the N. limit of **Egypt**, contrasting with **Syene** in the S. (Ezek. 29:10, 30:6), probably not far from **Pelusium** (Ezek. 30:15); possibly mod. *Tell el-Hêr*.

3. A city in **Egypt** (Jer. 44:1, 46:14); perhaps the same as 2.

MIGRON: 1. A place near **Gibeah** (1) (1 Sam. 14:2); probably mod. *Tell Miryam*, S.W. of **Michmash**.

2. A place on the route of the expected Assyrian approach to Jerusalem (Isa. 10:28); possibly mod. *Makrûn*, NW. of **Michmash**.

MILETUS: A seaport of Asia Minor, S. of **Ephesus**, where Paul stayed on his return from his third missionary journey (Ac. 20:15).

He sent for the elders of the church at Ephesus to meet him here (Ac. 20:17). He probably made another visit to Miletus, when he left Trophimus ill there (2 Tim. 4:20).

MINNI: A country mentioned in Jer. 51:27, known from Assyrian inscriptions. It was S. of Lake *Urmia*.

MINNITH: A place E. of the **Jordan**, to which Jephthah pursued the Ammonites (Jg. 11:33). It is mentioned in MT of Ezek. 27:17 (so JB) for its wheat, but RSV eliminates it.

MISHAL: An unidentified place in **Asher** (1) (Jos. 19:26), which became a Levitical city (Jos. 21:30); called **Mashal** in 1 Chr. 6:74.

MISREPHOTH-MAIM: A place to which Joshua pursued his foes (Jos. 11:8), but which was occupied by him (Jos. 13:6). It lay within the territory of **Sidon**, and is probably mod. *Khirbet el-Musheirefeh*.

MITHKAH: An unidentified stopping-place in the Wilderness wanderings (Num. 33:23f.).

MITYLENE: The chief city of the island of *Lesbos*. Paul put in here on his journey to **Jerusalem** after his third missionary journey (Ac. 20:14).

MIZAR: An unknown hill, possibly a peak of Mount **Hermon** (Ps. 42:6).

MIZPAH ('*watch-tower*'): 1. A place E. of the **Jordan**, where Laban overtook Jacob (Gen. 31:49). It must have been N. of the **Jabbok**, but its site is unknown.

2. A city in **Gilead** (1), where the Israelites encamped against the Ammonites (Jg. 10:17), and where there was a shrine at which Jephthah was made leader (Jg. 11:11). Here was the home of Jephthah (Jg. 11:34). This was most probably S. of the **Jabbok** and not far from **Aroer** (2) (Jg. 11:33), and is perhaps mod. *Khirbet Jel'ad*. This Mizpah is perhaps the one referred to in Hos. 5:1 and may be the same as **Ramath-mizpeh** (Jos. 13:26).

3. A city W. of the **Jordan**, where there was an important sanctuary. It was apparently in **Benjamin** (Jos. 18:26, here called

Mizpeh, 1), but it was the meeting place of the tribes assembled against Benjamin (Jg. 20:1ff., 21:1, 5, 8), and here Samuel assembled the people when the Philistines were thrown into confusion (1 Sam. 7:5ff.), and here he erected the stone **Ebenezer** (2) (1 Sam. 7:12). Samuel regularly judged at Mizpah (1 Sam. 7:16), and Saul was made king here (1 Sam. 10:17ff.). It was fortified by Asa (1 Kg. 15:22; 2 Chr. 16:6, and after the fall of **Jerusalem** Gedaliah's residence was here (2 Kg. 25:23ff.; Jer. 40:6ff., 41:1ff.). In post-exilic times it was an administrative centre (Neh. 3:15, 19) and its people helped in rebuilding the walls of Jerusalem (Neh. 3:7). After the desecration of the Temple by Antiochus Epiphanes, the people went to Mizpah to pray (1 Mac. 3:46ff.). It is probably mod. *Tell en-Naṣbeh*, though some scholars favour mod. *Nebi Samwil*.

MIZPAH, LAND OF: A district near Mount **Hermon** to which Jabin appealed for help (Jos. 11:3). Its location is uncertain.

MIZPEH (*'watch-tower'*): 1. A place in **Benjamin** (Jos. 18:26); probably the same as **Mizpah** (3).

2. A place in the lowland of **Judah** (Jow. 15:38); possibly mod. *Tell eṣ-Ṣāfiyeh*.

3. A place in **Moab**, to which David took his parents for safety (1 Sam. 22:3); its site is unknown.

MIZPEH, VALLEY OF: A valley in the **land of Mizpah**, near Mount **Hermon**, to which Joshua pursued his foes (Jos. 11:8). Its location is uncertain.

MOAB: The territory E. of the **Dead Sea**, with fluctuating boundaries, occupied by the Moabites and formerly by the Emim (Dt. 2:10f.). It was at one time invaded by the Midianites, who were defeated by **Edom** (Gen. 36:35). The Israelites avoided any interference with Moab during the Wilderness wandering (Dt. 2:8ff.; Jg. 11:15; 2 Chr. 20:10), but Moab was afraid of the Israelites (Exod. 15:15; Num. 23:3) and Balak, the king of Moab, hired Balaam to curse them (Num. 22ff.; Dt. 23:4). Jos. 24:9 says Balak fought against the Israelites, but Jg. 11:25 says he did not. Moabite cities N. of the **Arnon** (cf. Num. 21:13; Jg. 11.18) were allotted to Reuben (Jos. 13:15ff., **Aroer**, 1, **Medeba, Dibon**) or to Gad (Num. 32:34, Dibon, **Ataroth**, 1), but Moab later recovered them. Eglon, king of Moab, established some control W. of the **Jordan**, until he was assassinated by Ehud (Jg. 2:12ff.). Ruth, the great-grandmother of David, was a Moabitess (Ru. 4:17, 21f.), and David took his parents to Moab for safety (1 Sam. 22:3f.). Saul fought Moab (1 Sam. 14:47), and David conquered it (2 Sam. 8:2, 12). Solomon married Moabite wives (1 Kg. 11:1). Moab later recovered independence and lost it again, and served N. Israel for forty years (so the Moabite Stone), and then recovered independence once again. Israel and Judah tried to reconquer it, but failed (2 Kg. 3:4ff.). Later, marauding bands of Moabites invaded Israel (2 Kg. 13:20f.). Prophecies against Moab stand in Isa. 15f., 25:10ff.; Jer. 48; Ezek. 25:8ff.; Am. 2:1ff.; Zeph. 2:8ff. Moab harassed Judah when Jehoiakim rebelled against Babylon (2 Kg. 24:2).

MOAB, CITY OF: *See* Ar.

MOAB, PLAINS OF: A region frequently referred to (Num. 22:1, 33:49f., 35:1, 13; Dt. 34:1, 8; Jos. 13:22). It was the SE. part of the Jordan valley.

MOAB, WILDERNESS OF: The uncultivated pasture land to the E. of Moab, through which the Israelites passed to avoid conflict with the Moabites (Dt. 2:8).

MOCHMUR, BROOK: A torrent bed SE. of Dothan (Jdt. 7:18); possibly mod. *Wâdī el-Aḥmar*.

MODEIN: The home of Mattathias (1 Mac. 2:1), where the revolt against Antiochus Epiphanes began (1 Mac. 2:15ff.). Mattathias was buried here (1 Mac. 2:70) and so also Judas (1 Mac. 9:19) and Jonathan (1 Mac. 13:25). It is mod. *el-Midyeh*.

MOLADAH: A place in Simeon (Jos. 19:2; 1 Chr. 4:28) or in S. Judah (Jos. 15:26), which early absorbed Simeon. It was resettled after the exile (Neh. 11:26). It may be mod. *Tell el-Milḥ*.

MOREH: The location of an oak, near Shechem, where Abraham experienced a theophany (Gen. 12:6ff.). If the same place is referred to in Dt. 11:30, it was near Mounts Ebal and Gerizim. The oak is probably the one mentioned in Gen. 35:4; Jos. 24:26; Jg. 9:6.

MOREH, HILL OF: The place where the Midianites encamped against Gideon (Jg. 7:1); perhaps mod. *Jebel ed-Daḥī*.

MORESHETH: The home of Micah the prophet (Mic. 1:1; Jer. 26:18); called **Moresheth-gath** in Mic. 1:14. It is possibly mod. *Tell el-Judeideh.*

MORESHETH-GATH: *See* **Moresheth.**

MORIAH: Abraham went to the land of Moriah, and nearly sacrificed Isaac on one of the mountains there (Gen. 22:2). The Chronicler calls it Mount Moriah ,and identifies it with the site of the Temple (2 Chr. 3:1), this is followed by Jewish tradition. It is curious that there is no reference to this in the earlier record of Kings, or in any other early source. Some have connected the name with **Moreh**, near **Shechem**, and so with the Samaritan claim that **Gerizim** is the sacred mountain. But this is improbable, as Moreh is the location of a tree, certainly not on Gerizim, and the expression 'land of Moriah' is odd for the locality of a tree. The site of Moriah cannot be certainly identified.

MORTAR, THE: A commercial quarter of **Jerusalem**, near the **Second Quarter** and the **Fish Gate** (Zeph. 1:11); its exact location is unknown.

MOSERAH: An unlocated stopping-place in the Wilderness wanderings (Dt. 10:6). Here Aaron died and was buried. Elsewhere the death of Aaron is located on **Mount Hor** (1). It is probably the same as **Moserah.**

MOSEROTH: An unlocated stopping-place in the Wilderness wanderings (Num. 33:30f.). It is probably the same as **Moserah.**

MOSHECH: *See* **Meshech** (1).

MOZAH: A place in **Benjamin** (Jos. 18:26); perhaps mod. *Khirbet Beit Mizzeh*, W. of **Jerusalem.**

MUSTER GATE: A gate of **Jerusalem** on the E. side, restored in Nehemiah's time (Neh. 3:31). It is possibly the same as the **Benjamin Gate.**

MYNDOS: A city in **Caria** in Asia Minor, to which the Roman consul wrote announcing the Roman friendship for the Jews (1 Mac. 15:23).

MYRA: A city in **Lycia** in Asia Minor, where Paul transhipped on his journey to **Rome** as a prisoner (Ac. 27:5). It is mod. *Dembre*.

MYSIA: A region in NW. Asia Minor, through which Paul passed on his way to **Troas** on his second missionary journey (Ac. 16:7f.).

N

NAAMAH (*'pleasant'*): 1. A place in the lowland of **Judah** (Jos. 15:41); perhaps mod. *Khirbet Fered*.
2. The house of Zophar, the Naamathite (Job. 2:11 11:1, 20:1, 42:9). This is probably E. of **Palestine**, in **Arabia**.

NAARAH (*'girl'*): A place in **Ephraim** (1) (Jos. 16:7); called **Naaran** in 1 Chr. 7:28. It is possibly mod. *Tell el-Jiser*, near *'Ain Dûq*.

NAARAN: *See* Naarah.

NABATEA: The territory occupied by the Nabateans (1 Mac. 5:25, 9:35), who were an Arab people (cf. 2 Mac. 5:8, where Aretas, the king of the Nabateans, is called the ruler of the Arabs), who in the Persian and Hellenistic periods pressed from **Arabia** into **Edom**, and later controlled an area running E. of the **Jordan** up to and including **Damascus** (2 Cor. 11:32).

NACON: The name of the threshing floor where Uzzah died, or of its owner (2 Sam. 6:6); called **Chidon** in 1 Chr. 19:9.

NADABATH: A place E. of the **Jordan** where Jonathan and Simon avenged the murder of their brother John (1 Mac. 9:37). It is possibly mod. *Khirbet et-Teim*.

NAHALAL: A place in **Zebulun** (Jos. 19:15), which successfully resisted the Israelites (Jg. 1:30, here called **Nahalol**), but which later became a Levitical city (Jos. 21:35). It is perhaps mod. *Tell en-Nahl*.

NAHALIEL: A stopping-place in the Wilderness wanderings (Num. 21:19); possibly *Wâdî Zerqā Ma'în*.

NAHALOL: A Canaanite city whose inhabitants could not be dispossessed (Jg. 1:30); called **Nahalal** in Jos. 19:15, 21:35. It is perhaps mod. *Tell en Naḥl*.

NAIN: A city where Jesus raised a widow's son (Lk. 7:11ff.); mod. *Nein*, S.E. of Nazareth.

NAIOTH: A dwelling place of prophets in **Ramah** (4), where David fled to Samuel (1 Sam. 19:18ff.), and where Saul was seized with prophetic frenzy (1 Sam. 19:22ff.).

NAPHATH: This apparently stands for **Naphath-dor** in Jos. 17:11, where 'the third is Naphath' seems to mean the third city mentioned in the verse (Dor) is Naphath-dor, and so distinguished from **En-dor**, which is the fourth.

NAPHATH-DOR (*'height of Dor'*): Either an alternative name for **Dor** or for a part of Dor (Jos. 12:23). It was in Solomon's fourth district (1 Kg. 4:11). *See* **Naphath**.

NAPHOTH-DOR (*'heights of Dor'*): An alternative name for **Dor** (Jos. 11:2).

NAPHTALI: The territory occupied by the tribe of Naphtali. Its ideal limits are stated in Jos. 19:32ff. It was conquered by Benhadad (1 Kg. 15:20) and by Tiglath-pileser (2 Kg. 20:29).

NAZARETH: The village in which the angel visited Mary (Lk. 1:28) and where Jesus was brought up (Mt. 2:23; Lk. 2:39, 51, 4:16). from which He came to be baptized (Mk 1:9), and from which He moved to **Capernaum** when He began His ministry (Mt. 4:13). He spoke in the synagogue here (Lk. 4:16ff.), and so angered the people that they sought to kill Him (Lk. 4:28ff.). He is frequently called Jesus of Nazareth (Mk 1:24, 10:47, 16:6; Jn 1:45, 18:5; Ac. 2:22, 3:6, 4:10, 10:38, 22:8). It was an unimportant village (Jn 1:45f.), and is mod. *en-Nâṣirah*.

NEAH: A place in **Zebulun** (Jos. 19:13); its location is unknown.

NEAPOLIS: The port of **Philippi** (Ac. 16:11); mod. *Kavalla*.

NEBAIOTH: An Arab tribe (Gen. 25:13; 1 Chr. 1:29) affiliated to the Edomites (Gen. 28:8, 36:3) and perhaps the territory it occupied (Isa. 60:7). This tribe is frequently incorrectly identified with the Nabateans. *See* **Nabatea.**

NEBO: 1. A town in **Moab**, before which the Israelites encamped (Num. 33:47). It was assigned to **Reuben** (Num. 32:3; 1 Chr. 5:8), and rebuilt by the Reubenites (Num. 32:38). On the Moabite Stone, Mesha says he took it from the Israelites, and it is clearly Moabite in Isa. 15:2; Jer. 1:22. It is probably mod. *Khirbet el-Mekhayeṭ*.

2. A place in **Judah**, from which some who returned from exile traced their descent (Ezr. 2:29; Neh. 7:33). Some from here married foreign wives (Ezr. 10:43; 1 Esd. 9:35). It is possibly mod. *Beit Nûbā*, N.W. of **Jerusalem.**

NEBO, MOUNT: A mountain in **Moab** (Dt. 32:48), from which Moses viewed the Promised Land (Dt. 34:1ff.) and where he died (Dt. 32:50, 34:5). It is mod. *Jebel en-Nebā*.

NEGEB ('*dry land*'): An arid area (cf. Jos. 15:19; Jg. 1:15; Ps. 126:4) of **Palestine** (Dt. 1:7, 34:3; Jos. 10:40, 11:16, 12:8), in which the patriarchs moved (Gen. 20:1, 24:62). That it was in the S. is clear from Gen. 12:9, 13:1, 3. Here the Amalekites lived (Num. 13:29), and **Arad** was situated in this region (Num. 21:1, 33:40; Jg. 1:16). The spies went through the Negeb (Num. 13:17, 22). When it was conquered, it was allotted to **Simeon** or Judah (which early absorbed Simeon), but areas of it were distinguished as belonging to Judah, or the Jerahmeelites, or the Kenites (1 Sam. 27:10), or the Cherethites, or the Calebites (1 Sam. 30:14). Its dry winds were dreaded (Isa. 21:1), and it was infested with wild beasts (Isa. 30:6). Prophecies of trouble for this region are in Jer. 13:19; Ezek. 20:46f.; but more comforting words are in Jer. 17:26, 32:44, 33:13; Ob. 19f.

NEHELAM: Apparently a place name in Jer. 29:24, 31f., but this is doubtful. For 'of Nehelam' MT has the 'Nehelamite', which could be a patronymic. If Nehelam is a place, its location is unknown.

NEIEL: A place in **Asher** (1) (Jos. 19:27); perhaps mod. *Khirbet Ya'nûn*.

NEPHTOAH, WATERS OF: A spring on the border of **Judah** (Jos. 15:9) and **Benjamin** (Jos. 18:15); probably mod. *'Ain Liftā.*

NETAIM: An unidentified site in **Judah** (1 Chr. 4:23), apparently near **Gederah** (1).

NETOPHAH: A place from which two of David's heroes (2 Sam. 23:28f.; 1 Chr. 11:30, 27:13) and some other named persons (2 Kg. 25:43; Jer. 40:8; 1 Chr. 27:15) came. Some returning exiles traced their descent from here (Ezr. 2:22; Neh. 7:26; 1 Esd. 5:18). It is probably mod. *Khirbet Bedd Fālūḥ.*

NEW GATE: A gate of the Temple mentioned only in Jer. 36:10. Its situation is unknown.

NEZIB: A place in the lowland of **Judah** (Jos. 15:43); probably mod. *Khirbet Beit Naṣîb.*

NIBSHAN: A place in **Judah** in the wilderness (Jos. 15:62); possibly mod. *Khirbet el-Maqârī.*

NICOPOLIS: A city in *Epirus,* where Paul proposed to spend the winter and where he invited Titus to join him (Tit. 3:12). Whether Paul actually went there we do not know. It is mod. *Paleoprevaza.*

NILE, RIVER: The great river which flows through Egypt, on which its existence depends. It figured in Pharaoh's dreams (Gen. 41:1ff.), and the Hebrew male babies were to be cast into its waters (Exod. 1:22). Moses was saved by being put into a basket (Exod. 2:3ff.) It figures in the story of the plagues (Exod. 4:9, 7:17ff., 8:1ff.). The prophets frequently refer to it (Isa. 18:2, 19:5ff., 23:3, 10; Jer. 46:7f.; Ezek. 29:2, 9, 30:12; Am. 8:8, 9:5; Nah. 3:8; Zech. 10:11), and Jeremiah speaks of **Judah's** reliance on Egypt as drinking the waters of the Nile (Jer. 2:18).

NIMRAH: A place in **Gad** (Num. 32:3); called **Beth-nimrah** in Num. 32:36; Jos. 13:27. It is mod. *Tell el-Beleibil,* near *Tell Nimrîn.*

NIMRIM, WATERS OF: Waters in **Moab** mentioned in Isa. 15:6; Jer. 48:34; probably *Wâdī Numeirah.*

NINEVEH: A city of **Assyria,** said to have been founded by Nimrod (Gen. 10:11f.). It was made the capital of Assyria by Sennacherib, and is first mentioned in OT history in connection with him (2 Kg. 19:36; Isa. 37:37). When Assyria fell, it was taken by the Medes and the Babylonians, and its fall was fiercely hailed by Nahum (Nah. 1:1ff., 2:8, 3:7; cf. Zeph. 2:13). The book of Jonah relates the story of Jonah's mission to the city and its conversion, and this is referred to in Mt. 12:41; Lk. 11:30, 32. It figures in the stories of Tobit (Tob. 1:3, 10, 17, 19, 22, 11:1, 16f., 14:4, 8, 10, 15) and Judith, where Nebuchadnezzar is unhistorically said to have ruled in Nineveh (Jdt. 1:1, 2:21). It is mod. *Tell Quyunjiq* and *Tell Nebi Yûnus*.

NOB: The place where David came to Ahimelech and from which he took the sword of Goliath (1 Sam. 21:1ff.). Its priests were all afterwards slain by Doeg (1 Sam. 22:18ff.), with the exception of Abiathar (1 Sam. 22:20). It lay on the expected route of the Assyrian advance on **Jerusalem** (Isa. 10:32). It was repeopled after the exile (Neh. 11:32, where it is apparently near **Anathoth**). It is probably mod. *Râs Umm et-Ṭala'*.

NOBAH: 1. The name given to **Kenath** by its conqueror, Nobah (Num. 32:42); mod. *Qanawât*.
  2. A place mentioned with **Jogbehah** in **Gad** in the account of Gideon's pursuit of his enemies (Jg. 8:11). Its location is unknown.

NOD ('*wandering*'): The region to which Cain went (Gen. 4:16). Its location is unknown.

NOHAH: An unknown place in **Benjamin** mentioned in Jg. 20:43.

NOPHAH: An unidentified place mentioned in RSVm and JB in Num. 21:30, where RSV has 'until fire spreads' (*nuppaḥ 'esh*) for MT 'to Nophah which' (*nōphaḥ 'asher*).

O

OAK OF THE PILLAR: *See* **Pillar, Oak of the.**

OBOTH: A stopping-place in the Wilderness wanderings (Num. 21:10f., 33:43f.); perhaps mod. *'Ain el Weiba*.

OCINA: A town on the sea-coast of **Palestine**, mentioned in Jdt. 2:28. It cannot be certainly identified, but is possibly *Acco*.

OLD GATE: A gate in **Jerusalem**, repaired in Nehemiah's time (Neh. 3:6), and mentioned in the account of the procession (Neh. 12:39). This is thought by some to be the same as the **Ephraim Gate**.

OLIVES, MOUNT OF: A height E. of **Jerusalem**, beyond the **Kidron** valley. David passed over it when fleeing from Absalom (2 Sam. 15:30). Ezekiel saw the glory of the Lord go from Jerusalem to this mountain (Ezek. 11:23), and the eschatological battle was expected to start from here and the mountain itself to be split (Zech. 14:4). Jesus approached Jerusalem from this mountain, and sent disciples from here for the ass on which He entered the city (Mt. 21:1ff.; Mk 11:1ff.; Lk. 19:28ff.). Here He was hailed by the people (Lk. 19:37), and here He wept over the city (Lk. 19:41ff.). It was on the Mount that He spoke of the end of the age (Mt. 24:3ff.; Mk 13:1ff.), and here He lodged at nights during His visit to Jerusalem (Lk. 21:37.). Here He suffered his agony (Mt. 26:30ff.; Mk 14:26ff.; Lk. 22:39) in the Garden of **Gethsemane**. A night on this mountain during an earlier visit to Jerusalem is recorded in Jn 8:1. From this mountain the Ascension took place (Ac. 1:12). It is called **Olivet** in Lk. 19:19, 21:37; Ac. 1:12. It is mod. *Jebel eṭ-Ṭûr*.

OLIVET: *See* Olives, Mount of.

ON: The city in Egypt, the daughter of whose priest Joseph married (Gen. 41:45, 50, 46:20). It is mentioned in Ezek. 30:17, and is called **Heliopolis** in Jer. 52:13. It maybe referred to as the 'City of the Sun' in Isa 19:18. It is mod. *Tell Ḥuṣn*.

ONO: A place in **Benjamin** (1 Chr. 8:12), from which some returning exiles traced their descent (Ezr. 2:33; Neh. 7:37; 1 Esd. 5:22) and resettled when they returned (Neh. 11:35). Nehemiah's enemies invited him to meet them in one of the villages near here (Neh. 6:2). It is probably mod. *Kefr 'Anâ*.

OPHEL (*'swelling'*): The name of a hill in **Jerusalem**, where Jotham repaired the wall of the city (2 Chr. 27:3). Later Manasseh enclosed this hill in a very high wall (2 Chr. 33:14). On this hill the

Temple servants lived in the time of Nehemiah (Neh. 3:26, 11:21), and the wall of the city was repaired here (Neh. 3:27). Ophel corresponds to the city of Jerusalem that was captured by David, and is at the SE. end of the enlarged city that Jerusalem became. It had the valley of the Kidron on the E. side and the *Tyropoeon* valley on the W.

OPHIR: A country famous for the quality of its gold (1 Chr. 29:4; Job. 22:4, 28:16; Ps. 45:9; Isa. 13:12; Sir. 7:18). Solomon's ships sailed from Ezion-geber and brought back gold from there (1 Kg. 9:28, 10:11; 2 Chr. 8:18, 9:10), Jehoshaphat planned to do the same, but his plans ended in disaster (1 Kg. 22:48). Gen. 10:29, and 1 Chr. 1:23 would seem to locate Ophir in S. Arabia, but some think it was more probably in India or in E. Africa.

OPHNI: A place in Benjamin (Jos. 18:34); perhaps mod. *Jifnā*.

OPHRAH: 1. A town in Benjamin (Jos. 18:23). Philistine raiders from Michmash went in its direction (1 Sam. 13:17). It is perhaps the same as Ephraim (2) (2 Sam. 13:23) and Ephron (1) (2 Chr. 13:19), and is possibly mod. *eṭ-Ṭaiyibeh*.

2. The place where the angel met Gideon (Jg. 6:11), and where Gideon built an altar (Jg. 6:24) and placed his ephod (Jg. 8:27). Here Gideon was buried (Jg. 8:32), and here Abimelech slew all his brothers except Jotham (Jg. 9:5). Its location is unknown.

OREB, ROCK: The place where the Midianite prince Oreb was killed (Jg. 7:25), an incident referred to in Isa. 10:26. Its location is unknown.

ORTHOSIA: An unidentified place to which Trypho escaped (1 Mac. 15:37).

OVENS, TOWER OF THE: A tower in Jerusalem on the NW. side (Neh. 12:38), repaired by Malchijah and Hasshub (Neh. 3:11), and mentioned in the account of the procession (Neh. 12:38).

P

PADDEN: A shortened form of **Paddan-aram** (Gen. 48:7).

PADDAN-ARAM: A region of N. **Mesopotamia** in which Laban lived (Gen. 28:2, 5, 7, 31:18, 35:9, 26, 46:15).

PAI: The capital of Hadad in **Edom** (1 Chr. 1:50); called **Pau** in Gen. 36:39. Its site is unknown.

PALESTINA: *See* **Palestine**.

PALESTINE: A name for the Holy Land nowhere found in RSV. It is found in AV in Jl 3:4, and **Palestina** is in AV in Exod. 15:14; Isa. 14:29, 31. In all of these passages RSV has Philistia. The name of Palestine is derived from that of the Philistines. The common designation of the land in the Bible is **Canaan**.

PALMS, CITY OF: *See* **Jericho**.

PALON: An unknown place from which the gentilic **Pelonite** may have been formed. But this is doubtful. It is applied to Helez (1 Chr. 11:27), where the parallel 2 Sam. 23:26 has **Paltite**, and to Ahijah (1 Chr. 11:36), where the parallel 2 Sam. 23:24 has Eliam of **Gilo**.

PALTITE: A native of **Beth-pelet**.

PAMPHYLIA: A region in the S. of Asia Minor between **Lycia** and **Cilicia**. The Roman consul wrote here to declare the Roman friendship for the Jews (1 Mac. 15:23), and some Jews from here were in **Jerusalem** at Pentecost (Ac. 2:10). On his first missionary journey Paul came to **Perga** in Pamphylia (Ac. 13:13), and to it he returned (Ac. 14:24f.). On his voyage to **Rome** he sailed past its coast (Ac. 27:5).

PAPHOS: A city in the SW. of **Cyprus**, visited by Paul on his first missionary journey (Ac. 13:6). Here Paul encountered Bar-

Jesus, or Elymas (Ac. 13:6ff.) and converted Sergius Paulus, the proconsul (Ac. 13:12). It is mod. *Baffo*.

PARADISE: A Persian word, meaning '*park*', which is used in later Jewish thought for the abode of the righteous after death (Lk. 23:43; Rev. 2:7; 2 Esd. 8:52). Paul locates it in the third heaven (2 C. 12:4).

PARAN: A wilderness region inhabited by the descendants of Ishmael (Gen. 21:21), through which the Israelites passed after the Exodus (Num. 10:12, 12:16, 13:3; Dt. 1:1). From here the spies were sent into Canaan (Num. 13:3, 26). It is apparently connected with the **Wilderness of Zin** (Num. 13:21), in which **Kadesh** (1) was located (Num. 33:36), and is also associated with Mount **Seir** (Dt. 33:2; cf. Gen. 14:6), **El-paran** and **Teman** (Hab. 3:3). In this region Nabal lived (1 Sam. 25:1f.), and through it Hadad was taken on his escape to **Egypt** (1 Kg. 11:18).

PARBAR: A room or forecourt of the Temple (1 Chr. 26:18).

PARTHIA: A region which gained independence from the Seleucids in the third century B.C., and later gave much trouble to the Romans. Some Jews from here were present in **Jerusalem** at Pentecost (Ac. 2:9).

PARVAIM: A region from which gold used for Solomon's Temple came (2 Chr. 3:6).

PAS-DAMMIM: The scene of a battle between the Israelites and the Philistines (1 Chr. 11:13); called **Ephes-dammim** in 1 Sam. 17:1. Its site is unknown.

PATARA: A seaport of **Lycia**, from which Paul embarked for Tyre on his last journey to **Jerusalem** (Ac. 21:1f.); mod. *Gelemish*.

PATHROS: The name of Upper Egypt (Isa. 11:11; Jer. 44:1, 15; Ezek. 29:14, 30:14). The gentilic **Pathrusim** stands in Gen. 10:14; 1 Chr. 1:12.

PATHRUSIM: *See* **Pathros**.

PATMOS: An island off the coast of Asia Minor to which John was, according to tradition, banished by Domitian, and where he wrote Revelation (Rev. 1:9).

PAU: A city of **Edom**, the capital of Hadar (Gen. 36:39); called **Pai** in 1 Chr. 1:50. The site is unknown.

PAVEMENT, THE: The translation of the Greek name, *lithostrōton*, for the Aramaic **Gabbatha** (Jn 19:13).

PEKOD: A region of **Babylonia** inhabited by an Aramaean tribe, against which prophecies were uttered (Jer. 50:21; Ezek. 23:23).

PELONITE: *See* **Palon**.

PELUSIUM: A fortress on the frontier of **Egypt** (Ezek. 30:15f.); mod. *Tell Faramâ*.

PENIEL: The name given by Jacob to the place where he wrestled with the angel (Gen. 32:30); called **Penuel** in Gen. 32:31.

PENUEL: The place near the **Jabbok** where Jacob wrestled with the angel (Gen. 32:31); called **Peniel** in Gen. 32:30. It was destroyed by Gideon because its people withheld their aid against the Midianites (Jg. 8:8, 9, 17). It was fortified by Jeroboam I (1 Kg. 12:25). It is probably mod. *Tulûl edh-Dhahab*.

PEOR: 1. A mountain to which Balak took Balaam to curse Israel (Num. 23:28). Its location is unknown.

2. Used for **Beth-peor** in Jos. 22:17.

3. *See* **Baal-peor**.

4. A place in **Judah** (Jos. 15:59, in an addition in LXX and JB, not in MT and RSV). It is mod. *Khirbet Faghûr*.

PERAZIM, MOUNT: A mountain mentioned in Isa. 28:21; probably close to **Baal-perazim**.

PEREZ-UZZA: *See* **Perez-Uzzah**.

PEREZ-UZZAH (*'breach of Uzzah'*): The place where Uzzah died (2 Sam. 6:8); called **Perez-uzza** in 1 Chr. 13:11.

PERGA: A city in **Pamphylia**, visited by Paul on his first missionary journey (Ac. 13:13f.), and again on his return (Ac. 14:25); mod. *Murtana*.

PERGAMUM: A city of Mysia, where was one of the seven churches to which John wrote (Rev. 1:11, 2:12ff).. The city gave its name to parchment.

PERSEPOLIS: The chief capital of the Persian empire, mentioned in the Bible only in 2 Mac. 9:2, which tells how Antiochus Epiphanes attempted to rob its temples. It is mod. *Takht-i-Jamshíd.*

PERSIA: A country which, under the leadership of Cyrus, gained control of Media, and then conquered **Lydia** and **Babylonia**, and subsequently **Egypt**. This Persian empire continued until its conquest by Alexander the Great. Persia is mentioned in Ezek. 27:10, 38:5; Jdt. 1:7, and frequently together with Media (Est. 1:3, 14, 18, 10:2; Dan. 8:20 cf. 5:28, 6:8, 12, 15; 1 Esd. 3:1, 14). Of Persian kings the following are mentioned in the OT: Cyrus (2 Chr. 36:22f.; Ezr. 1:1, 2, 8, 3:7, 4:5, 6:3, 14; Isa. 44:23, 45:1; Dan. 1:21, 10:1); Darius I (Ezr. 4:5, 24, 5:5ff., 6:1ff.; Neh. 12:22; Hag. 1:1, 2:1, 10; Zech. 1:1, 7, 7:1); Artaxerxes I (Ezr. 4:7ff., 6:14; Neh. 2:1, 5:14, 13:6); possibly Artaxerxes II (Ezr. 7:1ff., 8:1); probably Darius III (Neh. 12:22; also 1 Mac. 1:1). The Ahasuerus of the book of Esther is usually identified with Xerxes I. In the Hellenistic period Persia was claimed by the Seleucids as part of their kingdom, but control was far from secure (1 Mac. 3:31, 6:1ff., 14:2ff.; 2 Mac. 1:12ff., 9:1ff.). Persia is unmentioned in the NT.

PETHOR: A place in N. **Mesopotamia** from which Balaam came (Num. 22:5; Dt. 23:4). Its location is unknown.

PHARATHON: A place named in 1 Mac. 9:50; possibly the same as OT **Pirathon**, mod. *Far'átá.*

PHARPAR: A river of **Damascus** (2 Kg. 5:12); possibly mod. *Nahr el-A'waj.*

PHASELIS: A city in **Lycia**, on the coast of Asia Minor, to which the Roman consul wrote declaring the Roman friendship for the Jews (1 Mac. 15:23); mod. *Tekirova.*

PHILADELPHIA: 1. A city of **Lydia**, in Asia Minor, where was one of the seven churches to which John wrote (Rev. 1:11, 3:7ff.); mod. *Alashehir.*

2. The Hellenistic name of **Rabbah** (1), a city in the **Decapolis**.

PHILIPPI: A Roman colony on the Via Egnatia in **Macedonia**, visited by Paul on his second missionary journey, and the first place in Europe where he established a church (Ac. 16:12). Here he converted Lydia (Ac. 16:14), and here Paul was illegally beaten and imprisoned without trial after performing a deed of mercy (Ac. 16:16ff.), and converted his jailor (Ac. 16:27ff.). A later visit to Philippi is mentioned in Ac. 20:6. One of Paul's letters was sent to the church here (Phil. 1:1), which generously ministered to his need (Phil. 4:10ff.). He refers to his shameful treatment in Philippi in 1 Th. 2:2.

PHILISTIA: The coastal region of **Palestine** occupied by the Philistines, who gave their name ultimately to the whole land. They are said to have come from **Caphtor** (Am. 9:7; Jer. 47:4), but they were not of Cretan origin. They were a non-Semitic people, and are frequently called uncircumcised because they did not practise circumcision. They settled on the coast of Palestine in the early twelfth century B.C., although there are anachronistic references to them in Genesis long before this (Gen. 21:32, 34, 26:1, 8, 14f., 18). They formed a confederacy of five cities. **Gaza, Ashkelon, Ashdod, Ekron,** and **Gath,** under 'lords' who bear a non-Semitic title. They figure in the stories of Samson (Jg. 13ff.), and it was doubtless indirectly due to the pressure of their expansion that the tribe of Dan was forced to migrate (Jg. 1:34, 18:1). In the time of Eli they defeated the Israelites and captured the Ark (1 Sam. 4), which they sent in turn to some of their cities (1 Sam. 5), until plague compelled them to return it (1 Sam. 6). Before the rise of the monarchy, they established their control in the heart of Israelite territory and kept the working of iron in their own hands (1 Sam. 13:19ff.). Saul achieved independence from them (1 Sam. 14) until the fatal field of **Gilboa** (1 Sam. 31). David reduced them to dependence (2 Sam. 5:17ff., 8:1), but after the disruption they became independent, and were more than once at war with Israel (1 Kg. 15:27, 16:15ff.). Sargon marched against Philistia and captured Ashdod (Isa. 20:1), and later Hezekiah smote the Philistines (2 Kg. 18:8). This was doubtless to compel them to join his rising against **Assyria**, and we learn from Sennacherib's inscription that Padi, the king of Ekron, was imprisoned in **Jerusalem** until Hezekiah was compelled to release him. Prophecies against Philistia are in Isa. 11:14, 14:29ff.; Jer. 25:20, 47:1ff.; Ezek. 25:15ff.; Jl 3:4ff.; Am. 1:6ff.; Zeph. 2:4ff.; Zech. 9:5ff.

PHILISTINES, SEA OF THE: The name for the Mediterranean Sea in Exod. 23:31.

PHOENICIA: The Greek name for a country on the coast of Syria, N. of Palestine. Its name is derived from the purple dye which was made here (cf. Canaan). Its principal towns were Tyre and Sidon, which are frequently referred to in the OT, but the name Phoenicia is found only in Ob. 20. It occurs many times in 1 Esdras (1 Esd. 2:17, 24f., 27, 4:48, 6:3, 7, 27, 29, 7:1, 8:19, 23, 67) and in 2 Maccabees (2 Mac. 3:5, 8, 4:4, 22, 8:8, 10:11). In the NT we read that Jesus healed the daughter of a Syrophoenician woman (Mk 7:24ff.), and after the marytrdom of Stephen some Christians went thither (Ac. 11:19). Paul and Barnabas passed through here on their way to Jerusalem (Ac. 15:3), and on Paul's final journey to Jerusalem he disembarked here (Ac. 21:2).

PHOENIX: A harbour on the S. coast of Crete, which the captain of the ship in which Paul was sailing to Rome tried in vain to reach to winter in (Ac. 27:12). It is mod. *Loutro*.

PHRYGIA: A region of Asia Minor from which some Jews were present at Pentecost (Ac. 2:10). Antioch of Pisidia and Iconium, visited by Paul on his first missionary journey (Ac. 13:14ff., 51) were ethnically in Phrygia, and on his second and third missionary journeys Paul is stated to have passed through Phrygia (Ac. 16:6, 18:23).

PI-BESETH: The Egyptian city of *Bubastis*, mentioned only in a prophecy against Egypt in Ezek. 30:17; mod. *Tell Baṣṭah*.

PI-HAHIROTH: A stopping-place in the Wilderness wanderings (Exod. 14:2, 9; Num. 33:7); called Hahiroth in Num. 33:8.

PILLAR, OAK OF THE: A sacred tree at Shechem beside which Abimelech was crowned (Jg. 9:6). The pillar was a sacred stone or *maṣṣēbhāh*, and is probably to be identified with that erected by Joshua (Jos. 24:26).

PIRATHON: A city in Ephraim (1), from which came Abdon (Jg. 12:13, 15) and one of David's heroes (2 Sam. 23:30; 1 Chr. 11:31, 27:14). It was later called Pharathon. It is probably mod. *Far'âtā*.

PISGAH: A mountain in **Moab,** commanding a view of the desert (Num. 21:30) and of the land W. of the **Jordan** (Dt. 3:27). Here Balak took Balaam and seven altars were built (Num. 23:14). Here also Moses viewed the Promised Land and died (Dt. 34:1ff.). It was assigned to **Reuben** (Dt. 3:17; Jos. 13:20). In Dt. 34:1 it is associated with **Mount Nebo** as a particular peak of the mountain, probably mod. *Râs es-Siâghah.*

PISHON: One of the four rivers of the **Garden of Eden** (Gen. 2:11). Neither it nor the land of **Havilah,** around which it flowed, can be identified.

PISIDIA: A mountainous region of Asia Minor through which Paul passed on his first missionary journey (Ac. 13:14, 14:24). **Antioch of Pisidia** was not strictly in, but near, Pisidia.

PITHOM: One of the two store cities which the Israelites built for Pharaoh (Exod. 1:11). It is probably mod. *Tell er-Reṭâbeh.*

PONTUS: The Black Sea, and also the country in Asia Minor bordering on it; or in particular the part of this region which formed the Roman province of Pontus. Jews from Pontus were in Jerusalem at Pentecost (Ac. 2:9), and Aquila was a native of Pontus (Ac. 18:2). 1 Peter was written to 'the exiles of the Dispersion' in Pontus and other regions (1 Pet. 1:1). It is probable that all these references are to the Roman province.

PORTICO OF SOLOMON: A colonnade on the E. side of the Temple (Jn 10:23; Ac. 3:11, 5:12). There was a similar colonnade of five porticoes at the pool of **Beth-zatha** (Jn 5:2).

POTSHERD GATE: A gate of **Jerusalem** leading to the **Valley of Hinnom** (Jer. 19:2).

POTTER'S FIELD: The field bought with Judas Iscariot's betrayal money (Mt. 27:7), and called **Akeldama.**

PRAETORIUM: The residence of the Roman *praetor* or governor (Mt. 27:27; Mk 15:16; Jn 18:28, 33, 19:9). In the Gospels it probably denotes Herod's palace, which the Roman governor occupied (cf. Ac. 23:35, where the meaning is probably the palace built by Herod in **Caesarea**). The term could also be used for the Praetorian guard, or the imperial bodyguard, and it is so translated in Phil. 1:13.

PTOLEMAIS: The Hellenistic name of **Acco**. Its people were hostile to the Maccabees (1 Mac. 5:15) and Simon pursued his foes to its gates (1 Mac. 5:22). It was occupied by Alexander Balas (1 Mac. 10:1), who promised it to the Jerusalem Temple (1 Mac. 10:39). Here Alexander met Ptolemy VI, and married Cleopatra (1 Mac. 10:57f.), and they were joined by Jonathan (1 Mac. 10:60). Subsequently Jonathan won the favour of Demetrius II here (1 Mac. 11:24), but later was treacherously seized here by Trypho (1 Mac. 12:45, 48), who made Ptolemais his base (1 Mac. 13:12). In the NT it is mentioned but once, to record a brief stay by Paul on his way to **Jerusalem** (Ac. 21:7).

PUNON: A stopping-place in the Wilderness wanderings (Num. 33:42f.); mod. *Feinân*.

PUT: An African country and its people, reckoned among the sons of Ham (Gen. 10:6; 1 Chr. 1:8), and mentioned by the prophets beside **Ethiopia** (Jer. 46:9), with **Persia** and **Lud** (2) (Ezek. 27:10), with Ethiopia, Lud (2), **Arabia**, and **Libya** (Ezek. 30:5), with Persia and **Cush** (Ezek. 38:5), and with Ethiopia, **Egypt**, and Libya (Nah. 3:9). The location of Put cannot be certainly made, but it is generally thought that it was some part of Libya, though its people may have been distinct from the Libyans.

PUTEOLI: A harbour of **Italy**, where Paul landed on the way to **Rome** (Ac. 28:13); mod. *Pozzuoli*.

Q

QUARTER, SECOND: A district of **Jerusalem**, on the N. side (Zeph. 1:10), where Huldah lived (2 Kg. 22:14; 2 Chr. 34:22). It led to the **Fish Gate**.

R

RABBAH: 1. The capital city of **Ammon**, and hence often called Rabbah of the Ammonites (Dt. 3:11; 2 Sam. 12:26, 17:27; Jer. 49:2; Ezek. 21:20). Og's bedstead was here (Dt. 3:11), and after the conquest Rabbah lay in the boundary of Gad (Jos. 13:25). It remained in Ammonite occupation, but was conquered by David (2 Sam. 11:1, 12:26ff.; 1 Chr. 20:1). When David fled before Absalom. Nahash sent him supplies by his own son (2 Sam. 17:27ff.). Prophecies against Rabbah stand in Jer. 49:2f.; Ezek. 21:20, 25:5; Am. 1:14. In the Hellenistic period it was called **Philadelphia** (2), and it became one of the cities of the **Decapolis**. It is mod. *'Ammân*.

2. A place in **Judah** (Jos. 15:60), near **Kiriath-jearim**; its exact site is unknown.

RABBITH: A town on the border of **Issachar** (Jos. 19:20). The name is possibly an error for **Daberath**.

RACAL: An unidentified place in **Judah** (1 Sam. 30:29). It is perhaps for **Carmel**, which LXX[B] reads.

RAGAE: *See* **Rages**.

RAGES: An important city in **Media** and the capital before **Ecbatana**. Tobit deposited money there (Tob. 1:14, 4:1, 20), which Tobias was sent to collect (Tob. 5:5), and which was in fact collected by the angel Raphael (Tob. 9:2ff.). It is mod. *Rai*. In Jdt. 1:5, 15 the district in which Rages lay is called **Ragae**, and here Nebuchadnezzar's battle with Arphaxad is located.

RAKKATH: A town of **Naphtali** (Jos. 19:35); perhaps mod. *Tell Eqlâfîyeh*.

RAKKON: A town of **Dan** (1) (Jos. 19:46); perhaps mod. *Tell er-Reqqeit*.

RAMAH ('*height*'): 1. A town in Asher (1) (Jos. 19:29); possibly mod. *Râmiah*.

2. A town in Naphtali (Jos. 19:36); possibly mod. *er-Râmeh*.

3. A town in Benjamin (Jos. 18:25), near which was Deborah's palm (Jg. 4:5). It lay N. of Gibeah (1), where the Levite and his concubine stayed (Jg. 19:13), and between Geba (1) and Gibeah (Isa. 10:29). It was fortified by Baasha (1 Kg. 15:17; 2 Chr. 16:1), but when Baasha was diverted to his own defence in the north, Asa used its materials to fortify Geba and Mizpah (3) (1 Kg. 15:22; 2 Chr. 16:6). Here Jeremiah was released from his chains (Jer. 40:1). Some returning exiles traced their descent from here (Ezr. 2:26; 1 Esd. 5:20), and it was resettled (Neh. 11:33). Rachel's tomb was located here by tradition (1 Sam. 10:2; Jer. 31:15; Mt. 2:18). It is probably mod. *er-Râm*.

4. A town in Ephraim (1) (1 Sam. 1:19), also called Ramathaim-zophim (1 Sam. 1:1). Here Elkanah lived and here Samuel was born, and it figures frequently in his story (1 Sam. 2:11, 7:17, 8:4, 15:34 +). It is probably mod. *Rentis*. It is called Rathamin in 1 Mac. 11:34, and is perhaps the same as Arimathea.

5. The shortened form of Ramoth-gilead in 2 Kg. 8:29; 2 Chr. 22:6.

RAMAH OF THE NEGEB: A town in Simeon, identified with Baalath-beer (Jos. 19:8); also called Ramoth of the Negeb in 1 Sam. 30:27, which shows that it had then been incorporated in Judah. Its site is unknown.

RAMATHAIM: *See* Rathamin

RAMATHAIM-ZOPHIM: The name of Ramah (4) in 1 Sam. 1:1. It probably stands for 'the two heights of the Zuphites'.

RAMATH-LEHI: The place where Samson slew the Philistines with a jawbone (Jg. 15:17); *see* Lehi.

RAMATH-MIZPEH: A town in Gad (Jos. 13:26); perhaps the same as Mizpah (2).

RAMOTH: A Levitical city in Issachar (1 Chr. 7:63); called Remeth in Jos. 19:21, and Jarmuth (2) in Jos. 21:29. It is possibly mod. *Kôkab el-Hawâ*.

RAMOTH-GILEAD: A Levitical city in **Gad** (Jos. 21:38; 1 Chr. 6:80) and a city of refuge (Dt. 4:43; Jos. 20:8). It was the chief town of one of Solomon's districts (1 Kg. 4:13). Ahab was killed in battle here (1 Kg. 22:3ff.; 2 Chr. 18:2ff.) and Jehu was anointed here when fresh fighting with **Syria** was going on (2 Kg. 8:28ff., 9:1ff.; 2 Chr. 22:5). It is sometimes called **Ramoth in Gilead** (Dt. 4:43; Jos. 20:8, 21:38; 1 Chr. 6:80). It is mod. *Tell Rāmîth*. It is called **Ramah** (5) in 2 Kg. 8:29; 2 Chr. 22:8.

RAMOTH IN GILEAD: *See* **Ramoth-gilead**.

RAMOTH OF THE NEGEB: *See* **Ramah of the Negeb**.

RAPHON: A town in **Bashan** where Judas defeated Timothy (1 Mac. 5:37ff.); possibly mod. *er-Râfeh*.

RATHAMIN: A district belonging to **Samaria** (2) transferred to Jonathan (1 Mac. 11:34). The name is probably corrupted from **Ramathaim** (so RV and JB). *See* **Ramah** (4)

RECAH: A place in **Judah** (1 Chr. 4:12); its site is unknown.

RED SEA: The Hebrew term which is so translated means 'sea of reeds'. In the story of the deliverance from **Egypt** it probably refers to the region of the Bitter Lakes (Exod. 13:18, 15:4, 22; Dt. 11:4; Jos. 2:10, 4:23, 24:6; Ps. 106:7, 9:22, 136:13, 15; Ac. 7:36; Heb. 11:29) It has, however, a wider use. In Num. 33:10f. the reference appears to be to the Gulf of *Suez*, and in several passages it clearly means the Gulf of *'Aqaba* (Dt. 1:40, 2:1; 1 Kg. 9:26). Whether it was also used more widely for what is today known as the Red Sea cannot be established.

REHOB (*'broad place'*): 1. A city in the N. of **Palestine**, marking the limit of the journey of the spies (Num. 13:21). It is mentioned also in 2 Sam. 10:8, where it is clearly the same as **Beth-rehob** (2 Sam. 10:6). Its exact site is unknown.

2. A town in **Asher** (1) (Jos. 19:28).

3. Another town in **Asher** (1) (Jos. 19:30). Either this or 2 was a Levitical city (Jos. 21:31; 1 Chr. 6:75) and is perhaps mod. *Tell el-Gharbi*. This is probably the town referred to in Jg. 1:31.

REHOBOTH (*'broad places'*): 1. The name of a well dug by Isaac (Gen. 26:22); perhaps mod. *Ruḥeibeh*.

2. The home of Shaul in **Edom** (Gen. 36:37; 1 Chr. 1:48). Its location is unknown.

REHOBOTH-IR: A city in **Assyria** built by Nimrod (Gen. 10:11). Its site is unknown.

REKEM: A place in **Benjamin** (Jos. 18:27), of unknown location.

REMETH: A town in **Issachar** (Jos. 19:21); called **Ramoth** in 1 Chr. 6:73 and **Jarmuth** (2) in Jos. 21:29. It is perhaps mod. *Kôkab el-Hawâ.*

REPHAIM, VALLEY OF: A valley or plain near **Jerusalem,** marking the boundary between **Judah** and **Benjamin** (Jos. 15:8, 18:16). Here David fought the Philistines (2 Sam. 5:18, 22, 23:13; 1 Chr. 11:15, 14:9). It is mentioned also in Isa. 17:5. It is probably mod. *el-Buqei'ah.*

REPHIDIM: A stopping-place in the Wilderness wanderings (Exod. 17:1, 8, 19:2; Num. 33:14f.). Here the Israelites fought the Amalekites (Exod. 17:8ff.). It was possibly in mod. *Wâdî Refâyid.*

RESEN: A city in **Assyria** built by Nimrod (Gen. 10:12), of unknown location.

REUBEN: The territory occupied by the tribe of Reuben. Its ideal limits are stated in Num. 33:32–38; Jos. 13:15–23. Much of it was only intermittently under Israelite control.

REZEPH: A city conquered by the Assyrians (2 Kg. 19:12; Isa. 37:12); possibly mod. *Ruṣâfeh.*

RHEGIUM: A port in SW. Italy at which the ship taking Paul to Rome put in (Ac. 28:13); mod. *Reggio.*

RHODES: An important Greek city on the island of the same name, mentioned as trading with **Tyre** (Ezek. 27:15, RSV). The Roman consul wrote here declaring the Roman friendship for the Jews (1 Mac. 15:23). Paul called here on his way to **Caesarea** (Ac. 21:1).

RIBLAH: 1. A city on the *Orontes,* where Pharaoh Neco had his military headquarters (2 Kg. 23:33), and where later Nebuchadrezzar established his (2 Kg. 25:6). Here Zedekiah's sons were slain before his eyes, and his eyes then put out (2 Kg. 25:7; Jer. 39:5f., 52:9f.); his ministers also were put to death (2 Kg. 25:20f.; Jer. 52:26f.). It is mod. *Ribleh*.

2. A place on the ideal eastern boundary of Israelite territory (Num. 34:11). It can hardly be the same as 1, but it cannot be identified.

RIDGE OF JUDEA: In Jdt. 3:9 it is said that when he encamped in the **Plain of Esdraelon** Holofernes faced 'the great ridge of Judea'. It is not clear what is meant by this, but it would appear to mean the central highlands.

RIMMON ('*pomegranate*'): 1. The name of a rock to which the Benjaminites fled (Jg. 20:45, 47, 21:13). In Isa. 27:10, RSV and JB follow an emended text, which, if correct, locates Rimmon on the expected line of the Assyrian advance on **Jerusalem**. It is probably mod. *Rammûn*, near **Bethel** (1).

2. A place in Judah (Jos. 15:32); called **En-rimmon** in Jos. 19:7, where it is assigned to **Simeon**, which was early absorbed in Judah. In 1 Chr. 4:2 'Ain, Rimmon' should be read En-rimmon. It is named as lying S. of **Jerusalem** (Zec. 14:10). It is mod. *Khirbet Ummer-Ramāmûn*.

3. A place in Zebulun (Jos. 19:13); called **Dimnah** in Jos. 21:35, where it is a Levitical city, and **Rimmono** in 1 Chr. 6:77. It is probably mod. *Rummâneh*.

RIMMONO: *See* **Rimmon** (3).

RIMMON-PEREZ: A stopping-place in the Wilderness wanderings (Num. 33:19f.); possibly mod. *Naqb el-Biyâr*.

RISSAH: A stopping-place in the Wilderness wanderings (Num. 33:21f.); perhaps mod. *Kuntilet el-Jerâfî*.

RITHMAH: A stopping-place in the Wilderness wanderings (Num. 33:18f.), of unknown location.

ROGELIM: A town in **Gilead** (1), the home of Barzillai (2 Sam. 17:27, 19:31); perhaps mod. *Bersîniyâ*.

ROME: The capital of the Roman republic and empire. It is unmentioned in the OT, but figures frequently in 1 Maccabees.

Antiochus Epiphanes was a hostage here (1 Mac. 1:10), and Demetrius I, who replaced him as a hostage, left Rome to claim the Seleucid throne (1 Mac. 7:1). Judas sent an embassy to Rome (1 Mac. 8:17ff.), and established an alliance, which Jonathan renewed (1 Mac. 12:1ff.); this alliance was renewed with Simon (1 Mac. 14:16ff.), and Numenius brought letters from Rome announcing the friendship of the Romans for the Jews (1 Mac. 15:15ff.). Jews from Rome were in Jerusalem at Pentecost (Ac. 2:10), but Claudius expelled all Jews from the city (Ac. 18:2). Paul later planned to visit Rome (Ac. 19:21; cf. 23:11; Rom. 1:15), but it was as a prisoner after his appeal to Caesar (Ac. 25:11) as a Roman citizen (Ac. 16:37f., 22:25ff.) that Paul came to the city (Ac. 28:14, 16), where he remained for two years (Ac. 28:30). Here he was visited by Onesiphorus (2 Tim. 1:16f.). One of his most important Letters was written to the Christians of Rome (Rom. 1:7).

RUMAH: The birthplace of Zebidah, the mother of Jehoiakim (2 Kg. 23:36); possibly mod. *Khirbet er-Rûmeh*.

S

SABTA: *See* Sabtah.

SABTAH: A region of **Arabia**, near **Havilah** (2) (Gen. 10:7); called **Sabta** in 1 Chr. 1:9. Its location is unknown.

SABTECA: A region of **Arabia** (Gen. 10:7; 1 Chr. 1:9), of unknown location.

SALAMIS: A city of **Cyprus**, visited by Paul on his first missionary journey (Ac. 13:5). Its ruins are N. of mod. *Famagusta*.

SALECAH: A town at the eastern extremity of **Bashan** (Dt. 3:10), taken from Og. (Jos. 12:5) and assigned to **Gad** (Jos. 13:11; 1 Chr. 5:11). It is mod. *Salkhad*.

SALEM: The city of Melchizedek (Gen. 14:18; Heb. 7:1f.). It is traditionally identified with **Jerusalem**, which is clearly called

Salem in Ps. 76:2. The identification has been challenged in modern times, but it has also been defended.

SALEM, VALLEY OF: An unknown valley mentioned in Jdt. 4:4.

SALIM: A place near **Aenon,** where John the Baptist baptized (Jn 3:23). Its location is unknown, but mod. *Umm el-'Amdân* is thought by many to be probable.

SALMONE: A cape in **Crete** off which the ship in which Paul was taken to **Rome** sailed (Ac. 27:7). It is mod. *Cape Sidero.*

SALT, CITY OF: A town in the **Wilderness of Judah** (Jos. 15:62); perhaps mod. *Khirbet Qumrân.*

SALT SEA: One of the names by which the **Dead Sea** is called in the Bible (Gen. 14:3; Num. 34:3, 12; Dt. 3:17; Jos. 3:16, 12:3, 15:2, 5, 18:19).

SALT, VALLEY OF: The arena of David's victory over the Edomites (2 Sam. 8:13; 1 Chr. 18:12; Ps. 60 heading). Here too Amaziah defeated the Edomites (2 Kg. 14:7; 2 Chr. 25:11). It is mod. *Wâdî el-Milḥ.*

SAMARIA: 1. A city built by Omri on a hill bought from Shemer and made his capital (1 Kg. 16:24). He was forced to cede trading facilities in the city to the Syrians (1 Kg. 20:34). Ahab erected a temple for the Tyrian Baal in the city (1 Kg. 16:32) and built a luxurious palace (1 Kg. 22:39). Samaria was besieged by Benhadad, but Ahab successfully resisted (1 Kg. 20). Jehoram removed a pillar of Baal which Ahab had made (2 Kg. 3:2), but a more radical attack on the Baal worship and its followers came after the revolution of Jehu (2 Kg. 10:15ff.). Meanwhile Samaria had suffered another Syrian siege, from which it had been delivered (2 Kg. 6:24ff., 7:1ff.). In the reign of Jeroboam II Samaria became wealthy and corrupt (Am. 3:9ff., 4:1ff., 6:1ff.). and in the years that followed there was constant revolution and reversals of policy (Hos. 6:11), until Shalmaneser attacked and besieged the city, and after three years of siege Sargon captured it and the northern kingdom came to an end (2 Kg. 17). Thereafter it was administered as an Assyrian province, and then as a Babylonian, and then again as a Persian. But from this time on Samaria becomes the name of the province and is commonly found in this sense (*see* 2). Little is known of the city, as distinct from the province, from this time. Alexander conquered it and brought Greek colonists here, and the city was hostile to the Maccabees (1 Mac. 3:10). It was conquered by John Hyrcanus, and Herod the Great rebuilt it and named it *Sebaste*. It is mod. *Sebastîyeh*.

2. The administrative region of which 1 was the centre. The term Samaritans is used of the people of all this region, and in post-exilic days hostility increasingly developed between them and the Jews of Judea. The 'adversaries' whose offer to share in the rebuilding of the Temple was refused (Ezr. 4:1ff.) are generally believed to have been Samaritans, and when Nehemiah rebuilt the walls of Jerusalem he faced the active hostility of Sanballat and the Samaritans (Neh. 2:10, 19, 4:1ff., 6:1ff.), with the result that, when Sanballat's daughter married the high priest's son, Nehemiah drove him out of the Temple (Neh. 13:28). The breach finally became complete (Jn 4:9), and the Samaritans established their own temple on **Mount Gerizim** (Jn 4:20), though they had the Pentateuch as their Scriptures. Samaria stands for the region in passages in the Apocrypha (Jdt, 4:4; 1 Mac. 3:10, 10:38; 2 Mac. 15:1) and in the NT (Lk. 17:11; Jn 4:4ff.; Ac. 1:8, 8:1ff., 9:31, 15:3).

SAMOS: An island in the Aegean to which the Roman consul wrote declaring the Roman friendship for the Jews (1 Mac. 15:23). Paul touched here on his return from his third missionary journey (Ac. 20:15).

SAMOTHRACE: An island in the N. Aegean on Paul's route from **Troas** to **Neapolis** (Ac. 16:11).

SAMPSAMES: One of the places to which the Roman consul wrote declaring the Roman friendship for the Jews (1 Mac. 15:23); possibly another name for *Amisus*, on the Black Sea; mod. *Samsun*.

SANSANNAH: A place in the S. of **Judah** (Jos. 15:31); mod. *Khirbet esh-Shamsâriyât*.

SARDIS: A city in Asia Minor, capital of the kingdom of **Lydia**. It is possibly referred to in Ob. 20 as **Sepharad**. Here was one of the seven churches to which John wrote (Rev. 1:11, 3:1ff.). It is mod. *Sart*.

SARID: A place on the border of **Zebulun** (Jos. 19:10, 12); probably mod. *Tell Shadûd*.

SCYTHOPOLIS: The Greek name of **Beth-shan** (2 Mac. 12:29f.; Jdt. 3:10).

SEBA: The territory occupied by a people associated with **Havilah** (2) (Gen. 10:7; 1 Chr. 1:9) and **Ethiopia** (Isa. 43:3), and also with **Sheba** (1) (Ps. 72:10). It is probable that they were a branch of the people of Sheba who migrated across the **Red Sea** to Africa.

SEBAM: A place in **Reuben** (Num. 32:3); called **Sibmah** in Num. 32:38; Jos. 13:19; Isa. 16:8f.; Jer. 48:12. It is possibly mod. *Qurn el-Kibsh*.

SECALAH: A place in the **Wilderness of Judah** (Jos. 15:61); perhaps *Khirbet es-Samrah*.

SECU: A place near **Ramah** (4), where there was a great well (1 Sam. 19:22), of unknown location.

SEIR: The country occupied by the Horites (Gen. 14:6, 36:21, 30) and then by the Edomites (Gen. 22:3, 33:14, 16, 36:8f.; Dt. 2:4, 8, 29; Jos. 24:4).

SEIR, MOUNT: 1. As the country of **Seir** is mountainous, it is frequently referred to as Mount Seir (Gen. 14:6; Dt. 1:2; 2:1, 5, 33:2; Jg. 5:4; 1 Chr. 20:10, 22f.; Ezek. 35:2ff.).
2. A mountain on the N. boundary of **Judah** (Jos. 15:10); possibly mod. *Sâris*.

SEITAH: The unknown location to which Ehud escaped (Jg. 3:26).

SELA (*'rock'*): 1. The Edomite capital captured by Amaziah and renamed **Joktheel** (2 Kg. 14:7). The rock from which the captives were hurled (2 Chr. 25:12) was probably that which gave its name to the place. Sela is mentioned in prophecy in Isa. 16:1ff. (here associated with **Moab**), 42:11, and is possibly referred to in Jer. 49:16; Ob. 3. It is probable that Sela was on the site of the later Nabataean city of *Petra*, mod. *Umm el-Bayârah*.
2. A place on the border of the Amorites (Jg. 1:36), of unknown location.

SELEUCIA: The port of **Antioch** (1), on the coast of **Syria**. Ptolemy VI gained control of it in his war with Alexander Balas (1 Mac. 11:8). Its only other mention in the Bible is as Paul's port of embarkation on his first missionary journey (Ac. 13:4).

SENEH: A crag, opposite **Bozez**, overlooking the **Michmash** gorge (1 Sam. 14:4).

SENIR: The Amorite name for Mount **Hermon** (Dt. 3:9), but a distinct, though associated, peak in 1 Chr. 5:23; Ca. 4:8. It was noted for fir trees (Ezek. 27:5).

SEPHAR: The limit of the territory of the descendants of Joktan (Gen. 10:30); of unknown location.

SEPHARAD: A place in which Jewish exiles were found (Ob. 20), probably **Sardis**.

SEPHARVAIM: A city conquered by **Assyria** (2 Kg. 18:34, 19:13; Isa. 36:19, 37:13), from which some people were brought to **Samaria** (1) (2 Kg. 17:24, 31). Possibly the same as **Sibraim**.

SERPENT'S STONE: A stone near **En-rogel** (1 Kg. 1:9), where Adonijah offered sacrifices at the time of his bid for the throne. It was clearly a sacred stone, and probably had something of the form of a serpent.

SHAALABBIN (*'place of foxes'*): A place in **Dan** (Jos. 19:42); the same as **Shaalbim**.

SHAALBIM (*'place of foxes'*): A town assigned to **Dan**, but from which the Amorites could not be ejected (Jg. 1:35). It became the centre of one of Solomon's administrative districts (1 Kg. 4:9); the same as **Shaalabbin**, and perhaps as **Shaalbon**. It is possibly mod. *Selbît*.

SHAALBON: The home of one of David's heroes (2 Sam. 23:32; 1 Chr. 11:33); perhaps the same as **Shaalbim**.

SHAALIM: A district of **Ephraim** (1), where Saul sought the lost asses (1 Sam. 9:4).

SHAARAIM (*'two gates'*): 1. A town in the lowland of Judah (Jos. 15:36), on the route of the fleeing Philistines (1 Sam. 17:52). The site is unknown.

2. A town in **Simeon** (1 Chr. 4:31); called **Sharuhen** in Jos. 19:6, and **Shilhim** in Jos. 15:32, where it is assigned to **Judah**, which early absorbed Simeon. It is probably mod. *Tell el-Fâr'ah*, S. of **Gaza**.

SHAHAZUMAH: A town of **Issachar** (Jos. 19:22), of unknown location.

SHALISHAH: A district of **Ephraim** (1), where Saul sought the lost asses (1 Sam. 9:4), and in which **Baal-shalishah** was probably located.

SHALLECHETH, GATE OF: A gate of the Temple, on the W. side (1 Chr. 26:16).

SHAMIR: 1. A place in **Judah** in the hill country (Jos. 15:48); possibly mod. *Khirbet el-Bireh*, near *Khirbet Sumara*, which preserves the name.

2. The home of Tola (Jg. 10:1f.); perhaps the site of the future **Samaria** (1).

SHAPHIR: A place mentioned only in Mic. 1:11; possibly mod. *Khirbet el-Kôm*, W. of **Hebron**.

SHARON: 1. The maritime plain extending from the neighbourhood of **Joppa** to **Mount Carmel**. It was noted for its pastures (1 Chr. 27:29; Isa. 65:10), its flowers (Ca. 2:1), its fertility (Isa. 33:9), and its general beauty (Isa. 35:2). Christian disciples were early won here (Ac. 9:35). *See* **Lasharon**.

2. The 'pasture lands of Sharon' (1 Chr. 5:16) are apparently E. of the **Jordan**. Nothing is known of a Sharon here.

SHARUHEN: A town in **Simeon** (Jos. 19:6); called **Shaaraim** (2) in 1 Chr. 4:31, and **Shilhim** in Jos. 15:32, where it is assigned to **Judah**, which early absorbed Simeon. It is probably mod. *Tell el-Fâr'ah*, S. of **Gaza**.

SHAVEH, VALLEY OF: A valley near **Salem**, where Abraham met the king of **Sodom** (Gen. 14:17). It is also called the **King's Valley**

(Gen. 14:17), and here Absalom set up a pillar (2 Sam. 18:18). It would appear to be near **Jerusalem**, but its precise location cannot be determined.

SHAVEH-KIRIATHAIM: The place where Chedorlaomer and his allies defeated the Emim (Gen. 14:5). It was apparently in Moab, and probably near **Kiriathaim (1)**.

SHEBA: 1. A region in **Arabia** (Gen. 10:7, 25:3; 1 Chr. 1:9, 32); the Queen of Sheba came to visit Solomon (1 Kg. 10:1ff.; 2 Chr. 9:1ff.). Its people are referred to as raiders (Job. 1:15) and slave traders (Jl 3:8), and also as merchants (Job 6:19; Ezek. 38:13). They traded in gold and frankincense (Isa. 60:6 Jer. 6:20; cf. Ps. 72:15), and other spices and precious stones (Ezek. 27:22). Sheba is mentioned with **Seba**, probably an African branch of the same people, in Ps. 72:10. It is probable that Sheba corresponded to mod. *Yemen*.

2. A place in **Simeon** (Jos. 19:2); possibly the same as **Shema** in Jos. 15:26. But since in Jos. 19:2–6 fourteen names are given and totalled as thirteen, it is possible that Sheba is a dittograph of part of **Beersheba**.

SHEBARIM: An unknown place to which the people of **Ai (1)** pursued the Israelites (Jos. 7:5).

SHECHEM: An ancient and important city near **Mount Gerizim**, associated with the traditions of Abraham (Gen. 12:6) and Jacob (Gen. 33:18). Simeon and Levi treacherously attacked its people (Gen. 34). Here Jacob buried all the idols of his household (Gen. 35:4), and near here his sons were pasturing their flocks when Joseph was sent to them (Gen. 37:12ff.). Joshua renewed the covenant here (Jos. 24:1ff.) and here Joseph was buried (Jos. 24:32). Shechem was assigned to **Manasseh** (Jos. 17:2), and later became a city of refuge (Jos. 20:7), and was reckoned to **Ephraim (1)** (1 Chr. 6:67, 7:28); but it was apparently still a Canaanite city in the time of Abimelech (Jg. 8:31, 9:1ff.). The temple of Baal-berith was here (Jg. 8:33, 9:4), and the city must have played a larger part in history than we can recover. For it was to Shechem that Rehoboam went to be acclaimed as king (1 Kg. 12:1; 2 Chron. 10:1), but in fact to disrupt the kingdom (1 Kg. 12:6f.; 2 Chr. 10:16), and Shechem was the first capital of the northern kingdom (1 Kg. 12:25). After the fall of **Jerusalem**

men of Shechem brought offerings to the Lord, but were killed by Ishmael (Jer. 41:5ff.). In Sir. 50:27 'the foolish people that dwell in Shechem' stands for the people of **Samaria** (2).

SHECHEM, TOWER OF: A fortress destroyed by Abimelech (Jg. 9:46ff.). This was probably the inner fortress of the city, to which the defenders retired after the fall of the city as a whole.

SHEEP GATE: One of the gates of **Jerusalem,** on the N. side, rebuilt by Nehemiah (Neh. 3:1, 32, 12:39). It is mentioned in Jn 5:2.

SHELAH, POOL OF: A pool in the **King's Garden** in **Jerusalem** (Neh. 3:15), probably the same as the **King's Pool** (Neh. 2:14). Water was brought from the spring **Gihon** by a surface conduit (Isa. 7:3), referred to as the **Waters of Shiloah** (Isa. 8:6), before Hezekiah made the **Siloam** tunnel to bring the water through the rock (2 Kg. 20:20; 2 Chr. 32:30; Sir. 48:17) to what then became known as the **Pool of Siloam** (Jn 9:7).

SHELEPH: The region occupied by an Arabian tribe (Gen. 10:26; 1 Chr. 1:20). It has not been identified, but it was in S. **Arabia.**

SHEMA: A town in **Judah** (Jos. 15:26); possibly the same as **Sheba** (2), there assigned to **Simeon,** which was early absorbed in Judah. Its site is unknown.

SHEPHAM: An unidentified place on the E. boundary of the Promised Land (Num. 34:10f.).

SHEPHELAH: The lowland region between the highlands of **Judah** and **Philistia.** It is often translated 'lowland' in RSV, but Shephelah is retained in 1 Kg. 10:27; 1 Chr. 27:28; 2 Chr. 1:15, 9:27, 26:10, 28:18; Jer. 17:26, 32:44, 33:13; Ob. 19. It also stands in 1 Mac. 12:38.

SHEPHER, MOUNT: A stopping-place in the Wilderness wanderings (Num. 33:23f.), of uncertain location.

SHIBAH: A well dug by Isaac (Gen. 26:33), which gave its name to **Beersheba.**

SHIHOR: A name associated in some way with Egypt. In Isa. 23:3 it is parallel to 'the Nile', where it might be a poetic synonym or another waterway; and in Jer. 2:18 it is used of Egyptian waters, where RSV renders by 'the Nile'. In 1 Chr. 13:5 it appears to mark the boundary between David's kingdom and Egypt, which is elsewhere marked by the **Brook** (or **River**) **of Egypt**. In Jos 13:3 it is said to be E. of Egypt. It may possibly denote the Pelusiac branch of the Nile.

SHIHOR-LIBNATH: A place on the boundary of **Asher** (1) (Jos. 19:26), apparently a stream; possibly *Nahr ez-Zerqā*.

SHIKKERON: A place on the N. boundary of **Judah** (Jos. 15:11); possibly *Tell el-Fûl*.

SHILHIM: A town in **Judah** (Jos. 15:32); possibly the same as **Shaaraim** (2) (1 Chr. 4:31), which is assigned to **Simeon**, which was early absorbed in Judah, and Sharuhen (Jos. 19:6). It is probably mod. *Tell el-Fâr'ah*, S. of **Gaza**.

SHILOAH, WATERS OF: A surface conduit (Isa. 7:3), bringing water from the spring **Gihon** into **Jerusalem** before Hezekiah made the **Siloam** tunnel to bring the water through the rock (2 Kg. 20:20; 2 Chr. 32:30; Sir. 48:17).

SHILOH: A city in **Ephraim** (1), N. of **Bethel** (1) (Jg. 21:19), where the Israelite tribes met (Jos. 18:1) and apportioned the land (Jos. 18:10, 19:51) and set aside the Levitical cities (Jos. 21:2ff.). Here the tribes assembled for war against the eastern tribes (Jos. 22:12). After the war with the Benjaminites the tribes again encamped here (Jg. 21:12), and the Benjaminites were encouraged to seize as brides the maidens who were sharing in the festival there (Jg. 21:19ff.). At the sanctuary in Shiloh Eli was priest (1 Sam. 1:3) when Hannah made her vow (1 Sam. 1:9ff.), and to Shiloh she brought Samuel (1 Sam. 1:24), where she left him (1 Sam. 2:11). Samuel received his call in Shiloh when a child (1 Sam. 3). The Ark was at Shiloh until it was taken to the battlefield at **Aphek** (1) (1 Sam. 4:1ff.), where it was captured, never to return to Shiloh. On hearing the news of its capture, Eli collapsed and died (1 Sam. 4:18). There are references to some disaster which befell the Shiloh shrine (Jer. 7:12, 14, 26:6, 9; cf. Ps. 78:60), and modern excavations have shown that Shiloh was destroyed about this time, making it probable that the Philistines destroyed it after their victory, and only a small settlement seems to have continued on the site. Ahijah the prophet lived here (1 Kg. 11:29, 14:2, 4), and after the fall of **Jerusalem** some men from Shiloh brought offerings to the Lord, but were killed by Ishmael (Jer. 41:5ff.). It is mod. *Seilûn*.

SHIMRON: A city which joined Jabin (Jos. 11:1), and which was assigned to **Zebulun** (Jos. 19:5); possibly mod. *Tell Semûniyeh*, W. of **Nazareth**.

SHIMRON-MERON: A Canaanite town whose king was defeated by Joshua (Jos. 12:20); probably the same as **Shimron**.

SHINAR: A name for **Babylonia**. The tower of **Babel** was in Shinar (Gen. 11:2), and Amraphel was its king (Gen. 14:1, 9). The return of exiles from Shinar is predicted (Isa. 11:11), and to Shinar Nebuchadnezzar is said to have taken the sacred vessels (Dan. 1:2). Zechariah saw in a vision an ephah which was to be taken there (Zech. 5:11). The older attempt to connect the word with 'Sumer' or with 'Sumer and Accad' is no longer favoured.

SHION: A place in **Issachar** (Jos. 19:19), of unknown location.

SHITTIM: A place in **Moab** where the Israelites encamped before crossing the **Jordan** (Jos. 3:1), from which the spies were sent to **Jericho** (Jos. 2:1). Here the people sinned with Moabite women (Num. 25:1ff.). It is called **Abel-shittim** in Num. 33:49. It was apparently while the people were at Shittim that the Balaam incident occurred (Num. 22ff.), and here the people were numbered (Num. 26:1ff.). Here, too, Joshua was commissioned to succeed Moses (Num. 27:23), and from here Moses viewed the land and died (Dt. 34:1ff.). Shittim is identified with mod. *Tell el-Ḥammâm*, S. of *Wâdī Kefrein*.

SHITTIM, VALLEY OF: A valley to be watered by the stream flowing from the Temple (Jl 3:18); possibly the lower **Kidron** valley, the *Wâdī en-Nâr*.

SHUAL, LAND OF: A region near **Ophrah** (1) raided by the Philistines (1 Sam. 13:17). Its exact location is unknown.

SHUNEM: A town of Issachar (Jos. 19:18), where the Philistines encamped before the battle of Gilboa (1 Sam. 28:4). Abishag was from Shunem (1 Kg. 1:3, 15), and Elisha was the guest of a woman of Shunem (2 Kg. 4:8ff.), whose child he restored to life (2 Kg. 4:32ff.), It is mod. *Sôlem.*

SHUR: A place, or a wilderness to which it gave its name, on the N.E. border of Egypt. Here Hagar was found by the angel (Gen. 16:7), and in this region Abraham sojourned (Gen. 20:1). It is said to be 'opposite Egypt in the direction of Assyria' (Gen. 25:18). Through this wilderness Moses led the Israelites after leaving the Red Sea (Exod. 15:22). It was inhabited by Amalekites (1 Sam. 15:7, 27:8). Its general location in the Egyptian border region is clear, but it cannot be precisely identified.

SIBRAIM: A place on the N. boundary of the ideal Israel (Ezek. 47:16); possibly the same as Sepharvaim. It is unidentified, but apparently in the neighbourhood of Hamath.

SICYON: One of the places to which the Roman consul wrote, declaring the Roman friendship for the Jews (1 Mac. 15:23). It lay on the Gulf of Corinth.

SIDDIM, VALLEY OF: A valley named only in Gen. 14:3, 8, 10 as the place where Chedorlaomer and his allies fought with Sodom and her allies. It is identified with the Salt Sea (Gen. 14:3), and is said to be 'full of bitumen pits' (Gen. 14:10). It probably lies today under the waters of the S. end of the Dead Sea.

SIDE: A city of Pamphylia to which the Roman consul wrote, declaring the Roman friendship for the Jews (1 Mac. 15:23); mod. *Eski Adalia.*

SIDON: A seaport of Phoenicia and its oldest city (Gen. 10:15); called Great Sidon in Jos. 11:8, 19:28. It lay near to the border of Zebulun, according to Gen. 49:13, and of Asher (1), according to Jos. 19:28 (cf. Jg. 1:31), but probably neither ever penetrated so far north. Laish seems to have had some link with Sidon before the Danites conquered it (Jg. 18:28), and Zarephath belonged to Sidon (1 Kg. 17:9; Lk. 4:26). It was renowned for its sea-borne trade (Isa. 23:2, 4), but it became dependent on Tyre, which outstripped it in importance (Ezek. 27:8). Prophecies against it stand in Jer. 25:22, 47:4; Ezek. 28:21ff.; Jl 3:4ff.; Zech. 9:2. It was visited by Jesus (Mt. 15:21; Mk 7:24, 31), and people from here came to hear Him (Lk. 6:17). The ship in which Paul sailed for Rome put in at Sidon (Ac. 27:3). It is mod. *Ṣaidā*.

SILOAM : A place where a tower fell, killing eighteen people (Lk. 13:4). This was probably just outside Jerusalem in the Kidron valley, near Gihon; mod. *Silwân*. It gave its name to the tunnel which carried water from Gihon to the Pool of Siloam inside the city.

SILOAM, POOL OF: A pool in Jerusalem, where Jesus healed a man born blind (Jn 9:7. 11). Water flowed through a tunnel, made in the time of Hezekiah (2 Kg. 20:20, 2 Chr. 32:30; Sir. 48:17), from Gihon to this pool. In the tunnel, carved in the living rock, was the famous Siloam inscription (now in *Istanbul*), recording the manner of its construction. *See* Shelah, Pool of, and Shiloah, Waters of.

SIN, WILDERNESS OF: A region passed through by the Israelites after leaving Elim (Exod. 16:1). It lay between Elim and Sinai (Exod. 16:1), but before Rephidim (Exod. 17:1). According to Num. 33:12ff., Dophkah and Alush also lay between the Wilderness of Sin and Rephidim. It is probably mod. *Debbet er-Ramleh*.

SINAI, MOUNT: The sacred mountain associated with the Covenant (Exod. 19:5) and the Law (Lev. 26:46, 27:34). Here God came down upon the mountain (Exod. 19:11, 18, 20), which was wrapped in smoke (Exod. 19:18) and cloud (Exod. 24:15f.), and which Moses was called to ascend (Exod. 19:24), while the people were warned to keep away from it (Exod. 19:12f., 23). Moses spent forty days and forty nights on the mountain (Exod. 24:18), and God gave him the two tables of stone (Exod. 31:18) which he broke on seeing the Golden Calf (Exod. 32:19). Moses again ascended (Exod. 34:2) with two new tables (Exod. 34:4). Traditionally Sinai is located at *Jebel Mûsā*, in the peninsula of Sinai, but this is disputed by some scholars, and various other locations have been proposed. In some passages the sacred mount is called Horeb, and again some think the two names were not originally synonymous, though they have become so.

SINAI, WILDERNESS OF: The Wilderness in which Mount Sinai stood (Exod. 19:1f.). Here the people were numbered (Num. 1:1, 19), and here Nadab and Abihu died (Num. 3:4). The Passover was kept here a year after leaving Egypt (Num. 9:1, 5). The stages of the journey after leaving the wilderness of Sinai are set out in Num. 33:16ff.

SIPHMOTH: A place in **Judah** to which David sent spoils taken from the Amalekites (1 Sam. 30:28). Its location is unknown.

SIRAH, CISTERN OF: The place where Joab's messengers overtook Abner and treacherously persuaded him to return (2 Sam. 3:26); perhaps mod. *'Ain Sâreh*.

SIRION: The Sidonian name for Mount **Hermon** (Dt. 3:9). It is used also in Dt. 4:48; Ps. 29:6; Jer. 18:14).

SITNAH (*'strife'*): A well dug by Isaac (Gen. 26:21), of unknown location.

SMYRNA: An important city on the W. coast of Asia Minor, in which was one of the seven churches to which John wrote (Rev. 1:11, 2:8ff.). It is mod. *Izmir*.

SOCO: 1. A town in **Judah** fortified by Rehoboam (2 Chr. 11:7) and raided by the Philistines (2 Chr. 28:18); called **Socoh** (1) in Jos. 15:35 and 1 Sam. 17:1.

2. In 1 Chr. 4:18 Heber is said to be the 'father of Soco', by which the founder of the town of Soco may be meant. If so, this is probably the same as **Socoh** (2).

SOCOH: 1. A town in the lowland of **Judah** (Jos. 15:35), where the Philistines gathered for battle (1 Sam. 17:1); called **Soco** (1) in 2 Chr. 11:7, 28:18. It is probably mod. *Khirbet 'Abbâd*.

2. A town in the hill country of **Judah** (Jos. 15:48); probably mod. *Khirbet esh-Shuweikeh*, SW. of **Hebron**. *See* **Soco** (2).

3. A city in Solomon's third administrative district (1 Kg. 4:10); mod. *Tell er-Râs*, N.W. of **Samaria** (1).

SODOM: One of the **Cities of the Valley** (Gen. 19:29), chosen by Lot for his residence (Gen. 13:10ff.). It fought with **Gomorrah** against Chedorlaomer and his allies (Gen. 14:2ff.), and was notorious for its wickedness (Gen. 13:13, 18:20, 19:4ff.; Jer. 23:14). It was destroyed with Gomorrah (Gen. 19:24ff.) in a disaster that was always remembered with horror (Dt. 29:23; Isa. 1:9f., 13:19; Jer. 49:18, 50:40; Lam. 4:6; Am. 4:11; Zeph. 2:9). It is alluded to in Wis. 10:6 and in many NT passages (Mt. 10:15, 11:23f.; Lk. 10:12, 17:29; Rom. 9:29; 2 Pet. 2:6; Jude 7). Its site is not known, but it is probably that it is submerged under the S. end of the **Dead Sea.**

SODOM, SEA OF: A name for the **Dead Sea** in 2 Esd. 5:7, where it is predicted that it will cast up fish as a miraculous sign. The Dead Sea is so salt that no fish can live in it.

SOLOMON, PORTICO OF: *See* **Portico of Solomon.**

SOREK, VALLEY OF: The valley in which Delilah's home was (Jg. 16:4); probably mod. *Wâdī eṣ-Ṣurâr.*

SORES: A place in the hill country of **Judah** (Jos. 15:59, in an addition in LXX and JB, not in MT and RSV).

SPAIN: Mentioned in the Bible only in 1 Mac. 8:3f., where the Roman penetration and control is referred to, and in Rom. 15:24, 28, where Paul expresses the hope of visiting Spain and journeying via **Rome**. Whether Paul ever went to Spain cannot be definitely known.

SPARTA: An important city in S. **Greece**, whose people are called Spartans or Lacedaemonians. Some Jews who escaped from the persecution of Jason migrated there (2 Mac. 5:9), and Jonathan wrote to the city to establish friendship and alliance (1 Mac. 12:2, 5ff.). When Jonathan died, Sparta grieved (1 Mac. 14:16) and wrote to Simon (1 Mac. 14:20ff.). Sparta was one of the places to which the Roman consul wrote, declaring the Roman friendship for the Jews (1 Mac. 15:23). It is mod. *Sparte.*

STAIRS OF THE CITY OF DAVID: A flight of steps near the **Fountain Gate** of Jerusalem (Neh. 3:15, 12:37). Such a flight cut in the rock has been discovered at the S. end of the city.

SUCCOTH: 1. The first stopping-place in the Wilderness wanderings (Exod. 12:37, 13:20; Num. 23:5f); possibly *Tell el-Maskhutah.*
2. A town in **Gad** (Jos. 13:27), where Jacob stopped after his

meeting with Esau (Gen. 33:17). It refused to help Gideon (Jg. 8:5ff.) and was punished on his return (Jg. 8:15f.), Here the bronze vessels for the Temple were made (1 Kg. 7:45ff.; 2 Chr. 4:11ff.). It is probably mod. *Tell Deir 'Alla*.

SUCCOTH, VALE OF: A valley near **Succoth (2)**, referred to in Ps. 60:6; 108:7.

SUPHAH: An unknown place referred to in a citation from the Book of the Wars of the Lord (Num. 21:14). It was apparently in Moab.

SUR: A place on the coast of **Syria** which sued for peace with Holofernes (Jdt. 2:28); of unknown location.

SUR, GATE: A gate in **Jerusalem** in the time of Athaliah (2 Kg. 11:6), possibly leading from the palace to the Temple. It is to be identified with the **Gate of the Foundation**.

SUSA: The capital of **Elam**, and a residence of the Persian kings (Ezr. 4:9; Neh. 1:1; Dan. 8:2). The story of the book of Esther is laid here (Est. 1:2, 5 +). It is mod. *Shush*.

SYCHAR: A city in **Samaria (2)**, mentioned only in Jn 4:5. Here was Jacob's Well (Jn 4:6), and it is said to be 'near the field that Jacob gave to his son Joseph' (Jn 4:5), where the reference would seem to be to Gen. 48:22, where RSV has 'mountain slope' (MT *shekhem*) with allusion to **Shechem**. It is uncertain whether Sychar is to be equated with Shechem, or identified with a nearby site, mod. *'Askar*.

SYENE: A place in **Egypt**, apparently on the S. border (Ezek. 29:10, 30:6), from which dispersed Jews are pictured as returning (Isa. 49:12). It is mod. *Aswân*. In the island of *Elephantine*, opposite *Aswân*, there was in the fifth century B.C. a Jewish military colony, with a temple of Jahu (Yahweh) which was in existence before 525 B.C. and from which the important Elephantine Papyri came.

SYRACUSE: An important city of Sicily, where Paul stayed for three days on his journey to **Rome** (Ac. 28:12); mod. *Siracusa*.

SYRIA: This is used most frequently in the OT for the kingdom whose capital was **Damascus** (1 Kg. 15:18, 19:15, 20:1 +), which is also referred to as **Aram** of Damascus (2 Sam. 8:6). In 1 Esd. 2:25 Syria corresponds to **Coelesyria** in 1 Esd. 2:17, 24, 27. Similarly in 1 Esd. 6:27, 8:19, 23 we have 'Syria and **Phoenicia**', but in 1 Esd. 6:29, 8:67 'Coelesyria and Phoenicia'. Here 'Coelesyria and Phoenicia' or 'Syria and Phoenicia' corresponds to the province 'Beyond the River' in Ezr. 4:11, and covers the whole area beyond the Upper **Euphrates**. In Jdt. 1:12 'Cilicia and Damascus and Syria' distinguishes Syria from Coelesyria, and means only the area lying to the north of the Damascus region, but including Phoenicia. In Jdt. 8:26 Jacob's sojourn with Laban is located 'in **Mesopotamia** in Syria', where again the northern part of the region is indicated. In 1 Maccabees Syria appears to stand for the part of the Seleucid kingdom which stretched from **Antioch** (1) to **Egypt** (1 Mac. 3:13, 41, 7:39, 11:2, 60). In the NT Syria means the Roman province, and could be used for the entire area including **Palestine** (Lk. 2:2; Ac. 18:18 (apparently including **Caesarea**, cf. 18:22) 20:3, 21:3 (including **Tyre**)), or, more specifically, for the northern area (Ac. 15:23, 41; Gal. 1:21), or apparently for the region bordering on **Galilee** (Mt. 4:24). There is therefore much fluidity in its use.

SYROPHOENICIA: A designation of **Phoenicia** in Mk 7:26, meaning the region of Phoenicia in the Roman province of **Syria**.

SYRTIS: The name of two shallow gulfs off the coast of N. Africa, where the captain of the ship on which Paul was a prisoner was afraid his vessel would be driven (Ac. 27:17).

T

TAANACH: A Canaanite royal city, whose king was defeated by Joshua (Jos. 12:21). Though it lay within the borders of **Issachar**, it was assigned to **Manasseh** (Jos. 17:11; 1 Chr. 7:29), but the Canaanites could not be dispossessed (Jg. 1:27). The battle with Sisera was fought near here (Jg. 5:19). It became a Levitical city (Jos. 21:25), and was in Solomon's fifth administrative district (1 Kg. 4:12). It is mod. *Tell Ta'annak*.

TAANATH-SHILOH: A place in **Ephraim** (1) (Jos. 16:6); probably mod. *Khirbet Ta'nah el-Fôqā*, SE. of **Shechem**.

TABBATH: A place E. of the **Jordan** to which Gideon pursued his foes (Jg. 7:22); possibly mod. *Râs Abū Ṭābât*.

TABERAH: A stopping-place in the Wilderness wanderings (Num. 11:3; Dt. 9:22), of unknown location. Here the people provoked the Lord and were punished (Num. 11:1f.).

TABOR: 1. A place in **Zebulun** (1 Chr. 6:77), probably near **Mount Tabor**; its location is unknown.
2. A place mentioned in Jg. 8:18 as the place where Zebah and Zalmunna slew Gideon's brothers. **Mount Tabor** may be intended, or it is quite unknown.

TABOR, MOUNT: A prominent mountain on the border of **Zebulun** (Jos. 19:22) in the **Valley of Jezreel**, where Barak gathered his army (Jg. 4:6, 12, 14). It is mentioned with **Mount Carmel** in Jer. 46:18, and with **Hermon** in Ps. 89:12. Here was a shrine denounced in Hos. 5:1, which may be alluded to in Dt. 33:19. It is the traditional mount of the Transfiguration (Mt. 17:1ff.; Mk 9:2ff.; Lk. 9:28ff.), but this is thought improbable.

TABOR, OAK OF: A tree in the vicinity of **Bethel** (1) (1 Sam. 10:3), of unknown location.

TADMOR: A city in the wilderness, built by Solomon (2 Chr. 8:4); called **Tamar** in the parallel (1 Kg. 9:18. It is not certain which is the correct reading. If the latter it is perhaps to be equated with **Hazazon-tamar**; if the former, it is perhaps the important desert oasis later known as *Palmyra*, mod. *Tudmur*.

TAHATH: An unidentified stopping-place in the Wilderness wanderings (Num. 33:26f.).

TAHPANHES: A city of Egypt (Jer. 2:16, 44:1, 46:14; Jdt. 1:9), to which Jeremiah was taken (Jer. 43:7ff.), and where we get our last glimpse of him. It is the Greek *Daphnae*, mod. *Tel Defneh*.

TAMAR: 1. A city in the wilderness built by Solomon (1 Kg. 9:18); called **Tadmor** in 2 Chr. 8:4. If Tamar is the correct reading, it should perhaps be identified with **Hazazon-tamar**.

2. A place on the boundary of the ideal Israel (Ezek. 47:18f., 48:28); possibly the same as Hazazon-tamar.

TAPPUAH: 1. A town in Judah in the lowland (Jos. 15:34); possibly mod. *Beit Nettîf.*

2. A town on the boundary of Ephraim (1) and Manasseh (Jos. 16:8, 17:8); probably the same as En-tappuah (Jos. 17:7), mod. *Tell esh-Sheikh Avū Zarad*. It was sacked by Menahem (2 Kg. 15:16, RSV; MT has Tiphsah and JB Tappush). *See* Tephon.

3. A Canaanite city whose king Joshua defeated (Jos. 12:17); perhaps the same as 2.

TAPPUSH: *See* Tappuah (2).

TARALAH: A town of Benjamin (Jos. 18:27), of unknown location.

TARSHISH: A far-off place to which ships sailed from Joppa (Jon. 1:3, 4:2) and Tyre (Isa. 23:6). It is frequently mentioned with distant places (Ps. 72:10; Isa. 66:19; Ezek. 38:13). It was a source of silver (Jer. 10:9), and iron, tin, and lead (Ezek. 27:12). It was formerly identified with *Tartessus*, in Spain. But 'ships of Tarshish' sailed to other places. They went apparently to Cyprus (Isa. 23:1), and Solomon's 'ships of Tarshish' must have sailed down the Red Sea to find their cargoes to bring back (1 Kg. 10:22; 2 Chr. 9:21), and Jehoshaphat's ill-starred fleet sailed from Ezion-geber (1 Kg. 22:48; 2 Chr. 20:36). It has been argued that the word *tarshîsh* meant 'metal-refinery' and then came to mean a metal-carrying vessel. The outgoing cargoes from Ezion-geber may have been from the metal refineries which are known to have been there. But as the cargoes were certainly not all metals, it may have come to mean a large ocean-going vessel, as distinct from a coaster, whatever it carried and wherever it sailed.

TARSUS: The capital of Cilicia, which revolted with Mallus against Antiochus Epiphanes (2 Mac. 4:30). It was the birthplace of Paul (Ac. 9:11, 21:39, 22:3), to which he returned after his conversion and cool reception in Jerusalem (Ac. 9:30), but from which he was brought by Barnabas to Antioch (1) (Ac. 11:25f.). It is mod. *Tersous.*

TATAM: A place in the hill country of Judah (Jos. 15:59, in an addition in LXX and JB, not in MT and RSV).

TAVERNS, THREE: A place 33 Roman miles from Rome on the Appian Way, to which many Christians from Rome went to meet Paul (Ac. 28:15).

TEHAPHNEHES: The spelling of Tahpanhes found in Ezek. 30:18.

TEKOA: A town in the hill country of Judah (Jos. 15:59, in an addition in LXX and JB, not in MT and RSV). The wise woman who pleaded for Absalom came from here (2 Sam. 14:2, 4, 9), as did one of David's heroes (2 Sam. 23:26; 1 Chr. 11:28). Rehoboam fortified it (2 Chr. 11:6), and in Jeremiah's time it was still a fortified town (Jer. 6:1). Amos had his home here (Am. 1:1). It is mod. *Khirbet Teqû'*.

TEKOA, WILDERNESS OF: A region near Tekoa (2 Chr. 20:20), to which Jonathan and Simon fled for refuge (1 Mac. 9:33).

TEL-ABIB: A place in Babylonia on the Chebar, in which were Jewish exiles (Ezek. 3:15). The site is unknown.

TELAIM: The place in Judah where Saul gathered his army to attack the Amalekites (1 Sam. 15:4); probably the same as Telem (Jos. 15:24).

TELAM: *See* Telem.

TELASSAR: A place in N. Mesopotamia conquered by Assyria (2 Kg. 19:12; Isa. 37:12). Its site is unknown.

TELEM: A place in the S. of Judah (Jos. 15:24), of uncertain location. It is probably the same as Telaim (1 Sam. 15:4). In 1 Sam. 27:8, LXX reads 'from Telem' for MT 'from of old', and JB follows ('from Telam'). The extent of Amalekite territory is then indicated.

TEL-HARSHA: A town of Babylonia (Ezr. 2:59; Neh. 7:61; 1 Esd. 5:36), of unknown location.

TEL-MELAH (*'mound of salt'*): A town of Babylonia (Ezr. 2:59; Neh. 7:61; 1 Esd. 5:36), of unknown location.

TEMA: A region of **Arabia** (Isa. 21:14; Jer. 25:23), whose inhabitants were Ishmaelites (Gen. 25:15; 1 Chr. 1:30), engaged in caravan trade (Job. 6:30). It is mod. *Teimā*.

TEMAN: A region of **Edom** (Jer. 49:7; Ezek. 25:13; Am. 1:12; Ob. 9) and its people, who were descendants of Esau (Gen. 36:11, 15, 42; 1 Chr. 1:36, 53). Its people were famous for wisdom (Jer. 49:7), and the oldest and wisest of Job's friends was a Temanite (Job 2:11). It is possibly mod. *Tawīlân*.

TEPHON: A town fortified by Bacchides (1 Mac. 9:50). This was probably the same as **Tappuah (2)**.

TERAH: A stopping-place in the Wilderness wanderings (Num. 33:27f.), of unknown location.

THEBES: The capital city of Upper **Egypt** (Jer. 46:25; Ezek. 30: 14ff.). It was conquered and sacked by Ashurbanipal (Nah. 3:8).

THEBEZ: A city N. of **Shechem**. Abimelech was killed when attacking it (Jg. 9:50; 2 Sam. 11:21). It is mod. *Ṭūbâṣ*.

THERAS: A river where Ezra encamped and proclaimed a fast (1 Esd. 8:41ff.). It corresponds to **Ahava** in Ezr. 8:21, 31.

THESSALONICA: A city in **Macedonia**, visited by Paul on his second missionary journey (Ac. 17:1). The opposition of Jews forced him to leave for **Beroea** (Ac. 17:10). He wrote two letters to the church there (1 Th. 1:1; 2 Th. 1:1). Aristarchus was from Thessalonica (Ac. 20:4, 27:2). The church at **Philippi** sent help to Paul in Thessalonica (Phil. 4:16). Paul wrote to Timothy that Demas had deserted him and gone to Thessalonica (2 Tim. 4:10). It is mod. *Salonika*.

THISBE: A place in **Galilee**, from which Tobit was carried captive by the Assyrians (Tob. 1:2). The site is unknown.

THRACE: A country E. of **Macedonia**, with coasts on the Aegean, the Sea of Marmara, and the Black Sea. A cavalryman from Thrace saved the life of Gorgias (2 Mac. 12:35).

THREE TAVERNS, *See* **Taverns, Three.**

THYATIRA: A city of **Lydia** in Asia Minor, from which Lydia, the first convert in **Philippi**, came (Ac. 16:14). The church here was one of the seven to which John wrote (Rev. 1:11, 2:18ff.). It is mod. *Akhisar*.

TIBERIAS: A town on the W. shore of the **Sea of Galilee**, built by Herod Antipas. Jesus seems never to have visited it, but there is a reference in the Fourth Gospel to boats from it (Jn 6:22). It is mod. *Tabariyeh*.

TIBERIAS, SEA OF: One of the names by which the **Sea of Galilee** is referred to (Jn 6:1, 21:1).

TIBHATH: A city belonging to **Zobah** (1 Chr. 18:8); called **Betah** in 2 Sam. 8:8. Its site is unknown.

TIGRIS: A river of Asia, which joins the **Euphrates** 40 miles N. of the Persian Gulf. It was one of the four rivers of the **Garden of Eden** (Gen. 2:14), and it is mentioned in Dan. 10:4, where Daniel had a vision of the angel Michael. Tobias and Raphael came to it on their journey (Tob. 6:1), and it is named in Jdt. 1:6 and Sir. 24:25. Its Hebrew name is **Hiddekel**, which in early editions of RSV stands in Gen. 2:14.

TIMNA: The region occupied by an Edomite clan bearing the same name (Gen. 36:40); its location is unknown.

TIMNAH: 1. A place in the hill country of **Judah** (Jos. 15:57); probably the place visited by Judah (Gen. 38:12ff.). It is perhaps mod. *Khirbet Tibnah*, W. of **Bethlehem**.
2. A place on the N. border of **Judah** (Jos. 15:10), assigned to **Dan** (1) in Jos. 19:43 and in Philistine possession in Samson's time (Jg. 14:1ff.). It later became Israelite, but was retaken by the Philistines in the reign of Ahaz (2 Chr. 28:18). It is mod. *Khirbet Tibnah*, S.W of **Beth-shemesh**.

TIMNATH: A town fortified by Bacchides (1 Mac. 9:50); probably the same as **Timnath-serah**.

TIMNATH-HERES: The place in the hill country of **Ephraim** (1) where Joshua was buried (Jg. 2:9); called **Timnath-serah** in Jos. 24:30.

TIMNATH-SERAH: A city given to Joshua (Jos. 19:50) and where he was buried (Jos. 24:30); called **Timnath-heres** in Jg. 2:9). It is believed to be *Khirbet Tibneh*, about 17 miles SW. of **Shechem**. It is probably the same as **Timnath** (1 Mac. 9:50, there reckoned to **Judea**. But note that **Beth-horon** is there also assigned to Judea.).

TIPHSAH: 1. A place marking the N. limit of Solomon's kingdom (1 Kg. 4:24). It is the classical *Thapsacus*, mod. *Dibseh*.

2. *See* **Tappuah** (2).

TIRZAH: A Canaanite city whose king was defeated by Joshua (Jos. 12:24). Jeroboam I made it his capital (1 Kg. 14:17) and it continued to be the capital of the northern kindgom (1 Kg. 15:21; 16:6, 8, 15, 17, 23) until Omri moved it to **Samaria** (1) (1 Kg. 16:24). From Tirzah Menahem rose against Shallum (2 Kg. 15:14, 16). It is a symbol of beauty in Ca. 6:4. It is mod. *Tell el-Fâr'ah*.

TISHBE: The home of Elijah (1 Kg. 17:1); possibly mod. *Khirbet Lisdib*.

TOB: A region S. of **Damascus**, where Jephthah lived when he was an outlaw (Jg. 11:3, 5). It helped **Ammon** against David (2 Sam. 10:6ff.). In the Maccabean period Jews were living there, and when many were killed by their enemies, Judas went to their aid (1 Mac. 5:13ff.; cf. 2 Mac. 12:17, where Toubiani are the inhabitants of Tob). Tob is probably mod. *et-Taiyibeh*, between **Edrei** (1) and **Bozrah** (3).

TOCHEN: A place in **Simeon** (1 Chr. 4:32); the site is unknown.

TOLAD: A place in **Simeon** (1 Chr. 4:29); called **Eltolad** in Jos. 19:4, which is assigned to **Judah** in Jos. 15:30. Its location is unknown.

TOPHEL: A place E. of the **Jordan** near where Moses addressed the people (Dt. 1:1); perhaps mod. *et-Tafîleh*, SE. of the **Dead Sea**.

TOPHETH: A place in the **Valley of Hinnom** where children were sacrificed (Jer. 7:31f.; 19:6, 11f.); it was defiled by Josiah (2 Kg. 23:10).

TRACHONITIS: A region governed by Herod Philip (Lk. 3:1). It was SE. of **Damascus**, mod. *Lejā*.

TRIPOLIS: A town in **Phoenicia**, where Demetrius I landed (2 Mac. 14:1). It was formed by colonies from **Tyre**, **Sidon** and **Arvad**, and thus got its name.

TROAS: A city in Asia Minor about 10 miles from ancient *Troy*, on the shore of the Aegean. Here Paul had his vision of the man of **Macedonia** (Ac. 16:9f.), and from here he sailed for Europe (Ac. 16:11). He seems to have met Luke here, as the 'we' sections of Acts begin at this point. Later Paul came to Troas from **Ephesus** on his third missionary journey and preached there before going to Macedonia (2 C. 2:12f.), and again on his return he stayed seven days at Troas (Ac. 20:6) and preached a sermon, during which Eutychus went to sleep and fell from a window (Ac. 20:7ff.). Luke appears to have rejoined Paul at **Philippi** for his journey to Troas (Ac. 20:6). It may have been at this time that Paul left his cloak and some books at Troas (2 Tim. 4:13). It is mod. *Eskistanbul*.

TROGYLLIUM: A promontory near **Samos**, mentioned in RSVm at Ac. 20:15, following the Western text of Acts, as a place where Paul made a temporary call.

TUBAL: A region and people of Asia Minor (Gen. 10:2; 1 Chr. 1:5; Isa. 66:19). Its people were warlike (Ezek. 32:26, 38:2) and traded with **Tyre** (Ezek. 27:13). Gog is its chief prince (Ezek. 38:2f., 39:1).

TYRE: A city of **Phoenicia** on an island, once overshadowed by **Sidon**, more than 20 miles to the N., but becoming the leading city of Phoenicia from about 1100 B.C. It was joined to the mainland by Alexander when he besieged it. In Jos. 19:29 it is said that the border of **Asher** (1) reached 'the fortified city of Tyre' (cf. 2 Sam. 24:7, where it would appear to be stated that Tyre was included in David's census, though Tyre was never under Israelite control). Tyre comes into prominence in the Bible in the time of David, when Hiram supplied David with timber (2 Sam. 5:11; 1 Chr. 14:1), and in Solomon's time, when the same king supplied technical help and materials for the building of the Temple (1 Kg. 5:1ff., 7:13f., 9:11; 2 Chr. 2:3ff.) in return for twenty cities of **Galilee** (1 Kg.

9:11ff.). Ahab married Jezebel, the daughter of Ethbaal, king of Tyre (1 Kg. 16:31, where 'king of the Sidonians' reflects the leadership which Sidon once had). Tyre figures frequently in psalm (Ps. 45:12, 83:7, 87:4) and prophecy (Isa. 23:1ff., 13ff.; Jer. 25:22, 27:3, 47:4; Ezek. 26:28; Jl 3:4; Am. 1:9f.; Zech. 9:2f.). In the Maccabean period Tyre was allied to the enemies of the Jews (1 Mac. 5:15), and Jason sent envoys to the king when he was attending games at Tyre (2 Mac. 4:18) and Menelaus sold some of the Temple vessels in Tyre (2 Mac. 4:32, 44ff.). Jesus visited the region of Tyre (Mt. 15:21; Mk 7:24, 31), and people from here came to hear Him (Lk. 6:17). Paul disembarked at Tyre on his return from his third missionary journey (Ac. 21:3). It is mod. *Ṣûr*.

TYRE, LADDER OF: The N. boundary of the region over which Simon was made governor by Antiochus VI (1 Mac. 11:59). A landmark in the neighbourhood of **Tyre**, probably a mountain or mountain range. Josephus says it was a mountain chain about 12 miles N. of **Ptolemais**.

U

ULAI: A river of **Elam**, beside which Daniel saw a vision (Dan. 8:2, 16). It is perhaps mod. *Kārûn* or *Kerkhā*.

UMMAH: A town of **Asher** (1) (Jos. 19:30). It is probably an error for **Acco** (so JB, with some MSS of LXX), which is surprisingly omitted from the list.

UPHAZ: A country or region from which gold came (Jer. 10:9; Dan. 10:5). It is perhaps a miswriting of **Ophir**.

UPPER GATE: A gate of the Temple built by Jotham (2 Kg. 15:35; 2 Chr. 27:3). It is possibly the same as the **Benjamin Gate** (Jer. 20:2).

UR OF THE CHALDEANS: The city from which the family of Abraham set out for **Haran** (Gen. 11:28ff., 15:7; Neh. 9:7). A famous city in S. **Babylonia**, mod. *el-Muqaiyar*. Some scholars have maintained that the Ur of the Abraham story was in N. **Mesopotamia**, in the neighbourhood of Haran. But this is very doubtful.

UZ: The country of Job (Job 1:1). This cannot be definitely located. Elsewhere in the OT, Uz is connected with **Edom** (Lam. 4:21), or mentioned separately from Edom but apparently near **Philistia** (Jer. 25:20). The name figures in Edomite (Gen. 36:28; 1 Chr. 1:42) and in Aramean (Gen. 10:23; 1 Chr. 1:17; cf. Gen. 22:21) genealogies, the former pointing to the S. and the latter to the N. In Job 1:3 Job is said to be 'the greatest of all the people of the east', and this suggests the region E. of **Palestine**. The result has been a great variety of opinions as the location of Job's home.

UZAL: 1. A region of **Arabia**, occupied by descendants of Joktan (Gen. 10:27; 1 Chr. 1:21).
  2. A district which traded with **Tyre** (Ezek. 27:19, based on an emended text). This was probably a district of **Arabia**, located by some in the region of *Mecca* and *Medina*, and by others in the *Yemen*. It is possibly to be identified with 1.

UZZA, THE GARDEN OF: A garden adjoining the palace of Manasseh, where Manasseh and Amon were buried (2 Kg. 21:18, 26).

UZZEN-SHEERAH: A town built by Sheerah, mentioned only in 1 Chr. 7:24; of uncertain location.

V

VALLEY, CITIES OF THE: A designation of the five wicked cities (Gen. 14:2): Sodom, Gomorrah, Admah, Zeboiim, and Bela (or Zoar) in Gen. 13:12, 19:29. They were defeated by Chedorlaomer and his allies (Gen. 14:8ff.), but the captives were rescued by Abraham (Gen. 14:13ff.). All of these cities save the last were destroyed in the disaster that overtook Sodom.

VALLEY GATE: One of the gates of **Jerusalem**. Here Uzziah built a tower (2 Chr. 26:9), and by this gate Nehemiah went out to inspect the walls (Neh. 2:13) and returned after his tour (Neh. 2:15).

It was repaired by the inhabitants of **Zaanah** (1) (Neh. 3:13). It led into the **Valley of Hinnom**.

W

WAHEB: An unknown place referred to in a citation from the Book of the Wars of the Lord (Neh. 21:14). It was apparently in **Moab**.

WALL, BROAD: A section of the wall of **Jerusalem** on the NW. side, mentioned in the account of Nehemiah's procession (Neh. 12:38).

WALLS, GATE BETWEEN THE TWO: The gate by which Zedekiah escaped from **Jerusalem** (2 Kg. 25:4; Jer. 39:4, 52:7). It was near the **King's Garden**, and was probably either the **Fountain Gate** or not far from it.

WATER GATE: A gate of **Jerusalem** repaired by Nehemiah (Neh. 3:26). In the square before this gate Ezra read the Law (Neh. 8:1, 3, 16). It was on the E. of the city (Neh. 12:37), above the spring of **Gihon**.

WESTERN SEA: A name for the Mediterranean Sea (Dt. 11:24; Jl 2:20; Zech. 14:8), in contrast to the **Eastern Sea**, i.e. the **Dead Sea**.

WILDGOATS' ROCKS: A place where David spared Saul's life (1 Sam. 24:2ff.). It was somewhere in the neighbourhood of **En-gedi** (1 Sam. 24:1).

WILLOWS, BROOK OF THE: A wady in **Moab** (Isa. 15:7); probably the **Zered**.

Y

YIRON: A town in **Naphtali** (Jos. 19:38); probably mod. *Yārûn*.

Z

ZAANAN: A place mentioned only in Mic. 1:11; probably the same as **Zenan** (Jos. 15:37).

ZAANANNIM: A place on the border of **Naphtali** (Jos. 19:33), marked by a well-known oak tree. It was near **Kedesh** (3) (Jg. 4:11), but its exact site is unknown.

ZABAD: The home of some Arabs called Zabadeans, defeated by Jonathan (1 Mac. 12:31f.); possibly mod. *Zebedâni*.

ZAIR: A place mentioned in the account of Joram's attack on **Edom** (2 Kg. 8:21). It is unmentioned in the parallel account in 2 Chr. 21:9. Possibly Zair is the same as **Zior** (Jos. 15:54).

ZAREPHATH: A town that belonged to Sidon (1 Kg. 17:9; Lk. 4:26), where Elijah stayed during the famine with a widow (1 Kg. 17:10ff.), whose son he restored to life (1 Kg. 17:17ff.). Obadiah prophesied that Jewish exiles would possess it (Ob. 20). It is mod. *Ṣarafand*.

ZARETHAN: A place near the **Jordan** (Jos. 3:16), not far from Succoth (2) (1 Kg. 7:46, where the parallel 2 Chr. 4:17 has **Zeredah,** 2). It is mentioned also in 1 Kg. 4:12. It is perhaps mod. *Tell es-Saʿîdîyeh. See* **Zererah.**

ZEBOIIM: One of the five **Cities of the Valley** (Gen. 10:19, 14:2, 8; Hos. 11:5), which shared the disaster that destroyed **Sodom.** Its site is unknown, and it is probably submerged beneath the waters of the S. end of the **Dead Sea.**

ZEBOIM: 1. A city resettled by the Benjaminites after the exile (Neh. 11:34). Its site is unknown.
  2. A place marking the direction taken by one party of the Philistine raiders (1 Sam. 13:18). It is probably mod. *Wâdi Abū Dabāʿ*.

ZEBULUN: The territory occupied by the tribe of Zebulun. Its ideal limits are stated in Jos. 19:10–16.

ZEDAD: A place on the ideal boundary of the Promised Land (Num. 34:8; Ezek. 47:15). It is probably mod. *Ṣedâd.*

ZEEB, WINEPRESS OF: A spot that took its name from the killing of the Midianite prince Zeeb there (Jg. 7:25). Its location is unknown.

ZELA: A town in **Benjamin** (Jos. 18:28). The name should probably be joined to the following name (so LXX), giving *Zela-haeleph* (so JB). Saul and Jonathan were buried in Zela (2 Sam. 21:14). It is possibly mod. *Khirbet Ṣalaḥ.*

ZELA-HAELEPH: *See* **Zela.**

ZELZAH: A place in **Benjamin**, where Rachel's tomb is said to have been (1 Sam. 10:2). This is supported by Jer. 31:15, which locates it near **Ramah** (3); but in Gen. 35:19f. Rachel's tomb appears to have been near **Bethlehem** (1). The location of Zelzah is unknown.

ZEMARAIM: A town of **Benjamin** (Jos. 18:22); possibly mod. *Râs ez-Zeimarah*, near *Ophrah* (1).

ZEMARAIM, MOUNT: A mountain in the hill country of **Ephraim** (1), where Abijah reproached Jeroboam I (2 Chr. 13:4). Its location is uncertain.

ZEMER: A city in **Phoenicia** (Ezek. 27:8). It was the home of the Zemarites (Gen. 10:18; 1 Chr. 1:16). Its location is uncertain.

ZENAN: A town in the lowland of **Judah** (Jos. 15:27); perhaps the same as **Zaanan** (Mic. 1:11). It is perhaps mod. *'Arâq el-Kharba*, W. of **Lachish.**

ZEPHATH: The earlier name of **Hormah** (Jg. 1:17), destroyed by the Israelites; probably mod. *Tell el-Mishâsh.*

ZEPHATHAH, VALLEY OF: A valley near **Mareshah**, where Asa defeated the Ethiopians (2 Chr. 14:10). Its location is unknown.

ZER: A city in Naphtali (Jos. 16:35); of unknown location.

ZERED, BROOK (or VALLEY) OF: A wady crossed in the Wilderness wanderings (Num. 21:12f.; Dt. 2:13f.). It is mod. *Wâdī el-Ḥesâ*, which flows into the Dead Sea near its SE. end.

ZEREDAH: 1. A town of Ephraim (1) and the birthplace of Jeroboam I (1 Kg. 11:26); perhaps mod. *Deir Ghassâneh*.
  2. A place mentioned in 2 Chr. 4:17; the parallel 1 Kg. 7:46 has Zarethan, which is to be preferred.

ZERERAH: A place on the route of the Midianite flight (Jg. 7:22). This should perhaps be read Zarethan (so JB).

ZERETH-SHAHAR: A town in Reuben (Jos. 13:19); perhaps mod. *Zârât*.

ZIDDIM: A fortified city in Naphtali (Jos. 19:35); possibly mod. *Ḥaṭṭîn el-Qadîm*.

ZIKLAG: A town allotted to Simeon (Jos. 19:5), but later reckoned to Judah (Jos. 15:31), which early absorbed Simeon. It became Philistine, belonging to Gath, and was assigned by Achish to David (1 Sam. 27:6), who was joined there by others from Israel (1 Chr. 12:1ff.). It was raided by Amalekites (1 Sam. 30:1f.) and David pursued them and recovered the captives and the spoil (1 Sam. 30:3ff.). On his return he learned of the death of Saul (2 Sam. 1:ff1.). Ziklag was resettled after the exile (Neh. 11:28). It is perhaps mod. *Tell el-Khuweilfeh*.

ZIN, WILDERNESS OF: A wilderness through which the wandering Israelites passed (Num. 13:21, 20:1, 27:14, 23:36, 34:3f.; Dt. 32:51; Jos. 15:1, 3). The spies set out from here (Num. 13:21), but in Num. 13:6, 26 from Paran. The wilderness of Zin was in the neighbourhood of Kadesh-barnea (Num. 27:14, 33:36; Dt. 32:51), with which Paran was also connected (Num. 13:26). The wilderness of Zin and Paran lay close together, therefore, and Kadesh could be reckoned to either.

ZION: The name of the fortified hill of pre-Israelite Jerusalem (2 Sam. 5:7, which was conquered by David (2 Sam. 5:6ff.; 1 Chr.

11:4ff.) and made his royal city (1 Kg. 8:1; 2 Chr. 5:2). The name is used very frequently in psalms and prophecy for Jerusalem, with particular reference to the Temple as God's sanctuary there.

ZIOR: A place in the hill country of Judah (Jos. 15:54; perhaps mod. *Sa'ir*, NNE. of Hebron. It is perhaps the same as Zair (2 Kg. 8:21).

ZIPH: 1. A city in the extreme S. of Judah (Jos. 15:24); perhaps mod. *Khirbet ez-Zeifeh*.

2. A town in the hill country of Judah (Jos. 15:55), which Rehoboam fortified (2 Chr. 11:8). The people of Ziph sought to betray David to Saul (1 Sam. 23:19ff., 26:1; Ps. 54 heading). It is mod. *Tell Zîf*, SE. of Hebron.

ZIPH, WILDERNESS OF: The region near Ziph (2), where David hid from Saul (1 Sam. 23:14f., 26:2).

ZIPHRON: An unknown place on the ideal N. boundary of the Land of Promise (Num. 34:9).

ZIZ, ASCENT OF: The route by which the Moabites and their allies approached from En-gedi to attack Jehoshaphat (2 Chr. 20:16). It is mod. *Wâdī Ḥaṣâṣah*.

ZOAN: A city of Egypt, built seven years after Hebron (Num. 13:22), and associated in tradition with the deliverance of the Israelites from Egypt (Ps. 78:12, 43). It is the ancient *Tanis*, mod. *Sân el-Ḥagar*, a royal residence of the Pharaohs Seti I and Rameses II, when it was called *Aviras*. It figures in prophetic oracles in Isa. 19:11, 13, 30:4; Ezek. 30:14.

ZOAR: One of the five Cities of the Valley (Gen. 13:10, 14:2, 8); also called Bela (Gen. 14:2, 8). It was spared the destruction that came upon Sodom and Gomorrah, as a refuge for Lot (Gen. 19:18ff.). References to Zoar stand in Dt. 34:3; Isa. 15:5; Jer. 48:4, 34. It was probably near the S. end of the Dead Sea, but its exact location cannot be known.

ZOBAH: An Aramean state on which Saul is said to have made an attack (1 Sam. 14:7), and which joined a coalition against David

(2 Sam. 8:3ff., 10:6ff.; 1 Chr. 19:6ff.), but was utterly defeated (2 Sam. 10:9ff.; 1 Chr. 18:3ff., 19:10ff.). In the time of Solomon, Rezon fled from Zobah to **Damascus**, where he established himself as king (1 Kg. 11:23ff.). Zobah must have been in the region in which **Hamath** and Damascus lay, but it cannot be precisely located. It is called **Aram-zobah** in Ps. 60 heading.

ZOPHIM, FIELD OF: One of the places to which Balaam was taken to curse the Israelites (Num. 23:14). It was in the neighbourhood of **Pisgah**, but its location is unknown.

ZORAH: A town in **Judah** (Jos. 15:33) or **Dan** (1) (Jos. 19:41; Jg. 18:2, 8, 11). Here Samson was born (Jg. 13:2, 25), and near here he was buried (Jg. 6:31). Rehoboam fortified it (2 Chr. 11:10), and it was resettled after the exile (Neh. 11:29). It is mod. *Ṣarʿah*.

ZUPH, LAND OF: A district where Saul sought the lost asses (1 Sam. 9:5); its precise location is unknown.

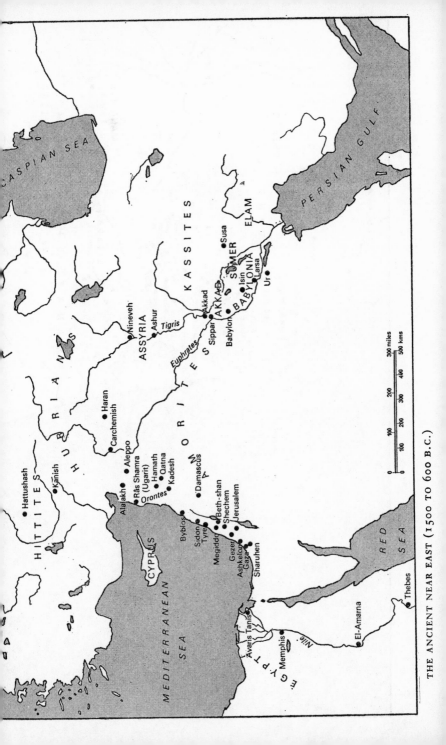

THE ANCIENT NEAR EAST (1500 TO 600 B.C.)

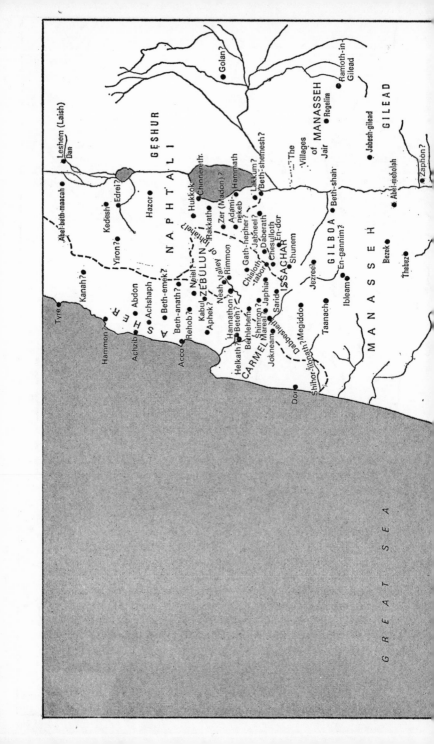

PALESTINE IN OLD TESTAMENT TIMES

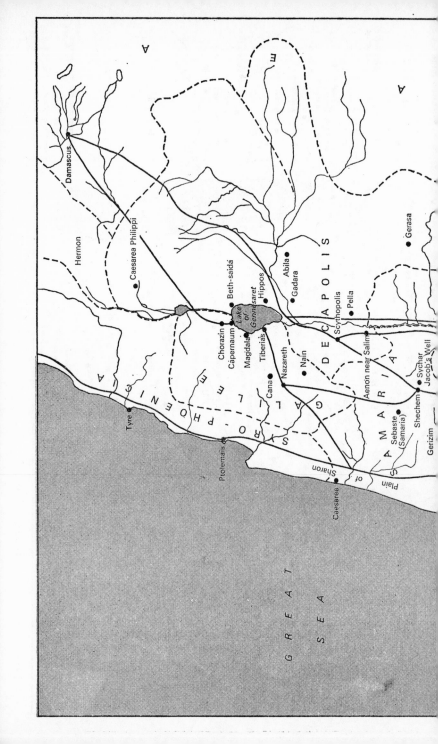

PALESTINE IN NEW TESTAMENT TIMES

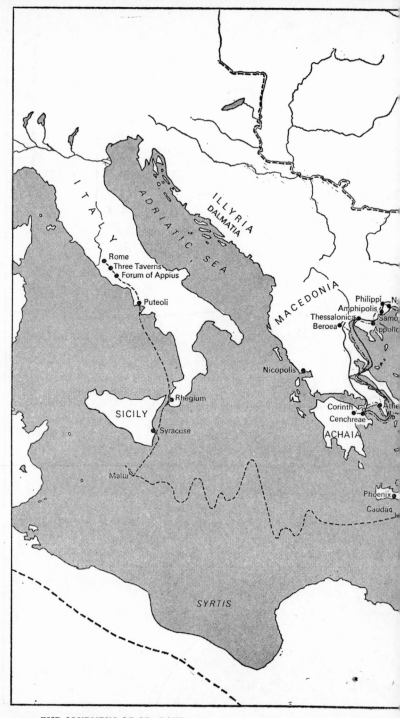

THE JOURNEYS OF ST. PAUL

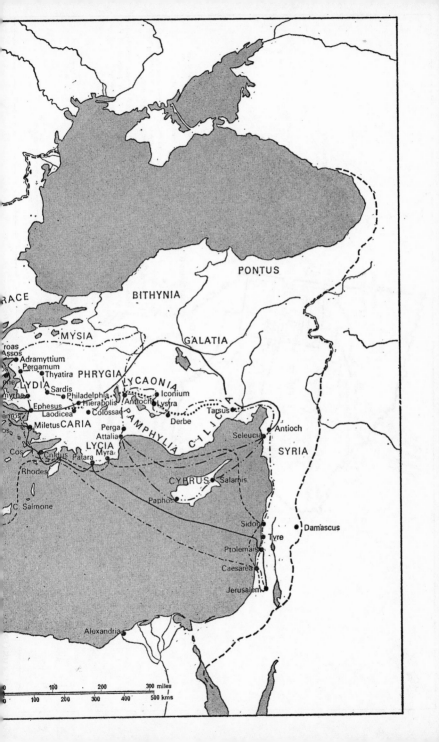

PONTUS

BITHYNIA

RACE

GALATIA

MYSIA

roas
Assos
Adramyttium
Pergamum
Thyatira
PHRYGIA
one
LYDIA
LYCAONIA
mytha
Sardis
Iconium
Philadelphia
Antioch Lystra
Tarsus
Ephesus
Hierapolis
antus
Laodicea
Colossae
Derbe
CILICIA
Miletus CARIA
Perga
PAMPHYLIA
Cos
LYCIA
Attalia
Antioch
Cos
Cnidus
Patara
Myra
Seleucia
SYRIA
Rhodes
CYPRUS
Salamis
C. Salmone
Paphos

Damascus

Sidon
Tyre
Ptolemais
Caesarea
Jerusalem

Alexandria

| 0 | 100 | 200 | 300 miles |
| 100 | 200 | 300 | 400 | 500 kms |

JERUSALEM IN THE TIME OF CHRIST